# iPhone SDK Programming

# iPhone SDK Programming

## Developing Mobile Applications for Apple iPhone and iPod touch

**Maher Ali, PhD**

*Bell Labs, Alcatel-Lucent*

A John Wiley and Sons, Ltd, Publication

### Other Wiley Editorial Offices

John Wiley & Sons Inc., 111 River Street, Hoboken, NJ 07030, USA

Jossey-Bass, 989 Market Street, San Francisco, CA 94103-1741, USA

Wiley-VCH Verlag GmbH, Boschstr. 12, D-69469 Weinheim, Germany

John Wiley & Sons Australia Ltd, 42 McDougall Street, Milton, Queensland 4064, Australia

John Wiley & Sons (Asia) Pte Ltd, 2 Clementi Loop #02-01, Jin Xing Distripark, Singapore 129809

John Wiley & Sons Canada Ltd, 6045 Freemont Blvd, Mississauga, ONT, L5R 4J3, Canada

Wiley also publishes its books in a variety of electronic formats. Some content that appears in print may not be available in
electronic books.

### British Library Cataloguing in Publication Data
A catalogue record for this book is available from the British Library.

ISBN 978-0-47074282-2 (PB)

Typeset by Sunrise Setting Ltd, Torquay, UK.
Printed and bound in Great Britain by Bell & Bain, Glasgow.

This book is printed on acid-free paper responsibly manufactured from sustainable forestry in which at least two trees are
planted for each one used for paper production.

# CONTENTS

**Preface**                                                          **xi**

**1   Objective-C and Cocoa**                                         **1**
  1.1   Classes                                                        1
        1.1.1   Class declaration                                      2
        1.1.2   How do I use other declarations?                       3
        1.1.3   Class definition                                       3
        1.1.4   Method definition and invocation                      4
        1.1.5   Important types                                        5
        1.1.6   Important Cocoa classes                                5
  1.2   Memory Management                                              6
  1.3   Protocols                                                      8
  1.4   Properties                                                    10
  1.5   Categories                                                    15
  1.6   Posing                                                        17
  1.7   Exceptions and Errors                                         17
        1.7.1   Exceptions                                            17
        1.7.2   Errors                                                22
  1.8   Key-value coding (KVC)                                        24
        1.8.1   An example illustrating KVC                           24
  1.9   Multithreading                                                30
  1.10  Summary                                                       34
  Problems                                                            35

**2   Collections**                                                  **39**
  2.1   Arrays                                                        39
        2.1.1   Immutable copy                                        42
        2.1.2   Mutable copy                                          44
        2.1.3   Deep copy                                             45
        2.1.4   Sorting an array                                      49
  2.2   Sets                                                          53
        2.2.1   Immutable sets                                        54
        2.2.2   Mutable sets                                          56

|  |  | 2.2.3 | Additional important methods | 57 |
|---|---|---|---|---|
|  | 2.3 | Dictionaries | | 58 |
|  |  | 2.3.1 | Additional important methods | 59 |
|  | 2.4 | Summary | | 60 |

**3  Anatomy of an iPhone Application                                61**

|  | 3.1 | `HelloWorld` Application | 61 |
|---|---|---|---|
|  | 3.2 | Building the `HelloWorld` Application | 64 |

**4  The View                                                        69**

|  | 4.1 | View Geometry | | 69 |
|---|---|---|---|---|
|  |  | 4.1.1 | Useful geometric type definitions | 69 |
|  |  | 4.1.2 | The UIScreen class | 71 |
|  |  | 4.1.3 | The `frame` and `center` properties | 72 |
|  |  | 4.1.4 | The `bounds` property | 73 |
|  | 4.2 | The View Hierarchy | | 74 |
|  | 4.3 | The Multitouch Interface | | 75 |
|  |  | 4.3.1 | The `UITouch` class | 76 |
|  |  | 4.3.2 | The `UIEvent` class | 76 |
|  |  | 4.3.3 | The `UIResponder` class | 77 |
|  |  | 4.3.4 | Handling a swipe | 81 |
|  |  | 4.3.5 | More advanced gesture recognition | 86 |
|  | 4.4 | Animation | | 91 |
|  |  | 4.4.1 | Using the `UIView` class animation support | 92 |
|  |  | 4.4.2 | Transition animation | 96 |
|  | 4.5 | Drawing | | 99 |

**5  Controls                                                        103**

|  | 5.1 | The Foundation of All Controls | | 103 |
|---|---|---|---|---|
|  |  | 5.1.1 | UIControl attributes | 103 |
|  |  | 5.1.2 | Target-action mechanism | 104 |
|  | 5.2 | UITextField | | 107 |
|  |  | 5.2.1 | Interacting with the keyboard | 108 |
|  |  | 5.2.2 | The delegate | 111 |
|  |  | 5.2.3 | Creating of, and working with, a `UITextField` | 112 |
|  | 5.3 | Sliders | | 113 |
|  | 5.4 | Switches | | 115 |
|  | 5.5 | Buttons | | 116 |
|  | 5.6 | Segmented Controls | | 117 |
|  | 5.7 | Page Controls | | 120 |
|  | 5.8 | Date Pickers | | 121 |
|  | 5.9 | Summary | | 123 |

**6   View Controllers**                                                        **125**
  6.1   The Simplest View Controller                                   125
      6.1.1   The view controller                              125
      6.1.2   The view                                         128
      6.1.3   The application delegate                         128
      6.1.4   Summary                                          129
  6.2   Radio Interfaces                                               131
      6.2.1   A detailed example                               131
      6.2.2   Some comments on tab bar controllers             136
  6.3   Navigation Controllers                                         140
      6.3.1   A detailed example                               141
      6.3.2   Customization                                    149
  6.4   Modal View Controllers                                         152
      6.4.1   A detailed example                               153
  6.5   Summary                                                        159

**7   Special-Purpose Views**                                                   **161**
  7.1   Picker View                                                    161
      7.1.1   The delegate                                     161
      7.1.2   An example                                       163
  7.2   Progress Views                                                 168
      7.2.1   An example                                       169
  7.3   Text View                                                      172
      7.3.1   The delegate                                     172
      7.3.2   An example                                       173
  7.4   Alert View                                                     176
  7.5   Action Sheet                                                   178
  7.6   Web View                                                       180
      7.6.1   A simple web view application                    180
      7.6.2   Viewing local files                              185
      7.6.3   Evaluating Javascript                            189
      7.6.4   The web view delegate                            196

**8   Table View**                                                              **205**
  8.1   Overview                                                       205
  8.2   The Simplest Table View Application                            206
  8.3   A Table View with both Images and Text                         209
  8.4   A Table View with Sections Headers and Footers                 211
  8.5   A Table View with the Ability to Delete Rows                   213
  8.6   A Table View with the Ability to Insert Rows                   219
  8.7   Reordering Table Rows                                          227
  8.8   Presenting Hierarchical Information                            233
      8.8.1   Detailed example                                 235
  8.9   Grouped Table Views                                            245

8.10  Indexed Table Views                                              248
8.11  Summary                                                          254

**9   File Management                                                  257**
9.1   The Home Directory                                               257
9.2   Enumerating a Directory                                          258
9.3   Creating and Deleting a Directory                                259
9.4   Creating Files                                                   261
9.5   Retrieving and Changing Attributes                               265
9.6   Working with Resources and Low-Level File Access                 269
9.7   Summary                                                          273

**10  Working with Databases                                           275**
10.1  Basic Database Operations                                        275
10.2  Processing Row Results                                           279
10.3  Prepared Statements                                              282
      10.3.1  Preparation                                              282
      10.3.2  Execution                                                282
      10.3.3  Finalization                                             283
10.4  User-defined Functions                                           285
10.5  Storing BLOBs                                                    289
10.6  Retrieving BLOBs                                                 293
10.7  Summary                                                          295

**11  XML Processing                                                   297**
11.1  XML and RSS                                                      297
      11.1.1  XML                                                      297
      11.1.2  RSS                                                      298
11.2  Document Object Model (DOM)                                      301
11.3  Simple API for XML (SAX)                                         307
11.4  An RSS Reader Application                                        317
11.5  Summary                                                          320
Problems                                                               322

**12  Location Awareness                                               325**
12.1  The Core Location Framework                                      325
      12.1.1  The `CLLocation` class                                   327
12.2  A Simple Location-aware Application                              329
12.3  Google Maps API                                                 334
      12.3.1  A geocoding application                                  334
12.4  A Tracking Application with Maps                                 340
12.5  Working with ZIP Codes                                          347
12.6  Summary                                                          350

**13 Working with Devices**                                              **351**
   13.1 Working with the Accelerometer                              351
      13.1.1 Example                                           352
   13.2 Audio                                                       356
      13.2.1 Example                                           357
   13.3 Video                                                       358
   13.4 Device Information                                          359
   13.5 Taking and Selecting Pictures                               360
      13.5.1 Overall approach                                  360
      13.5.2 Detailed example                                  361
   13.6 Summary                                                     367

**Appendices**                                                          **369**

**A  Saving and Restoring App State**                                   **371**

**B  Invoking External Applications**                                   **375**

**References and Bibliography**                                         **377**

**Index**                                                               **379**

# PREFACE

Welcome to *iPhone SDK Programming*, an introductory text to the development of mobile applications for the iPhone and the iPod Touch. This text covers a wide variety of essential topics, including:

- The Objective-C programming language

- Collections

- Cocoa Touch

- Building advanced mobile user interfaces

- Core Animation and Quartz 2D

- Model-view-controller (MVC) designs

- Table views

- File management

- Parsing XML documents using SAX and DOM

- Working with Google Maps API

- Consuming RESTful web services

- Building advanced location-based applications

- Developing database applications using SQLite engine

- Building multimedia applications

## Is this book for you?

The book's intended audience is primarily application developers with a basic understanding of the C language and object orientation concepts such as encapsulation and polymorphism. You don't need to be an expert C coder to follow this book. All you need is a basic understanding of structures, pointers, and functions. The text does cover general topics such as databases and XML processing. These topics are covered assuming minimal or no prior knowledge.

## What else do you need?

To master iPhone SDK programming, you will need the following:

- Intel-based Mac running Mac OS X Leopard.

- iPhone SDK. Download from: `http://developer.apple.com/iphone`.

- Optional: membership of the iPhone Developer Program. To use the device for development, you will need to pay a fee for membership of the iPhone Developer Program.

- Source code. The source code of the applications illustrated in this book is available online at: `http://code.google.com/p/iphone-sdk-programming-book-code-samples/downloads/list`.

## Organization

**Chapter 1** This chapter presents the main features of the Objective-C language under the Cocoa environment. We introduce the main concepts behind classes in Objective-C. You will learn how to declare a new class, define it, and use it from within other classes. You will also be exposed to important Cocoa classes and data types. You will learn about memory management in the iPhone OS. You will learn about how to create new objects as well as how to deallocate them. You will also learn about your responsibility when obtaining objects from Cocoa frameworks or other frameworks. We also introduce the topic of Objective-C protocols. You will learn how to adopt protocols and how to declare new ones as well. This chapter also covers language features such as properties, categories, and posing. Exceptions and error handling techniques are both covered in this chapter, and you will be exposed to the concept of key-value coding (KVC). Finally, you will learn how to use multithreading in your iPhone application.

**Chapter 2** This chapter addresses the topic of collections in Cocoa. It discusses arrays, sets, and dictionaries. You will learn about immutable and mutable collections, the different approaches used for copying collections, and several sorting techniques.

**Chapter 3** In this chapter, we discuss the basic steps needed to build a simple iPhone application. First, we demonstrate the basic structure of a simple iPhone application and then we show the steps needed to develop the application using XCode.

**Chapter 4** This chapter explains the main concepts behind views. You will learn about view geometry, view hierarchy, the multitouch interface, animation, and basic Quartz 2D drawing.

**Chapter 5** In this chapter, you will learn about the base class for all controls, `UIControl`, and the important *target-action* mechanism. This chapter also presents several important graphical controls that can be used in building attractive iPhone applications.

**Chapter 6** In this chapter, you will learn about the available view controllers that are provided to you in the iPhone SDK. Although you can build iPhone applications without the use of these view controllers, you shouldn't. As you will see in this chapter, view controllers greatly simplify your application. This chapter provides a gentle introduction to view controllers. After that, detailed treatment of tab bar controllers, navigation controllers, and modal view controllers is provided.

**Chapter 7**  In this chapter, we present several important subclasses of the `UIView` class. We discuss picker views and show how they can be used for item selection. We investigate progress views and also talk about activity indicator views. We present text views used in displaying multiline text. We show how to use alert views for the display of alert messages to the user. Similar to alert views are action sheets which are also discussed. We also discuss several aspects of web views.

**Chapter 8**  This chapter will take you through a step-by-step journey to the world of table views. We start by presenting an overview of the main concepts behind table views. After that, we present a simple table view application and discuss the mandatory methods you need to implement in order to populate and respond to users' interactions with the table view. We show how easy it is to add images to table rows. We introduce the concept of sections and provide a table view application that has sections, with section headers and footers. We introduce the concept of editing a table view. An application that allows the user to delete rows is presented and the main ideas are clarified. We address the insertion of new rows in a table view. An application is discussed that presents a data entry view to the user and adds that new data to the table's rows. We continue our discussion of the editing mode and present an application for reordering table entries. The main concepts of reordering rows are presented. We discuss the mechanism for presenting hierarchical information to the user. An application that uses table views to present three levels of hierarchy is discussed. We deal with grouped table views through an example. After that, we present the main concepts behind indexed table views.

**Chapter 9**  This chapter covers the topic of file management. Here, you will learn how to use both high- and low-level techniques for storing/retrieving data to/from files. First, we talk about the `Home` directory of the application. Next, we show how to enumerate the contents of a given directory using the high-level methods of `NSFileManager`. You will learn more about the structure of the `Home` directory and where you can store files. After that, you will learn how to create and delete directories. Next, we cover the creation of files. We also cover the topic of file and directory attributes. You will learn how to retrieve and set specific file/directory attributes in this chapter. We also demonstrate the use of application bundles and low-level file access.

**Chapter 10**  In this chapter, we will cover the basics of the SQLite database engine that is available to you using the iPhone SDK. SQLite is an embedded database in the sense that there is no server running, and the database engine is linked to your application. First, we describe basic SQL statements and their implementation using SQLite function calls. Second, we discuss handling of result sets generated by SQL statements. Third, we address the topic of prepared statements. Fourth, we talk about extensions to the SQLite API through the use of user-defined functions. Finally, we present a detailed example for storing and retrieving BLOBs to/from the database.

**Chapter 11** In this chapter, you will learn how to effectively use XML in your iPhone application. The chapter follows the same theme used in other chapters and exposes the main concepts through a working iPhone application: an RSS feed reader. First, we explain the main concepts behind XML and RSS. Next, we present a detailed discussion of DOM and SAX parsing. After that, we present a table-based RSS reader application. Finally, we provide a summary of the main steps you need to take in order to effectively harness the power of XML from within your native iPhone application.

**Chapter 12** In this chapter, we will address the topic of location awareness. First, we will talk about the Core Location framework and how to use it to build location-aware applications. After that, we will discuss a simple location-aware application. Next, we cover the topic of geocoding. You will learn how to translate postal addresses into geographical locations. You will also learn how to sample movement of the device and display that information on maps. Finally, we discuss how to relate ZIP codes to geographical information.

**Chapter 13** In this chapter, we demonstrate the use of the several devices available on the iPhone. We discuss the use of the accelerometer, show how to play small sound files, and show how to play video files. After that, we discuss how to obtain iPhone/iPod touch device information. Using the built-in camera and the photo library is also discussed in this chapter.

**Appendix A** In this appendix, you will learn how to use property lists for saving and restoring the application state. This will give the user the illusion that your application does not quit when he/she hits the Home button.

**Appendix B** Here, you will learn how to programatically invoke iPhone applications from within your application. In addition, you will learn how to publish services that other iPhone applications can utilize.

# 1

# Objective-C and Cocoa

This chapter presents the main features of the Objective-C language under the Cocoa environment. The organization of this chapter is as follows. In Section 1.1, we introduce the main concepts behind classes in Objective-C. In that section, you will learn how to declare a new class, define it, and use it from within other classes. You will also be exposed to important Cocoa classes and data types.

After that, you will learn in Section 1.2 about memory management in the iPhone OS. You will learn about how to create new objects as well as how to deallocate them, and you will also learn about your responsibility when obtaining objects from Cocoa frameworks or other frameworks.

Section 1.3 introduces the topic of Objective-C protocols. You will learn how to adopt protocols and how to declare new ones as well. You will learn in Section 1.4 about properties, an Objective-C language feature that allows you to access instance variables using the dot notation. The concept of categories is the subject of Section 1.5. These allow you to extend existing classes by adding new methods. Posing is another technique that is slightly different from categories. Posing allows you to replace a given class with one of its descendants. This is discussed in Section 1.6.

Exceptions and error handling are important features in any modern language. Section 1.7 covers both of these techniques and shows you the appropriate use of each feature. After covering exceptions and errors you will be exposed to the concept of key-value coding (KVC) in Section 1.8. KVC is an important and widely used technique in Cocoa. KVC allows you to indirectly access object properties.

Next, you will learn how to use multithreading in your iPhone application (Section 1.9). Cocoa makes it very easy to use multithreading and you will discover, using a step-by-step approach, how to make a task run in the background. Finally, we provide a summary of this chapter in Section 1.10.

We have a lot to cover, so let's get started.

## 1.1 Classes

In object-oriented languages, such as Java, an object encapsulates attributes and provides methods. These methods can be used by the outside world (i.e., other objects) to change the object's state as well as to interact with the object. All this can be achieved without opening the actual implementation of the object's behavior to the outside world.

In Objective-C, in order to create a new class, you first need to declare it using an *interface* and then define it using an *implementation*. The declaration and the definition are usually written

*iPhone SDK Programming*   Maher Ali
© 2009 John Wiley & Sons, Ltd

in two separate files. The declaration part is customarily done in a .h file having the same name as the class, while the implementation (also having the same name as the class) is in a .m file. Both the declaration and the definition parts use compiler directives. A compiler directive is an instruction to the Objective-C compiler and it is prefixed by the @ sign. The declaration is signaled to the compiler using the @interface directive, while the actual definition is signaled using the @implementation directive.

### 1.1.1   Class declaration

To declare a class, MyClassName, as a subclass of class MyParentName, you simply write:

```
@interface   MyClassName : MyParentName
{
     attribute  declarations
}
     method  declarations
@end
```

Here, we are telling the compiler that a new class type, MyClassName, is being declared. MyClassName is a subclass of MyParentName class. In addition, we list the definition of all instance variables between the curly brackets. The methods are declared between the end of the curly bracket and the @end compiler directive.

There are a few important aspects of the @interface declaration:

1. The attributes declared between the curly brackets are *instance* variables. At runtime, every class has a unique *class* object and zero or more instances of the class. Every instance (object) of MyClassName has its own values of these attributes. The unique class object has no access to these instance variables.

2. Methods declared can be either: a) instance methods, or b) class methods. An instance method is called by sending a *message* to an actual instance (i.e., an object) of the class. A class method does not require an object instance. You call a class method by sending a message to the unique class object. In Objective-C, every class has exactly one class object during the runtime of the program. An instance method is declared/defined by a "–" prefix, while the class method is declared/defined by a "+" prefix.

   For example:

   ```
   -(Address *) getAddress;
   ```

   is an instance method, while

   ```
   +(id) getANewInstance;
   ```

   is a class method.

3. Objective-C does not support class variables. However, you can use the familiar static keyword in an implementation file of a given class. This will allow instance methods (i.e., those with a "–" prefix in their definition) to have access to the single value of this variable

shared by all instances of that declared class. If you define a `static` variable inside a method, then that method is the *only* method that has access to that variable. If you put the definition of the `static` variable outside the class implementation, then all methods have access to that variable.

## 1.1.2   How do I use other declarations?

As a Cocoa developer, you will need to be able to use classes that other developers have written. In addition, if the declaration and the definition of your classes are in separate files, you will need to inform the compiler about the location of the class declaration in the implementation file.

If you use the name of a class without accessing its methods or instance variables, you can just use the `@class` directive. This gives the compiler enough information to successfully compile the code. Usually the `@class` directive is used in class declarations. For example, consider the following declaration:

```
@class Address;
@interface Person
{
    Address *address;
}
@end
```

Here, we have a `Person` class declaration that uses the `Address` class. The compiler only needs to know that the `Address` is a class type. No details about the actual methods and attributes are needed since we just use the type.

If, on the other hand, you use the methods and/or the attributes of a given class, then you need to point the compiler to the location of the file that contains the declaration. There are two ways to do that: (1) using `#include`, and (2) using `#import`. `#include` and `#import` are almost identical, except that `#import` loads the given file only once during the compilation process. The `#import` directive is much simpler, fully supported by Apple, and produces potentially fewer problems. Bottom line: use `#import`.

## 1.1.3   Class definition

To actually define a class, you need to specify the actual implementation of the class/instance methods declared in the `@interface` part. To define the class, you write:

```
#import "MyClassName.h"
@implementation MyClassName
    method definitions
@end
```

Notice that we needed to import the declaration file. This import allowed us to skip repeating the parent's class name as well as the instance variables. Both can be deduced by the compiler so there is no need to repeat them.

## *1.1.4   Method definition and invocation*

In Java, a method is invoked using its name followed by a pair of left and right round brackets. If the method requires parameters, the values of these parameters are inserted inside the brackets and separated by commas. For example, if aPoint is a Java object representing a point in 3D, setLocation (float x, float y, float z) can represent a method for changing the location of this point object. aPoint.setlocation(3, 6, 9) asks the aPoint object to change its location to (3, 6, 9). One problem with this notation is readability. If you come across such a statement written by another programmer, you cannot know for sure what these values represent. You have to go to the interface of this class and read about what each position in the parameters list represents.

Objective-C is an object-oriented language. It, too, provides data encapsulation. The outside world interacts with an object by sending *messages* to that object. To send an object, aObject, a message, aMessage, you use square brackets and write [aObject aMessage]. A message is composed of two parts: (1) keywords, and (2) parameters. Every message has at least one keyword. A keyword is an identifier followed by a colon.

Let's make these definitions concrete by writing the setlocation method invocation in Objective-C. In Objective-C, you write something like:

    [aPoint setLocationX:3 andY:6 andZ:9];

Notice the improved readability of the invocation of the method. Just by looking at it, we know that 6 is used to change the y-coordinate. This message has three keywords: setlocationX:, andY:, andZ:. The method is represented by setLocationX:andY:andZ:. This representation is called a *selector*. A selector is a unique name (within a class) of a method used by the runtime to locate the code implementing that method. The method is declared in the interface as:

−(**void**)setLocationX: (**float**) x andY:(**float**) y andZ:(**float**) z;

The statement [aPoint setLocationX:3 andY:6 andZ:9] as a whole is called a *message expression*. If this expression evaluates to an object, then it, too, can also receive a message. Objective-C allows nested message invocation. For example, you can write:

[[ addressBook getEntryAtIndex:0] printYourself ];

First, the message getEntryAtIndex:0 is sent to the addressBook object. The method identified by the selector getEntryAtIndex: returns an object. This object is then sent a printYourself message.

It's worth noting that if a method has zero parameters, you should not use the ":" when the method is invoked. This notation can be difficult to deal with at first, but after a time it becomes natural.

Methods in Objective-C are always *public*. There is no such thing as a private method. Instance variables are defaulted to *protected*, a setting that works well for you most of the time.

## 1.1.5   Important types

We mentioned before that every class in a Cocoa application has a singleton class object. The type of this class object is `Class`. A null class pointer is of type `Nill`. `Nill` is basically `(Class)0`. We also learned that a class can be instantiated. An instance of a class `A` is declared as:

A        *anObject;

There is, however, a defined type in Cocoa that represents an arbitrary object. This type is named `id`. If an `anObject` does not point to any object, its value is `nil`. A `nil` is basically `(id)0`.

SEL is a defined type that represents a selector. To obtain the `SEL` of a method, `aMethod:`, use the directive `@selector` as follows.

SEL  mySelector  =  **@selector**(aMethod:);

If you want `mySelector` to point to a null selector, assign it `NULL`.

You can also obtain the `SEL` of a method from a string representation of its name. The function to use is `NSSelectorFromString()` which is declared as:

SEL  NSSelectorFromString  (
    NSString  *aSelectorName
);

`NSSelectorFromString` will always return a `SEL` named by a non-nil `aSelectorName` even if the selector is not found. If there is no selector with the name `aSelectorName`, a new selector is registered with this name and returned. If the parameter `aSelectorName` is `nil` or the function faces memory problems, it will return `NULL` (basically `(SEL)0`.)

## 1.1.6   Important Cocoa classes

There are several important Cocoa classes that you will often use in your iPhone application. In this section, we will discuss just the ones needed in this chapter. Other classes will be covered throughout this text.

- `NSObject`. This is the base class of most Cocoa classes. An object is not considered a Cocoa object if it is not an instance of `NSObject` or any class that inherits from `NSObject`. This class defines the runtime methods required for allocating and deallocating objects.

- `NSString`. This is the main class representing strings in Cocoa. Using this class, you can store an arbitrary text. However, once you store a value in an object of this type, you cannot change it. This kind of class is referred to as *immutable*. To be able to change a string's value (e.g., append text to it, etc.), you need the *mutable* string class `NSMutableString`. You can create a constant string using the "@" sign. For example, `@"Plano"` represents an `NSString` instance.

- `NSArray`. Instances of this class represents Cocoa array objects. The mutable version of this class is `NSMutableArray`. See Section 2.1 for more information on arrays in Cocoa.

- `NSSet`. Instances of this class represents Cocoa set objects. The mutable version is `NSMutableSet`. See Section 2.2 for more information on sets in Cocoa.

## 1.2  Memory Management

Modern computer languages employ *garbage collection*. A garbage collector is a runtime algorithm that scans the allocated objects in your program and reclaims (deallocates) objects that you have lost contact with. For example, if you have created an object and have stored its location in a variable pointer named `ptr` and later you set `ptr` to `nil`, the memory block allocated, and whose address was stored in `ptr`, is no longer accessible by your code. The garbage collector, at a time of its choosing, intervenes on your behalf and deallocates this memory so that future allocation requests can use it.

Cocoa under the iPhone OS does not employ a garbage collector. Instead, Cocoa applications must use *managed memory*. Applications running on this platform should clean up after themselves. Since iPhone applications run in a memory-constrained environment, you, as a developer, should pay extra attention to memory usage.

You have learned in the previous section that `NSObject` is the root class in the Cocoa programming environment. `NSObject` defines the methods required for memory management and much more. One of the most important methods of `NSObject` is the `alloc` method. When you send an `alloc` message to a class object, the class object allocates memory for a new object instance of the class and sets its attributes to zero. For a class instance to start receiving messages, the `init` method usually needs to be invoked. Every class implements at least one `init` method either explicitly or implicitly through the inheritance chain. If you override `init`, then you should call your parent's `init` first and then perform your initialization. This can be achieved using the `super` keyword. The keyword `super` makes the search for the method (here, `init`) start from the parent class rather than the class of the object, while the variable name `self` makes the search start from the class of the object where this statement is being executed. You can change the value of `self` at runtime, but you cannot change `super`. To change `super`, you have to change the parent class in the interface and then build your code.

We have talked about how a new object is born, but how can we know when we can get rid of it? The solution to this problem is simple: keep a counter per object. This counter tells us how many other objects are interested in this object. When an object wants to put a claim on our object, it increments this counter. When it wants to remove this claim, it decrements the counter.

This counter is maintained by the `NSObject` and is called the *retain count*. When you allocate the object, the retain count is set to 1. Any time another object wants to put a claim on this object, it sends it a `retain` message, thus increasing the retain count by 1. If the object wants to remove the claim, it sends it a `release` message, which in effect decrements the retain count by 1. When the retain count reaches 0, the object is deallocated by the system.

To keep your program from leaking memory, you need to release any object for whose memory you are responsible after it is no longer needed. You are mainly responsible for an object's memory in the following three scenarios:

1. You allocated the object using `alloc`. If you `alloc`ated the object, you have to `release` it at the end.

2. The object is a result of a `copy` made by you. If you create an object by `copy`ing it from another object, you are responsible for releasing it at the end.

3. The object was `retained` by you. If you express your desire to keep a given object alive, you have to express your desire that the object should die when you are no longer in need of it.

We are left with one problem which can be illustrated by the following code.

```
// In one of your methods
// Ask an object to create a new object for you
NSMutableString *aString = [anObject giveMeANewString];
```

In the above code, you are asking `anObject` to give you a brand new object of type `NSMutableString`. The question is: who is responsible for releasing this new object when you are no longer in need of it?

One solution to this problem is to delay the release of the object. Basically, the `giveMeANewString` method creates a brand new `NSMutableString` object (e.g., using `alloc`) and puts that object in a pool for later release. When the time comes and you want to free up some memory, you release this pool and the pool will go over its content and send a `release` message to each and every object added to it.

The Foundation framework provides the `NSAutoreleasePool` class for managing delayed releases. Every thread in your program needs to have at least one instance of this class.

You create an instance of the class as follows:

```
NSAutoreleasePool *pool = [[NSAutoreleasePool alloc] init];
```

This line will make `pool` the active autorelease pool for the code that follows. Any time your code or any of Cocoa's framework functions send an `autorelease` message to an object, a reference to that object is added to this pool. You can think of an autorelease pool as a list of entries. Each entry consists of a reference to an object (i.e., its address) and an integer counting the number of autorelease messages sent to this object on this pool.

To dispose of a pool, you send a release message to it, e.g., `[pool release]`. This will cause the pool to send `release` messages to every object it has a reference to. The number of `release` messages is equal to the number of `autorelease` messages sent to this object on this pool (a variable kept in the object's entry in the pool). Therefore, the retain count of every object will be reduced by the same number of delayed releases (i.e., autoreleases) it has received.

Autorelease pools can be nested. When you create a pool, this pool is pushed onto a stack. Any time an object receives an `autorelease` message, the runtime will send a reference to that object to the pool on top of the stack.

Having nested pools allows the developer to optimize memory usage. Let's assume, as an example, that `giveMeANewString` creates a large number of temporary objects in order to compute the return value. At the end of this method, these temporary objects are not needed. If you have only one autorelease pool in your application, these objects will linger until the end of the current run-loop and then get released.

To be able to reclaim the memory used by these temporary objects, you can create a new autorelease pool at the beginning of this method. All autoreleased objects generated by the method code (or calls made by the method) will go to this pool as it is on top of the pool stack. Before you return from this method, you `release` this local pool, thereby causing all these temporary objects to be released as well.

Listing 1.1 shows how the `giveMeANewString` method can be implemented. Here, we assume that producing the string is a rather involved process which requires extensive memory allocation of temporary objects.

**Listing 1.1**    Demonstration of local autorelease pools.

```
-(NSMutableString *) giveMeANewString
{
    NSAutoreleasePool *pool =
            [[NSAutoreleasePool alloc] init];
    NSMutableString *returnString =
            [[NSMutableString alloc] init];
    // code that generates large amount of
    // autoreleased objects.
    .
    .
    .
    // update the returnString with calculated data
    [returnString appendString:computedData];
    [pool release];
    return [returnString autorelease];
}
```

All temporary objects created inside the method will be deallocated. The value returned is autoreleased and will be available to the caller as long as its immediate pool is not released.

If your class retains or allocates other objects, you need to make sure that these objects are released when your instance is released. The `dealloc` method is used for this purpose. It is called before the instance of an object is released. You should release any object that you are responsible for and propagate the deallocation up the inheritance chain by calling [**super** dealloc ] as the last statement in this method.

## 1.3   Protocols

A protocol is an important language feature in Objective-C. Protocols allow, among other things, the ability to realize multiple inheritance in a single-inheritance language.

Think of a protocol as an interface in the Java language. Just as classes in Java can implement multiple interfaces, so can classes in Objective-C adopt multiple protocols.

A protocol is just a list of methods. Each method in this list can be tagged as either required (`@required`, the default) or optional (`@optional`). If a class adopts a protocol, it must implement, at least, all required methods in that protocol. For example, to define a `Litigating` protocol, you would write something like this:

```
@protocol Litigating
-(int)sue:(id<Litigating >)someone;
-(int)getSuedBy:(id<Litigating >)someone;
@end
```

Any class can adopt this protocol by listing it, using angle brackets, in its declaration after the superclass name. For example,

@**interface** Citizen : Human <Litigating >

A class can adopt multiple protocols. For example, one could write[1]:

@**interface** Citizen : Human
<Litigating , MilitaryService , TransferFunds>

Two classes with different inheritance chains can implement the same protocol. For example,

@**interface** DemocraticCountry : Country<Litigating >

A democratic country does adopt the Litigating protocol; it can be sued and it can sue others. A dictatorship or a fascist country, on the other hand, does not adopt such a protocol.

Suppose you want to model a system where citizens travel to different countries and can be potential candidates to be sued or to sue the host country. How can you, elegantly, test to see if a country can be sued? You cannot just send a message to the country instance and hope it will respond favorably[2].

Objective-C provides an elegant solution for this: protocols. You can test, at runtime, whether an object is an instance of a class that adopts a given protocol. You do that by sending that object a conformsToProtocol: message. For example, to test that a given country, aCountry, can be sued, you write:

```
if ([ aCountry conformsToProtocol : @protocol( Litigating )]){
    [ aCountry getSuedBy : self ];
else
    [ self letItGo ];
}
```

The conformsToProtocol: method is defined in NSObject twice, once as a class method (with a "+" sign) and another as an instance method (with a "–" sign). Both are identical and are provided for convenience. For example, the class version is defined as:

+ (BOOL) conformsToProtocol :( Protocol ∗) aProtocol

It takes one argument: a protocol object. We can use @protocol (protocol-name) to get an instance of the protocol protocol-name. This instance is most of the time a unique instance during the lifetime of your program. However, it is safer to assume that it is not and not cache the protocol object.

conformsToProtocol: returns YES if the class of the receiving object adopts the protocol-name, and NO, otherwise. It is important to note that conformance is defined based on the declaration of the receiver's class, and not based on whether the methods of the protocols have actually been implemented. For example, if you have:

---

[1]In the USA, even non-citizens must serve in case of a draft.
[2]In real life, this can be very dangerous!

```
@interface DemocraticCountry : Country<Litigating>
@end
```

```
@implementation DemocraticCountry
@end
```

And you have:

```
DemocraticCountry *aCountry =
    [[DemocraticCountry alloc] init];
```

the statement:

```
[aCountry conformsToProtocol:@protocol(Litigating)]
```

will return YES (1). However, the statement:

```
[aCountry getSuedBy:self];
```

will result in an application crash.

It is also worth noting that a protocol can incorporate other protocols. For example:

```
@protocol LegalEntity <Taxable>
```

A class that adopts a protocol, must implement all required methods of that protocol as well as the required methods of protocols incorporated by that protocol (and so on recursively). Moreover, protocol methods are inherited by subclasses, i.e., a subclass conforms to a given protocol if its superclass also conforms to that protocol.

## 1.4  Properties

A property is a neat feature of Objective-C that allows you to generate setter/getter methods for your instance variables. These setter and getter methods can be invoked without you even specifying them. To get/set the value of the instance variable, you use the `dot` notation. For example, if you have a defined `NSString*` property, `name`, in an object, `aObject`, you can write: `aObject.name = @"Plano"`. This statement is actually translated by the compiler to something like: `[aObject setName:@"Plano"]`. Note that the instance variable, `name`, is still a non-public variable, but it appears as if we are accessing the variable directly from the outside.

You use the `@property` directive in the class declaration in order to declare a property. To actually generate the getter and/or setter method(s), you use the `@synthesize` directive in the class definition (i.e., implementation). This feature of Objective-C allows you to request only getter methods for instance variables that are read-only.

Properties are declared in the methods' section (i.e., after the curly bracket) of the `@interface` part of your class. The format for property declaration is:

```
@property(property-attributes) property-type property-name;
```

The property attributes are used to influence how the compiler generates the getter/setter methods. You can use the following attributes:

- `nonatomic`. By using this attribute, you tell the compiler that it does not need to generate extra code for guaranteeing thread safety. If you do not specify `nonatomic`, the compiler will generate that extra code. If you know that the property will be accessed from a single thread, then specifying `nonatomic` can improve performance. Having an atomic accessor means that the setter/getter are thread-safe; it does not necessarily mean, however, that your code, as a whole, is correct. Having a code that is thread-safe involves more work from your side than guaranteeing the atomicity of a single operation such as a getter or a setter method. See Section 1.9 for more information on multithreading.

- `readonly`. This attributes tells the compiler that the property can be read but it cannot be set. The compiler will generate only a getter method. If you attempt to write code that will assign value to the property via the dot notation, the compiler will generate a warning.

- `readwrite`. This is the default. Both a getter and a setter will be generated for you by the compiler when you use the `@synthesize` directive.

- `assign`. The value you use to set the property is directly assigned to the instance variable. This is the default.

- `copy`. You use this attribute when you want to store a copy of the object being assigned to your instance variable rather than the reference to that object. The value being assigned has to be an object that knows how to copy itself (i.e., implements the `NSCopying` protocol).

- `retain`. Specifies that you are interested in putting an ownership claim on this object. The compiler will invoke a `retain` on this object and assign it to the instance variable. If the caller later `released` this object, it does not get deallocated since you `retain`ed it. You need to `release` it, either when you are finished with it, or in the `dealloc` method of your object.

- `getter=getterName, setter=setterName`. By default, the name of the automatically generated setter of a property, `prob`, is `setProb`, and the getter is `prob`. You can change this naming convention of either the setter, the getter or both.

After declaring the property, you have two choices: a) ask the compiler to generate the getter/setter methods by using the `@synthesize` directive, or b) implement the methods yourself by using the `@dynamic` directive.

Let's look at an example demonstrating these concepts. Consider the `Employee` class declared and defined in Listing 1.2.

**Listing 1.2** The `Employee` class declaration and definition demonstrating Objective-C properties.

```
@interface Employee : NSObject
{
  NSString      *name;
  NSString      *address;
  NSMutableArray   *achievements;
  BOOL         married;
  Employee     *manager;
  NSString     *_disability;
}
```

```
@property  (nonatomic, copy)    NSString* name;
@property  (nonatomic, retain) Employee* manager;
@property  (nonatomic, assign) NSString* address;
@property  (nonatomic, copy)    NSMutableArray* achievements;
@property  (nonatomic, getter=isMarried) BOOL married;
@property  (nonatomic, copy) NSString* disability;
@end

@implementation Employee
@synthesize name, address, manager, achievements, married,
            disability=_disability;
@end
```

The first property declaration:
```
@property (nonatomic, copy) NSString* name
```
can be realized by the compiler as follows:

```
-(NSString*) name
{
  return name;
}
-(void) setName:(NSString*) aName
{
  if(name != aName)
  {
    [name release];
    name = [aName copy];
  }
}
```

The getter accessor returns a reference to the name instance variable. The setter accessor first checks to see if the new value for name is not the same as the current name value. If they are different, then the old object is released and a copy (as instructed by the @property directive) of the aName is made and stored in the name instance variable. Note that in the dealloc method, you need to release name.

The second property declaration:
```
@property (nonatomic, retain) Employee* manager
```
can be realized by the compiler as follows:

```
-(Employee*) manager
{
  return manager;
}

-(void) setManager:(Employee*) theManager
```

```
{
  if(manager != theManager){
    [manager release];
    manager = [theManager retain];
  }
}
```

The setter first checks to see if theManager is not the same as the instance variable manager. If they are different objects, the old manager object is released and the manager instance variable is set to a retained theManager. Note that you need to release manager in the dealloc method.

The third property declaration:

@property (nonatomic, assign) NSString* address

can be realized by the compiler as follows:

```
-(NSString*) address
{
  return address;
}

-(void) setAddress:(NSString*)anAddress
{
  address = anAddress;
}
```

Notice that, since the property directive is assign, the setter just stores the memory address of anAddress in the instance variable.

The fourth property declaration is:

@property (nonatomic, copy) NSMutableArray* achievements

When dealing with mutable collections such as NSMutableArray, the compiler-provided setter/getter might not be appropriate. Let us see a possible synthesis of the achievements property.

```
-(NSMutableArray*) achievements{
  return achievements;
}
-(void) setAchievements:(NSMutableArray*) newAchievements{
  if(achievements != newAchievements){
    [achievements release];
    achievements = [newAchievements copy];
  }
}
```

There are two problems with such a synthesis:

1. The caller of the getter will receive a reference to the actual achievements array. That means that the caller will be able to modify the state of the Employee instance. In some cases, you might not want such a behavior.

You might try to rewrite the getter yourself as:

```
-(NSArray*) achievements{
  return achievements;
}
```

This, however, will not solve the problem as the returned reference, although made to be an immutable array, is still an NSMutableArray and can be changed by the caller. One solution to this problem is to return an autoreleased copy of the collection as follows:

```
-(NSArray*) achievements{
  return [[achievements copy] autorelease];
}
```

This way, the caller will receive an immutable array. Note that, following the memory management convention, the caller is not responsible for deallocating the returned value; thus we autoreleased it before returning it. If it seems confusing to you, at present, please return to this discussion after reading Chapter 2.

2. The synthesized setter will assign an immutable copy to the mutable array instance variable. You will not be able to add/remove objects to/from this array. Therefore, you have to write the setter yourself. The following is a possible valid implementation:

```
-(void) setAchievements:(NSMutableArray*)
  newAchievements{
  if(achievements != newAchievements){
    [achievements release];
    achievements = [newAchievements mutableCopy];
  }
}
```

Notice the use of the mutableCopy instead of the copy. Refer to Chapter 2 for further information on arrays and collections in general.

The fifth property:

```
@property (nonatomic, getter=isMarried) BOOL married
```

instructs the compiler to change the name of the getter accessor to isMarried instead of the conventional name married. The following is a possible implementation of the property:

```
-(BOOL) isMarried
{
  return married;
}

-(void) setMarried:(BOOL)newMarried
{
  married = newMarried;
}
```

The sixth property:

```
@property (nonatomic, copy) NSString* disability
```

has a synthesis directive as `@synthesize disability=_disability`. It will be synthesized exactly as we saw the synthesis of the first property, except that we tell the compiler to associate the `disability` property with the `_disability` instance variable.

A possible synthesis of this property is as follows:

```
-(NSString *) disability
{
  return _disability;
}


-(void) setDisability :(NSString *) newDisability
{
  if (_disability != newDisability){
    [_disability release];
    _disability = [newDisability copy];
  }
}
```

We have seen how we can realize the different types of property declarations. Of course, you will, for most of the time, rely on the compiler to generate the accessor methods and not write them yourself. In some special cases, such as mutable collections, and depending on your application's requirements, you may want to write some of these accessor methods yourself.

## 1.5   Categories

A category is an Objective-C feature that allows you to extend the capabilities of a given class. This feature works even if you do not have access to the source code of the class you are extending.

When you extend a given class through a category, the extension is inherited by all its subclasses. Of course, the additional methods defined by the category are only seen by your program.

To illustrate this powerful feature, let us extend the NSObject class by adding an instance method to it:

```
@interface NSObject(EnhancedObject)
-(NSComparisonResult) rankSelf :(NSObject *) anotherObject;
@end

@implementation NSObject(EnhancedObject)
-(NSComparisonResult) rankSelf :(NSObject *) anotherObject
{
  if ([self retainCount] > [anotherObject retainCount]){
    return NSOrderedDescending;
  }
  else if ([self retainCount] < [anotherObject retainCount]){
```

```
    return NSOrderedAscending;
  }
  else return NSOrderedSame;
}
@end
```

To declare a category on an existing class such as NSObject, you add the name of the category in brackets after the class name. The actual definition of the category follows a similar form. You define the category methods in the methods' section as you define regular methods.

The following illustrates the usage of this category. Since all objects are descendants of NSObject, all objects, in your application, will be able to rank themselves.

```
NSMutableString *string =
   [[ NSMutableString alloc ] initWithString :@"string" ];
Employee *emp1 = [[ Employee alloc ] init ];
[ emp1 retain ];
NSComparisonResult result = [ emp1 rankSelf : string ];
```

Here, we ask the emp1 object of type Employee to rank itself with the string object of type NSMutableString. Neither Employee class nor NSMutableString class defines the rankSelf: method. The category EnhancedObject defined on NSObject, the ancestor of both, however, does define such a method. When emp1 receives the message rankSelf:, the message is propagated up the inheritance chain to NSObject.

This feature is widely used in Cocoa. For example, the UIStringDrawing.h file defines a category UIStringDrawing (see Listing 1.3) on NSString, thus making every NSString object capable of drawing itself.

**Listing 1.3**   An example of a Cocoa category defined on NSString for the purpose of drawing.

```
@interface NSString ( UIStringDrawing )
- ( CGSize )
drawAtPoint :( CGPoint ) point
withFont :( UIFont *) font ;
- ( CGSize )
drawAtPoint :( CGPoint ) point
forWidth :( CGFloat ) width
withFont :( UIFont *) font
lineBreakMode :( UILineBreakMode ) lineBreakMode ;
  .
  .
  .

@end
```

## 1.6   Posing

Posing is an Objective-C programming feature that allows you to swap one class, A, with another class, B. Swapping will result in all active instances that are subclasses of A, as well as all future instances of A or its subclasses, to use B instead of A. Therefore, after posing, all messages sent to A will, instead, be sent to B. This requires that B be a subclass of A. B can override existing methods, and add new methods, but it cannot add new instance variables.

Unlike categories, where the same method defined in the category replaces the one defined in the original class, a posing class that overrides one of its parent's methods can still call the overridden method using super. Posing is customarily used in testing scenarios.

The posing is achieved by a single call to the NSObject's class method defined as:

```
+ (void)poseAsClass:(Class)aClass
```

For example,

```
[B poseAsClass: [A class]];
```

This should be done at the beginning of the program before any instance of A is created.

## 1.7   Exceptions and Errors

As a developer, even the simplest of your applications will some day face an unexpected event resulting in a change in the normal execution of your code. This event could simply be a division-by-zero, sending an undefined message to an object, or adding an element to an immutable collection. Regardless of the type of the error, your application needs to be aware of the possibility of its occurrence so that it can handle it gracefully when it does occur.

Cocoa divides these unexpected events into two categories: (1) those that are the developer's fault, and (2) those that are the user's fault. The problems that the developer is responsible for are called *exceptions*, while the problems that are user-specific are called *errors*. In Cocoa, exceptions are dealt with during the development of the application, and errors are used during the lifetime of the application. Cocoa frameworks use exceptions and errors. Therefore, as a Cocoa developer, you are expected to master both techniques.

### 1.7.1   Exceptions

Modern languages, such as Java and C++, provide language constructs for exception handling. Objective-C is no exception, for it too provides the same capabilities. To capture a possible exception, you enclose the problematic code with a try block. To process the actual exception, you use a catch() block. If you want to execute some statements regardless of whether an exception occurred or not (e.g., releasing memory, etc.), you enclose these statements in a finally block.

But what is an exception and how it is signaled? An exception can be any Cocoa object. However, as a Cocoa developer, you should use NSException or any subclass of it. An exception is signaled by being *thrown* or *raised*. Objective-C provides the @throw directive for throwing an exception and the NSException class defines a raise instance method for raising an exception. Using the @throw directive, you can throw any Cocoa object, not just an instance of NSException.

However, using the `raise` method, you can only throw an NSException object. Other than that, both techniques accomplish the same thing.

The structure of exception handling follows the following pattern:

```
@try {
    // statements that may cause an exception
}
@catch (NSException *e) {
    // statements that handle an exception
    @throw; // optionally re-throwing the exception
}
@finally {
    // statements that should be executed regardless
    // of having an exception or not
}
```

You basically surround the potentially problematic code with a @try directive. To actually process the exception, you use an @catch() block. The catch block takes the exception object as its only parameter. As we mentioned above, the exception object does not have to be an instance of NSException; any Cocoa object can be thrown/caught. For example, you can have code like the following, where an instance of NSString is being caught.

```
@catch(NSString *str){
.
.
.
}
```

However, as we mentioned above, you should stick with NSException or any of its subclasses.

Optionally, you can have a finally block where you put in it any code that is required to be executed regardless of the occurrence of an exception. This code usually releases memory and closes opened files.

You can optionally re-throw the exception to the next level on the call stack. You use the @throw directive to do that. You do not need to specify the exception object, however, as it is implied. Note that, if you re-throw an exception, the @finally block gets executed before actually throwing the exception to the lower level.

Let's illustrate these concepts with a concrete example as shown below.

```
#import <Foundation/Foundation.h>
int main(int argc, char *argv[]) {
  NSAutoreleasePool * pool =
        [[NSAutoreleasePool alloc] init];
  NSMutableArray *myArray =
      [[NSMutableArray alloc] initWithCapacity:0];
  [myArray addObject:@"an object"];
  [myArray replaceObjectAtIndex:1
          withObject:@"another object"];
```

```
[myArray release];
[pool release];
return 0;
}
```

The code above creates an array, then adds an element to it, and after that it attempts to replace that element with another object. If we run this code, an exception will occur and the program will be terminated with an error message similar to the following:

```
Exception Type:  EXC_BREAKPOINT (SIGTRAP)
Exception Codes: 0x0000000000000002, 0x0000000000000000
Crashed Thread:  0

Application Specific Information:
*** Terminating app due to uncaught exception 'NSRangeException',
reason: '*** -[NSCFArray replaceObjectAtIndex:withObject:]:
index (1) beyond bounds (1)'
```

What has happened here is that we are using an invalid index (1) on an array of size 1. The method `replaceObjectAtIndex:withObject:` raised an exception upon seeing this invalid index. This method is declared as:

```
- (void)replaceObjectAtIndex:(NSUInteger)index
       withObject:(id)anObject
```

If you look at the documentation of this method, you will notice that the method can potentially raise two exceptions: (1) it raises an `NSRangeException` if `index` is beyond the end of the receiver, and (2) it raises an `NSInvalidArgumentException` if `anObject` is `nil`.

Let's rewrite the `main()` function adding an exception handler.

```
int
main(int argc, char *argv[]) {
  NSAutoreleasePool * pool =
       [[NSAutoreleasePool alloc] init];
  NSMutableArray *myArray = nil;
  @try {
    myArray = [[NSMutableArray alloc] initWithCapacity:0];
    [myArray addObject:@"an object"];
    [myArray replaceObjectAtIndex:1
       withObject:@"another object"];
  }
  @catch (NSException *e) {
    printf("Exception Name: %s. Reason: %s",
        [[e name] cString],
        [[e reason] cString] );
  }
  @finally {
```

```
    [ myArray release ];
    [ pool release ];
  }
  return 0;
}
```

We surrounded the problematic code with a `try` block. In catching the exception, we just print an error message. The `finally` block is important as we need to release the allocated memory. Instead of the application being terminated, it outputs the following useful message but, most importantly, exits gracefully.

```
Exception Name: NSRangeException.
Reason: *** -[NSCFArray replaceObjectAtIndex:withObject:]:
index (1) beyond bounds (1)
```

There are three important pieces of information that every instance of NSException has:

1. name. A string that identifies the exception. This name has to be unique, relatively short, and never nil. You should never start the names of your exceptions with "NS", but rather start names with something unique to your application and organization.

2. reason. This string attribute is also mandatory. It stores a human-readable explanation of the exception.

3. userInfo. This attribute is an optional dictionary (see Section 2.3). Using this dictionary, the code that generates the exception can communicate with the exception handler.

If you are writing a method and you would like to communicate with the caller via exceptions, you need to be able to create exceptions and then throw them. To create an exception, you can use NSException's class method exceptionWithName:reason:userInfo: declared as:

```
+ (NSException *)exceptionWithName:(NSString *)name
                reason:(NSString *)reason
                userInfo:(NSDictionary *)userInfo
```

This method returns an autoreleased NSException object having the specified attributes. It returns nil if no such exception can be created.

In the following, we present an example for creating and throwing an exception.

```
-(void) myMethod:(NSString *) string {
  if (string == nil){
    NSException *anException =
        [NSException
          exceptionWithName:@"NSInvalidArgument"
          reason:@"Argument is nil"
          userInfo:nil ];
        @throw anException;
        // OR [anException raise];
  }
```

```
  else {
    // proceed normally
  }
}
```

### Nesting exceptions

Because an exception handler can optionally re-throw the exception (or a new one), exceptions can be nested. For example, consider the scenario where you have a method that adds a record to a database. This method calls another low-level method that handles the actual physical insertion of the record in a file. The following two listings show the database `addRecord:` and the `insertRecord:` methods.

```
-(void) addRecord:(Record *) record {
  @try {
    [file insertRecord:record];
  }
  @catch (NSException * e) {
    // create a new exception, db,
    // name=MYDBException
    @throw db;
  }
  @finally {
    // close files, etc.
    // release memory
  }
}

-(void) insertRecord:(Record *) record {
  @try {
    // open the file
    // seek
    // insert record
  }
  @catch (NSException * e) {
    // locally handle exception
    @throw;
  }
  @finally {
    //close file
    // release memory
  }
}
```

Here, we see the nested exceptions. If an exception occur while accessing the file, that exception is caught in the `insertRecord:` method, dealt with locally, and re-thrown. The `addRecord:` method has an exception handler that catches the re-thrown exception. It creates a new exception, named `MYDBException`, and throws it. This last exception is communicated to the caller of the `addRecord:` method. In case of a failure, the caller of `addRecord:` sees a meaningful *database* exception rather than the low-level *file* access exception. Note that nesting levels can be arbitrary.

## 1.7.2   Errors

As a C-programmer, you must be used to using error codes as a means to conveying errors to the caller. This approach is limited in that you can only convey a single piece of information (a number) to the caller.

Cocoa uses objects of type `NSError` (or subclasses of it) as the main mechanism to convey runtime errors to users.

A Cocoa method follows a pattern in conveying errors:

1. The return value of a method is used to indicate failure or success. If the return value is of type `BOOL`, a `NO` indicates an error. If, on the other hand, the return value is of type `id`, a `nil` indicates a failure.

2. As a secondary mechanism to further elaborate on the error, the user can pass a pointer to an `NSError` object as the last parameter of the method. If this parameter is not `NULL`, the method stores a new autoreleased `NSError` object using that pointer.

An `NSError` object stores three important attributes:

1. `domain` – a string representing the error domain. Different frameworks, libraries, and even classes, have different error domains. Examples of error domains are `NSPOSIXErrorDomain` and `NSCocoaErrorDomain`. Applications can, and should, create their own unique error domains. If you are creating an error domain, make sure it is unique by prefixing the domain name with the name of the application and your organization's name.

2. `code` – an integer error code that has meaning within the domain. Two `NSError` objects with the same error code but different domains are different.

3. `userInfo` – a dictionary (see Section 2.3) containing objects related to the error.

Let's illustrate error handling in Cocoa. The following example deliberately causes an error. It handles the error by displaying the three attributes of the error described above.

```
NSError *myError = nil;
NSURL *myUrl    =
    [NSURL URLWithString:@"http://fox.gov"];
NSString *str =  [NSString
            stringWithContentsOfURL:myUrl
            encoding:NSUTF8StringEncoding
            error:&myError];
```

```
if( str == nil ){
    printf("Domain: %s. Code: %d \n",
        [[myError domain] cString],
        [myError code]);
    NSDictionary *dic = [myError userInfo];
    printf("Dictionary: %s\n", [[dic description] cString]);
}
```

You do not necessarily need to know URL loading at this stage as we will go over it in detail, later in this text. What you need to know is that we make a call to a Cocoa method to obtain an object (here, this object is the page as an NSString object). The method returns nil if there was an error, and allows the user to specify a pointer to an NSError object for further information on the error. We pass a pointer to an NSError object and make the call. Since the site http://fox.gov does not exist, the returned value of the method is nil, and the NSError object is created and autoreleased by the Cocoa method.

The output of this code snippet is the error domain, code, and the contents of the dictionary.

```
Domain: NSCocoaErrorDomain. Code: 260
Dictionary: {
    NSURL = http://fox.gov;
    NSUnderlyingError = Error Domain=NSURLErrorDomain
    Code=-1003
    UserInfo=0x4183a0 "can\325t find host";
}
```

We notice that the domain is NSCocoaErrorDomain with code 260. The userInfo dictionary contains two entries: (1) the NSURL with value http://fox.gov, and (2) the NSUnderlyingError with value Error Domain=NSURLErrorDomain Code=-1003 UserInfo=0x4183a0 "can't find host".

### Creating an NSError instance

We have seen how we can handle an error object that was created for us, but oftentimes, we are required to write methods that return an autoreleased error object to our clients. To create an NSError object, you can use one of the several class/instance methods available. For example, the class method errorWithDomain:code:userInfo: returns an autoreleased error object. Another way for obtaining an error object is to allocate it using alloc and initialize it using initWithDomain:code:userInfo:. For example, assuming the last argument of your method, error, is of type NSError**, the following will create a new NSError object for the caller.

```
*error = [[NSError alloc]
    initWithDomain:CompanyCustomDomain
    code:12 userInfo:dictionary];
```

## 1.8   Key-value coding (KVC)

Upto now, we have seen two ways of accessing the instance variables in an object: either using accessor methods, or directly. Cocoa defines a third way that allows you to access the instance variables of a class indirectly. This technique is called key-value coding (KVC).

KVC is, declared in the protocol NSKeyValueCoding. This protocol is implemented by NSObject the root of all Cocoa objects. At the heart of this protocol, there are two basic methods that you use: (1) setValue:forKey: sets the value of a given key, and (2) valueForKey: retrieves the value of a given key.

The valueForKey: method is declared in the protocol as:

− (**id**)valueForKey:(NSString *)key

where key is an ASCII encoded string that starts with a lowercase letter and does not contain whitespace.

The setValue:forKey method is declared in the protocol as:

− (**void**)setValue:(**id**)value forKey:(NSString *)key

where value is a Cocoa object (i.e., a subclass from NSObject), and key is an instance of NSString with the same restrictions as stated above.

For KVC to work, you need to follow some Cocoa conventions in naming accessor methods. Given a key xyz, there should be an accessor named xyz or isXyz defined in your class in order to use the valueForKey: method. Similarly, to use the setValue:forKey: method, your class should define a setter named setXyz:.

Several keys can be dot-separated to form what is called a *key path*. The key path defines the sequence of object properties to traverse. For example, the key path key1.key2.key3 says: obtain the object specified by key1 from the receiver, then obtain the object specified by key2 from the object you have just obtained from the receiver, and finally, obtain the object specified by key3 from the last object you have obtained using key2.

To retrieve the value of a given key path, use the method valueForKeyPath:. To set the value for a key path, use the setValue:forKeyPath: method.

### 1.8.1   An example illustrating KVC

Let's illustrate KVC with an example: consider the Person class declared and defined as follows:

```
@interface Person: NSObject{
    NSString *name;
    NSArray *allies;
    Person *lover;
}
@property NSString *name;
@property NSArray *allies;
@property Person *lover;
−(id)initWithName:(NSString*) theName;
@end
```

```
@implementation Person
@synthesize name, allies, lover;
-(id)initWithName:(NSString*) theName{
  if(self = [super init]){
    name = theName;
  }
  return self;
}
@end
```

In addition, consider the `Community` class declared and defined as follows:

```
@interface Community : NSObject
{
    NSArray *population;
}
@property NSArray *population;
@end
```

```
@implementation Community
@synthesize population;
@end
```

Before delving into the KVC example, you need to notice how the `initWithName:` method is implemented. First, notice how we invoke the `super`'s `init` first and use the result as the value of the variable `self`. Second, notice that we assign the instance variable, `name`, directly. The reason we do that has nothing to do with our KVC example. It just shows that if you want the assignment to use the synthesized setter, you should use:

```
self.name = theName
```

The setter is `assign` (default), so we skip it and assign the instance variable directly. Be careful when you set instance variables inside your class. If you do not use `self`, you end up assigning the value rather than invoking the setter. Also, be careful when you implement the setter yourself. If, in your setter, you set the instance variable using `self`, you end up with an infinite loop which results in a stack overflow and an application crash.

Let's use the above two classes to put KVC into action. Listing 1.4 shows the main function that demonstrates KVC. We first create and initialize seven `Person` instances and one `Community` instance. Next, we use KVC to set the `allies` array. KVC is used after that to set the `lover` attribute. Then we set the `population` of the lost `Community` instance with an array instance containing the seven `Person` instances.

Now, we would like to use KVC to retrieve values using keys and key paths. The line

```
[lost valueForKeyPath:@"population"];
```

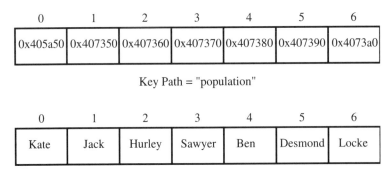

Figure 1.1  Using keys and key paths to retrieve the population array and an array of names of population from the lost instance.

retrieves the population array in the lost object. The key population is applied to the lost instance producing the array of Person instances returned to the caller. Figure 1.1 shows the result graphically.

Next, the line

```
[lost  valueForKeyPath:@"population.name"];
```

retrieves an array of names representing the population in the lost instance. This is a key path example. First, the key population is applied to the receiver, lost. This will produce an array of Person instances. Next, the key name is applied to each and every entry in this array. This will produce an instance of NSString. The array of NSString instances will be returned as the result. Figure 1.1 shows the result graphically.

The line:

```
[lost  valueForKeyPath:@"population.allies"];
```

is an interesting one. Let's follow it to come up with the result. First, the population key is applied to the receiver lost. This will produce an array of Person instances. Next, the key allies is applied to each and every Person instance in that array. This will produce an array of Person instances. So, now we have an array of an array of Person instances. This will be the result and will be returned to the caller. Figure 1.2 shows the result graphically.

The line:

```
[lost  valueForKeyPath:@"population.allies.allies"];
```

goes even further. The subkey path population.allies produces the exact result as above, but now we apply another key, allies, to the result. This will produce an array of an array of an array of Person instances as shown in Fig. 1.3.

The line:

```
[lost  valueForKeyPath:@"population.allies.allies.name"];
```

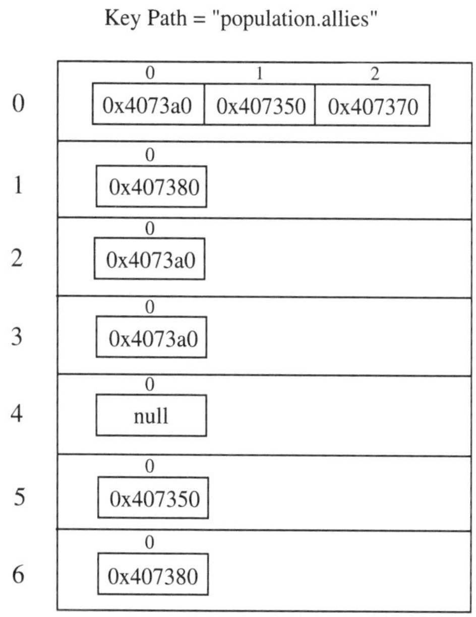

Key Path = "population.allies"

**Figure 1.2** Graphical representation of the result obtained from applying the key path `popula-`
`tion.allies` to the `lost` instance.

does the same as above, except that it further applies the key `name` to every `Person` instance in the
array of an array of an array of `Person` instances.

The code:

```
theArray =
      [lost    valueForKeyPath:
           @"population.allies.name"];
  NSMutableSet     *uniqueAllies =
        [NSMutableSet setWithCapacity:5];
  for(NSArray *a in theArray){
    if(![a isMemberOfClass:[NSNull class]]){
      for(NSString *n in a){
        printf("%s ", [n   cString]);
        [uniqueAllies addObject:n];
      }
      printf("\n");
    }
  }
```

Key Path = "population.allies.allies"

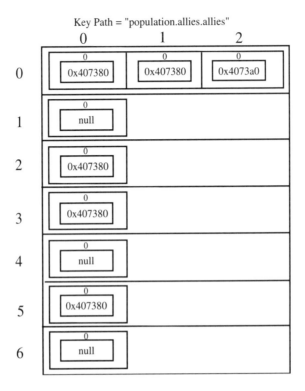

**Figure 1.3** Graphical representation of the result from applying the key path `popula-tion.allies.allies` to the `lost` instance.

demonstrates the structure of the result from applying the key path `population.allies.name`. It enumerates all names, and produces a set of unique names. See Chapter 2 for more information on arrays and sets.

One thing you need to be aware of is the `nil` problem. Since some of the instance variables of objects can be `nil`, and collections in Cocoa cannot have `nil` entries, Cocoa uses the `NSNull` class to represent `nil` entries. In the above code, we just check to see if the entry is an instance of `NSNull`. If so, we skip it.

Some may confuse collections and key paths, thinking that a key path always results in a collection instance. But that is not true as these two concepts are orthogonal. The statement:

```
NSString *luckyPerson  =
        [jack valueForKeyPath :@"lover.lover.lover.name" ];
```

will result in an instance of `NSString` with the value `@"Hurley"`.

**Listing 1.4**   Demonstration code for key-value coding (KVC).

```
int main(int argc, char *argv[]) {

  NSAutoreleasePool * pool =
          [[NSAutoreleasePool alloc] init];

  Person  *kate=
     [[Person alloc] initWithName:@"Kate"];
    Person  *jack=
        [[Person alloc] initWithName:@"Jack"];
    Person  *hurley=
        [[Person alloc] initWithName:@"Hurley"];
    Person  *sawyer=
        [[Person alloc] initWithName:@"Sawyer"];
    Person  *ben =
        [[Person alloc] initWithName:@"Ben"];
    Person  *desmond=
        [[Person alloc] initWithName:@"Desmond"];
    Person  *locke=
        [[Person alloc] initWithName:@"Locke"];

  Community *lost = [[Community  alloc] init];

  [kate   setValue:[NSArray
     arrayWithObjects:locke, jack, sawyer, nil]
  forKey:@"allies"];
  [hurley setValue:[NSArray
     arrayWithObjects:locke, nil] forKey:@"allies"];
  [sawyer setValue:[NSArray
     arrayWithObjects:locke, nil] forKey:@"allies"];
  [desmond setValue:[NSArray
     arrayWithObjects:jack, nil] forKey:@"allies"];
  [locke setValue:[NSArray
     arrayWithObjects:ben, nil] forKey:@"allies"];
  [jack setValue:[NSArray
     arrayWithObjects:ben, nil] forKey:@"allies"];

  [jack setValue:kate   forKey:@"lover"];
  [kate setValue:sawyer forKey:@"lover"];
  [sawyer setValue:hurley forKey:@"lover"];

  [lost setValue:[NSArray
     arrayWithObjects: kate, jack, hurley,
                 sawyer, ben, desmond,
```

```
                    locke,  nil ]  forKey :@"population" ];

   NSArray  *theArray  =
            [ lost    valueForKeyPath :@"population" ];
  theArray  =  [ lost    valueForKeyPath :@"population.name" ];
  theArray  =  [ lost    valueForKeyPath :@"population.allies" ];
  theArray  =
       [ lost    valueForKeyPath :@"population.allies.allies" ];
  theArray  =
     [ lost    valueForKeyPath :
          @"population.allies.allies.name" ];
  theArray  =
     [ lost    valueForKeyPath :
            @"population.allies.name" ];
  NSMutableSet      *uniqueAllies  =
          [ NSMutableSet  setWithCapacity :5 ];
  for ( NSArray  *a  in  theArray ){
    if ( ![ a  isMemberOfClass :[ NSNull  class ]]){
      for ( NSString  *n  in  a ){
        printf ( "%s  ",  [ n    cString ]);
        [ uniqueAllies  addObject :n ];
      }
      printf ( "\n" );
    }
  }
  NSString  *luckyPerson  =
          [ jack  valueForKeyPath :@"lover.lover.lover.name" ];
  [ kate  release ];
  [ jack  release ];
  [ hurley  release ];
  [ sawyer  release ];
  [ ben  release ];
  [ desmond  release ];
  [ locke  release ];
  [ pool  release ];
  return  0;
}
```

## 1.9   Multithreading

Multithreading is an important subject in computing. In a single-core system, multithreading gives the user the illusion of concurrent processing. It allows the developer to have an application with a responsive user interface while performing time-consuming tasks in the background. In a multicore system, the importance of multithreading is highlighted even further. Developers want to design applications to utilize the multicore computers more efficiently. Even if the computer system is a single-core, they still want to design the application to be user-centric and to have maximum flexibility.

Multithreading in Cocoa is very simple to achieve. All you have to do is to make sure that you design the multithreaded tasks[3] to have minimal interaction with either the main thread or among the other threads. When threads interact with each other by using shared data structures, problems manifest themselves in the form of corrupted data or difficult-to-find bugs.

A simple approach for multithreading is the use of *operation objects*. You can use operation objects by either subclassing the NSOperation class or by using a concrete subclass of it called NSInvocationOperation. Using the latter approach makes transforming your code into a concurrent application even easier.

Let's assume that you have a method, possibly calling other methods, in a class, and you want to run this method in the background. Without multithreading, the structure of your code will look something like the following.

In one of your objects, you have, in one of the methods:

```
[myComputationallyIntensiveTaskObject  compute:data];
```

In the class that actually does the job (i.e., the class of myComputationallyIntensive-TaskObject) which defines the compute: method, you have:

```
-(void)  compute:(id)data{

  // do some computationally-intensive calculations on data
  // store the either partial or final results
  // in some data structure, ds, for others to use
}
```

The compute: method operates on data and performs computationally intensive calculations. It either stores partial results in an instance variable for other threads to consume, or waits until it finishes the computation to present the final results for consumers. It all depends on the application.

Here are the steps you need to take in order to put the compute: method in the background, thus making the main thread responsive to the user while performing this task.

1. Create a launching method. Create a method in the class of myComputationally-IntensiveTaskObject. This method will be the one used by other objects if they choose to run the task in the background. Call it something meaningful such as initiateCompute: or computeInBackground:.

2. In computeInBackground:, create an operation queue. An operation queue is an object of type NSOperationQueue that holds operation objects. You do not necessarily have to create the operation queue here, as long as you have a queue created somewhere in the program.

---

[3]A task is a piece of code that accomplishes a specific goal (e.g., find the square root of a number).

3. Create an `NSInvocationOperation` object. This will be your operation object. You configure this object with enough information so that the new thread will know where to start executing.

4. Add the newly created operation object to the queue so that it starts running.

5. Since every thread requires its own autorelease pool, in the original `compute:` method, add a new autorelease pool at the beginning and `release` it at the end.

6. If the `compute:` method produces data to be used by other threads, synchronize access to this data using locks. Use locks to access this data in *all* places within your program that use (either read or write) this data.

And that's all! Let's apply these steps to our example and see how easy it is to use multithreading in Cocoa. Listing 1.5 shows the updated code.

We added two instance variables in the class, one for the operation and the other for the operation queue. We also added three methods: the `computeInBackground:` for initiating background computation, the `computationFinished` to check if the final result is ready, and `computationResult` for retrieving the final result. This is the simplest inter-thread communication. Depending on your application requirements, you might opt for more sophisticated protocols. In the method that initiates the background thread, `computeInBackground:`, we start by allocating the operation queue. Next, we allocate the `NSInvocationOperation` and initialize it with the tasks object, main method, and the input data. The initialization method, `initWithTarget:selector:object:` is declared as:

— (**id**) initWithTarget:(**id**) target  selector:(SEL)sel
            object:(**id**) arg

The `target` is the object defining the selector `sel`. The selector `sel` is the method that is invoked when the operation is run. You can pass at most one parameter object to the selector through the `arg` argument. Note that the selector has exactly one parameter. In the cases where you do not have a need to pass an argument, you can pass a `nil`.

After setting up the operation queue and creating and initializing the new operation object, we add the operation object to the queue so that it starts executing. This is done using the `addOperation:` method of the `NSInvocationOperation` object.

As we have mentioned before, autorelease pools are not shared across threads. Since our `compute:` method will be run in its own thread, we create and initialize an `NSAutoreleasePool` object at the beginning and release it at the end of the method. We keep the original `compute:` method intact.

Any time the shared data, `ds`, is accessed, we use a locking mechanism in order to guarantee data integrity. The shared data can be an instance variable of the object defining the method `compute:` or it can be in another object. Regardless of what shared data you have, if it is accessed from more than one thread, use a lock.

Locking is made easy with the `@synchronized()` directive. The `@synchronized()` directive is used to guarantee exclusive access to a block of code for only one thread. It takes one object as an argument. This object will act as the lock to that piece of code. It is not necessary that the data you are trying to protect is used as a lock. You can use `self`, another object, or even the `Class` object itself as the lock. It is important to note that if the sensitive data structure you are trying to protect is accessed from other parts of your program, the *same* locking object must be used. To enhance the concurrency of your program, delay access to the shared data till the end (i.e., when it needs to be written) and use different locking objects for different unrelated sections of your code.

**Listing 1.5**    A multithreaded application using operation objects.

```objc
// Changes to interface
@interface MyComputationallyIntensiveTask {

...
  NSInvocationOperation  *computeOp;
  NSOperationQueue        *operationQueue;
}
...
-(void) computeInBackground:(id)data;
-(BOOL) computationFinished;
-(DS*) computationResult;
@end

@implementation MyComputationallyIntensiveTask
...
// additional methods
-(void) computeInBackground:(id)data{
  operationQueue = [[NSOperationQueue alloc] init];
  computeOp = [[[NSInvocationOperation alloc]
         initWithTarget:self
         selector:@selector(compute:)
         object:data] autorelease];
  [operationQueue addOperation: computeOp];
}

-(BOOL) computationFinished{
  @synchronized(ds){
    // if ds is complete return YES, else return NO
  }
}

-(DS*) computationResult{
  if([self computationFinished] == YES){
    return ds;
  }
  else
    return nil;
}
```

```
// changes to original method
-(void) compute:(id)data{

NSAutoreleasePool * threadPool =
      [[NSAutoreleasePool alloc] init];

  // do some computationally-intensive calculations
  // on data store the (either partial or final) results
  // in  some data structure, ds, for others to you
  @synchronized(ds){
    // store result in ds
  }
  [threadPool release];
}


// Usage from another object
-(void)someOtherMethod{
...
[myComputationallyIntensiveTaskObject
  computeInBackground:data];
// be responsive to user GUI
...
  //If you need some results or all results
  if(myComputationallyIntensiveTaskObject
  computationFinished]  == YES){
     result =
     [myComputationallyIntensiveTaskObject computationResult];
  }
}
@end
```

## 1.10   Summary

We have certainly covered a lot of ground in this chapter. In Section 1.1, we introduced the mechanism for declaring and defining classes. Then, we talked about how an object interacts with other objects by sending messages to them. In Section 1.2, we covered the topic of memory management. We illustrated how to allocate objects and how to initialize these objects. We discussed the concept of retain count and how every object maintains one such counter. We also covered the topic of autorelease pools and outlined the responsibilities that clients have with respect to releasing objects. In Section 1.3, we discussed the protocols feature of Objective-C. Protocols were shown to be a powerful feature that allows, among other things, the ability to realize multiple-inheritance in a single-inheritance language. In Section 1.4, we discussed properties. A property is a feature of Objective-C that allows you to declaratively generate setter/getter accessor methods for instance variables. After that, we covered the topic of categories in Section 1.5. Using the category feature, we showed how you can extend the capabilities of existing classes without even having their source code. Posing was covered in Section 1.6. This facilitates the replacement of one class by another class that is a descendant of it and it is mostly useful as a testing feature. Exceptions and errors were covered in Section 1.7. Exceptions are usually used by the developer in finding bugs, while errors are used in production code for conveying runtime errors due to the user's environment. In Section 1.8, we introduced the concept of key-value coding (KVC). KVC provides the ability to access object properties indirectly. KVC is widely used in Cocoa and we gave a lengthy treatment of the subject. Finally, multithreading was discussed. In particular, we outlined a simple approach for multithreading using operation objects.

## Problems

(1) Consider the following class declaration, definition, and usage:

```
@interface A
-(int)doSomething;
@end
@implementation A
-(int)doSomething{
    return 1;
}
@end
int main(int argc, char *argv[])
{
  A *a = [[A alloc] init];
  int v = [a doSomething];
  [a release];
}
```

Study the above code and comment on the outcome of the main() function.

(2) Consider the following class and its usage in the main() function. What is the last statement executed and why?

```
1  @interface B : NSObject{
2      NSString *myString;
3  }
4  @property(nonatomic) NSString * myString;
5  -(unichar)getFirstCharacter;
6  @end
7
8  @implementation B
9  @synthesize myString;
10 -(unichar)getFirstCharacter{
```

```
11    return [myString characterAtIndex:0];
12  }
13  @end
14
15  int main(int argc, char *argv[])
16  {
17    NSAutoreleasePool * pool1 =
18          [[NSAutoreleasePool alloc] init];
19    NSMutableString *str =
20        [NSMutableString stringWithString:@"Where am I?"];
21    B *b = [[B alloc] init];
22    b.myString = str;
23    [pool1 release];
24    unichar x = [b getFirstCharacter];
25    [b release];
26  }
```

(3) The following code declares and defines a `Person` and a `Dog`, and then uses the two classes.

```
@interface Person: NSObject{}
-(void)bark;
@end

@implementation Person
-(void)bark{
  printf("Woof\n");
}
@end

@interface Dog : NSObject{}
-(void)bark;
-(void)bark:(NSString *)a;
@end

@implementation Dog
-(void)bark:(NSString *)a{
  printf("Woof\n");
}
-(void) bark{
  printf("Woof woof\n");}
@end

int main(int argc, char *argv[]) {

  NSAutoreleasePool * pool =
```

```
                  [[ NSAutoreleasePool alloc ] init ];
        SEL sel = @selector( bark );
        SEL sel1 = @selector( bark : );
        Person *aPerson = [[ Person alloc ] init ];
        Dog *aDog = [[ Dog alloc ] init ];
        .
        .
        .

  }
```

Answer the following questions:

(a) What is the value of `equal` after the following statement?

```
   BOOL equal = sel == sel1 ;
```

(b) What happens when the following statement is executed?

```
   [ aPerson performSelector : sel ];
```

(c) What happens when the following two statements are executed?

```
   [ aDog bark ];
   [ aDog bark :@" " ];
```

(d) What is the result of the following statement?

```
   [ aPerson
       performSelector : NSSelectorFromString (@"bark : ") ];
```

(e) What does the following statement do?

```
   [ aDog bark : ];
```

(4) Consider the following code. Describe the outcome of each line. What is the last line executed?

```
1   NSAutoreleasePool * pool1 =
2          [[ NSAutoreleasePool alloc ] init ];
3   NSMutableArray *arr ;
4   arr = [ NSMutableArray arrayWithCapacity : 0 ];
5   NSAutoreleasePool * pool2 =
6          [[ NSAutoreleasePool alloc ] init ];
7   NSMutableString *str =
8     [ NSMutableString stringWithString :@"Howdy! " ];
9   [ arr addObject : str ];
10  [ pool2 release ];
11  int n = [ arr count ];
12  str = [ arr objectAtIndex : 0 ];
```

```
13    [ arr release ];
14    n = [ str length ];
15    [ pool1 release ];
```

(5) The following function will cause an application crash. Why? Hint: a large percentage of iPhone application crashes have to do with illegal memory access.

```
1  void function(){
2    NSAutoreleasePool *pool =
3        [[ NSAutoreleasePool alloc ] init ];
4    NSString    *myString =
5            [[[ NSString alloc ]
6            initWithString:@"Hello!"] autorelease ];
7    @try {
8      [ myString appendString:@"Hi!" ];
9    }
10   @catch (NSException * e) {
11     @throw;
12   }
13   @finally {
14     [ pool release ];
15   }
16 }
```

# 2

# Collections

As a Cocoa developer, you are provided with many classes that can help you group several of your objects together in specific ways. In this chapter, we discuss the main collection classes available to you.

The chapter is organized as follows. In Section 2.1, we address the topic of arrays. You will learn about immutable and mutable arrays, the different approaches used for copying arrays, and several sorting techniques. Section 2.2 covers the topic of sets. Sets are collections that do not impose ordering on the objects they contain. You will learn about immutable and mutable sets as well as several interesting operations on sets. In Section 2.3, we discuss dictionaries. Dictionaries allow you to store objects and retrieve them using keys. As you have seen in Section 1.7, dictionaries are widely used in Cocoa frameworks and understanding them is essential. Finally, we provide a summary in Section 2.4.

## 2.1 Arrays

You use `NSArray` and `NSMutableArray` if you would like to store/access your objects in an ordered way. `NSArray` is the immutable version of the array, allowing you to store your objects only once (during initialization). `NSMutableArray` is a subclass of `NSArray` that allows you to add/remove objects even after initialization of the collection.

To help illustrate the main concepts behind these two classes, let us use the simple class `Person` shown in Listing 2.1.

**Listing 2.1**   The class `Person` used in the arrays examples.

```
#import <Foundation/Foundation.h>

@interface Person : NSObject
{
  NSString  *name;
  NSString  *address;
}
@property(copy) NSString  *name;
@property(copy) NSString  *address;
-(id)initWithName:(NSString *)  theName
```

```
    andAddress:(NSString*) theAddress;
-(id)init;
@end

@implementation Person
@synthesize name;
@synthesize address;
-(id)initWithName:(NSString*) theName
andAddress:(NSString*) theAddress{
    self = [super init];
    if(self){
        self.name    =    theName;
        self.address =    theAddress;
    }
    return self;
}
-(id)init{
    return [self initWithName:@""
            andAddress:@""
        ];
}
-(void)dealloc{
    [name      release];
    [address   release];
    [super    dealloc];
}
@end
```

Listing 2.2 demonstrates how you can configure a static array using the NSArray class. We start by creating five instances of the class Person. Figure 2.1 shows the state of these five objects before being added to the array.

**Listing 2.2** Creating a simple immutable array.

```
int main(int argc, char *argv[])
{
    NSAutoreleasePool * pool =
                [[NSAutoreleasePool alloc] init];
    Person   *a  = [[Person alloc] init];
    Person   *b  = [[Person alloc] init];
    Person   *c  = [[Person alloc] init];
    Person   *d  = [[Person alloc] init];
    Person   *e  = [[Person alloc] init];
    NSArray *arr1 = [NSArray arrayWithObjects: a,b,c,d,e,nil];
    [pool release];
    [a release];
```

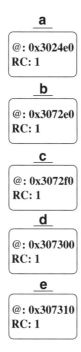

**Figure 2.1**    Five instances of `Person` before being added to an `NSArray` instance. "@" denotes an address, and "RC" denotes retain count.

```
    [b release];
    [c release];
    [d release];
    [e release];
    return 0;
}
```

There are several ways to create and initialize an `NSArray` instance. Here, we use the class method `arrayWithObjects:` and list the objects we want to initialize the array with in a comma-separated form. The last parameter must be `nil`, which means that an `NSArray` instance cannot have a `nil` element. Since the creation method used does not contain `alloc` or `new` in its name, nor do we use a `copy` method to obtain the new instance, this `NSArray` instance is not owned by us and we are not responsible for releasing it. Once the `NSArray` instance is initialized, you cannot remove/add elements from/to it. It remains static until it is deallocated.

One thing you need to be aware of is that if an object is added to a collection, its retain count is incremented by that collection. In our example, the five objects will each have a retain count of 2, right after the initialization of the `NSArray` instance as shown in Fig. 2.2. Notice how the array just holds pointers to its elements.

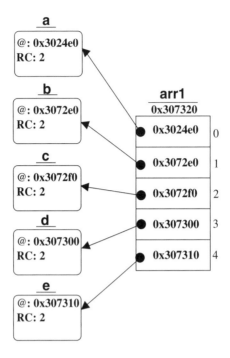

**Figure 2.2**    State of the five instances of Person after being added to an instance of NSArray. "@" denotes an address, and "RC" denotes retain count.

Once we are finished with a collection, we can release it. When you release an instance of NSArray, that instance sends a release message to each of its elements (remember that collections retain their objects when the objects are added). Since we do not own arr1, just releasing the autorelease pool will release arr1 and our five Person instances. We still have to send a release message to these five objects since we own them.

### 2.1.1   Immutable copy

Now that we know the basics of NSArray, let us look at the syntax and the semantics of making a copy of an NSArray instance. Listing 2.3 shows a sample code demonstrating this behavior. We create and add our five Person instances as we did before. After that, we ask arr1 to make a copy of itself and we store that new copy into an NSArray* local variable.

**Listing 2.3**    Immutable copy of an NSArray instance.

```
int main(int argc, char *argv[])
{
  NSAutoreleasePool *pool =
                [[NSAutoreleasePool alloc] init];
```

```
Person   *a  = [[ Person  alloc ]  init ];
Person   *b  = [[ Person  alloc ]  init ];
Person   *c  = [[ Person  alloc ]  init ];
Person   *d  = [[ Person  alloc ]  init ];
Person   *e  = [[ Person  alloc ]  init ];

NSArray  *arr1 =
             [NSArray   arrayWithObjects:  a,b,c,d,e,nil ];
NSArray  *arr2 = [ arr1  copy ];

Person   *aPerson  = [ arr1  objectAtIndex :0];
aPerson.name   = @"Marge Simpson";
aPerson.address = @"Springfield";

// Result of the following line is:
// Person at 0 is: Name: Marge Simpson, Addr: Springfield
printf("Person at %d is: Name: %s, Addr: %s\n",
    0,
    [[[ arr2  objectAtIndex :0]  name]
            cStringUsingEncoding :NSUTF8StringEncoding],
    [[[ arr2  objectAtIndex :0]  address]
            cStringUsingEncoding :NSUTF8StringEncoding ]);
// Must release arr2 since we created it using copy.
[ arr2  release ];
// must release all objects
[ a  release ];
[ b  release ];
[ c  release ];
[ d  release ];
[ e  release ];
[ pool  release ];
return  0;
}
```

After making a copy of the array, we change the first element of the original array, `arr1`. Remember that `NSArray` and `NSMutableArray` are ordered collections. Each stored element has a specific location or index. To retrieve the first element, we use the `objectAtIndex:` method with the index 0.

After we change the first element in the original array, we inspect the first element in the copy, and we discover that that element was also changed. The documented semantics of how an `NSArray` makes a copy of itself is as follows. First, `NSArray` makes a shallow copy of its elements. This means that only the pointers to these elements are copied. Second, the new instance of the `NSArray` is owned by the caller and is not autoreleased. Figure 2.3 shows the state of our five objects after making a copy of the `NSArray`.

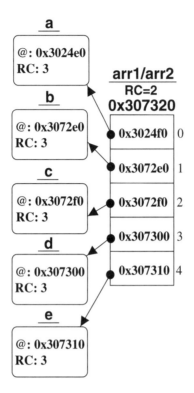

**Figure 2.3**   State of an NSArray and its immutable copy.

What we notice is that we did not even obtain a new instance of NSArray. All that happened is that: (1) arr2 got a copy of the address of arr1, which is basically a simple assignment, (2) arr1 retain count was incremented by 1, and (3) the retain count of all five objects was incremented by 1. This behavior of immutable copy makes sense as the original array object is static and does not change.

Finally, even though arr2 is just arr1, we did obtain it using a method that has copy in it. Therefore, we have to release it when we are finished with it.

### 2.1.2   Mutable copy

Until now, we have been working exclusively with NSArray and its static behavior. NSMutableArray is a mutable version of this class, which means that the number of objects stored in it can grow and shrink during the lifetime of the program. As shown in Listing 2.4, we can obtain a mutable copy of an immutable source. However, instead of using copy, we use mutableCopy.

**Listing 2.4**  Illustration of how you can obtain a mutable copy of an immutable instance of `NSArray`.

```
int main(int argc, char *argv[])
{
  NSAutoreleasePool *pool =
                    [[NSAutoreleasePool alloc] init];
  Person  *a = [[Person alloc] init];
  Person  *b = [[Person alloc] init];
  Person  *c = [[Person alloc] init];
  Person  *d = [[Person alloc] init];
  Person  *e = [[Person alloc] init];
  NSArray *arr1 =
              [NSArray arrayWithObjects: a,b,c,d,e,nil];
  NSMutableArray  *arr2 = [arr1 mutableCopy];
  Person  *f =[[Person alloc] init];
  [arr2 addObject:f];
  [arr2 removeObject:a];
  [arr2 release];
  [a release];
  [b release];
  [c release];
  [d release];
  [e release];
  [f release];
  [pool release];
  return 0;
}
```

Having an `NSMutableArray` instance allows you to dynamically remove and add objects from to it. In the code example, we add a new object, `f`, and remove an existing object, `a`[1]. Besides the change in the existing elements' positions within the array and their retain count, the retain count of `f` is incremented by 1 and that of `a` is decremented by 1. Figure 2.4 illustrates the state of the objects at this stage. Notice that, although the two arrays are now distinct, they still share pointers to the same elements.

### 2.1.3  Deep copy

Until now, we have been dealing with shallow copies. Shallow copying is the default behavior of `NSArray` and `NSMutableArray` regardless of the type of copy (i.e., whether the copy is mutable or immutable). However, sometimes you want to have a copy of an object that is independent of the original. Such a copy is referred to as a *deep copy*.

For an object to be able to make a clone of itself, its class has to implement the `NSCopying` protocol. `NSCopying` protocol defines only one method: `copyWithZone:`. This method must be

---

[1]`removeObject:` removes all occurrences of the object in the collection.

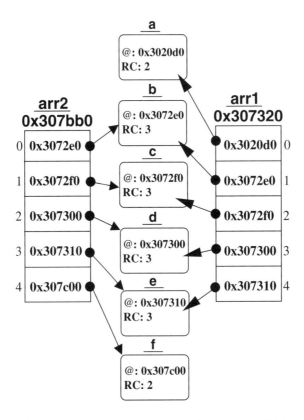

**Figure 2.4**    Illustration of a mutable copy of an immutable NSArray.

implemented by the adopting class. It should return an independent, functionally equivalent copy of an object whose instance variables have identical values of the object at the time of copying.

The following summarizes how copying is done.

1. Your class must be a descendant of NSObject and it must adopt the NSCopying protocol.

2. It must implement the copyWithZone: method. Unless the superclass is NSObject, a call to the super's copyWithZone: (with the same zone that you have received) should be the first statement in your implementation of copyWithZone:.

3. Inside copyWithZone:, you create a new instance of your class and initialize it with the same state that your instance is in. Depending on how deep a copy you want to achieve, you may want to propagate the copying to the instance variables themselves. It all depends on the requirements of your code.

4. The copyWithZone: returns the new copy instance to the caller. The caller owns that copy and is the one responsible for its eventual release.

These are the basic steps you can take in order to generate a new copy of the original object.

One question remains. How does sending a copy message to an instance end up in sending it a copyWithZone: message? The answer to this question is simple. The NSObject has a convenience copy method which calls copyWithZone: with a nil zone. Note that NSObject does not adopt the NSCopying protocol itself. Obviously, if none of the classes in the inheritance chain implement a copyWithZone: method, an exception (see Section 1.7.1) is raised. Therefore, it is important to understand that sending a copy message to an array object will always result in a shallow copy regardless of whether the objects it contains adopt the NSCopying protocol or not.

Listing 2.5 shows the updated Person class with the added NSCopying protocol adoption. You can easily notice that this class follows a deep copying approach. We generate a new instance of the object containing new instance variables and are not just copying pointers. The new instance variables come from the property attribute "copy" used for both instance variables, name and address.

**Listing 2.5**    Enhanced Person class adopting the NSCopying protocol.

```
#import <Foundation/Foundation.h>

@interface Person : NSObject<NSCopying>
{
  NSString  *name;
  NSString  *address;
}
@property(copy) NSString  *name;
@property(copy) NSString  *address;
-(id)initWithName:(NSString*) theName
             andAddress:(NSString*) theAddress;
-(id)init;
-(id)copyWithZone:(NSZone *)zone;
@end

@implementation Person
@synthesize name;
@synthesize address;
-(id)initWithName:(NSString*) theName
             andAddress:(NSString*) theAddress{
  self = [super init];
  if(self){
    self.name    =   theName;
    self.address  =   theAddress;
  }
  return self;
}
-(id)init{
  return [self initWithName:@"" andAddress:@""];
}
```

```
−(void)dealloc{
  [name     release];
  [address     release];
  [super     dealloc];
}
```

```
// Implementing copyWithZone: declared   in NSCopying
−(id)copyWithZone:(NSZone *)zone
{
    Person *aPerson = [[[self class] allocWithZone: zone]
            initWithName:[self name]
            andAddress:[self address]];
    return aPerson;
}
@end
```

Listing 2.6 shows the demonstration code for acquiring a deep copy of an NSArray object. We use the same class method, arrayWithObjects:, that we used before to get a new instance of NSArray. The objects, however, are now copies of the original objects: a, b, c, d, and e.

Since the copy message returns a new object that we own, we send an autorelease message to the copy object before adding it to the new array. At the end of creating and initializing the new array, the state of the objects is as depicted in Fig. 2.5.

**Listing 2.6**   Implementing a deep copy of an array of objects.

```
int main(int argc, char *argv[])
{
  NSAutoreleasePool *pool =
                    [[NSAutoreleasePool alloc] init];
  Person   *a  = [[Person alloc] init];
  Person   *b  = [[Person alloc] init];
  Person   *c  = [[Person alloc] init];
  Person   *d  = [[Person alloc] init];
  Person   *e  = [[Person alloc] init];

  NSArray *arr1 =
              [NSArray   arrayWithObjects: a,b,c,d,e,nil];
  NSArray *arr2 =
    [NSArray   arrayWithObjects:
      [[a copy] autorelease],
      [[b copy] autorelease],
      [[c copy] autorelease],
      [[d copy] autorelease],
      [[e copy] autorelease],
      nil
    ];
```

```
Person  *aPerson  =  [arr1   objectAtIndex:0];
aPerson.name  = @"Marge Simpson";
aPerson.address = @"Springfield";

// Result of the following line is:
// Person at 0 is: Name: , Addr:
printf("Person at %d is: Name: %s, Addr: %s\n",
    0,
    [[[arr2 objectAtIndex:0] name]
            cStringUsingEncoding:NSUTF8StringEncoding],
    [[[arr2 objectAtIndex:0] address]
            cStringUsingEncoding:NSUTF8StringEncoding]);
// must release all objects
[a release];
[b release];
[c release];
[d release];
[e release];
[pool release];
return 0;
}
```

As the figure illustrates, the arrays are independent of each other. Every object involved is unique and has its own identity. If we change an element in `arr1`, no change occurs in `arr2`, and vice versa. This is illustrated in the code when we change the state of the object at index 0 in `arr1` and observe no change in `arr2` nor in its contained objects.

To clean up, we only need to release the objects a, b, c, d, e, and `pool`. All other objects are autoreleased and will be released when we release the autorelease pool at the end.

## 2.1.4   Sorting an array

There are several approaches available to you for sorting an array. The two main options available are: a) write a function that finds the proper order of two objects, and b) add a method to your class that enables an instance to compare itself with another instance of the same class.

In Listing 2.7, we have updated the `Person` class as follows. First, we added a new instance variable called `personID` of type `NSInteger` (which is basically an `int`), and second, we added a new method `nameAscCompare:` which enables a `Person` object to compare itself with another `Person` instance.

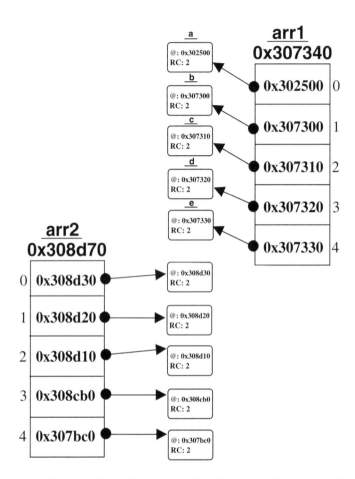

**Figure 2.5**   Illustration of the state of the objects involved in a deep copy of the contents of an array of objects.

**Listing 2.7**   The updated `Person` class with a sorting method.

```
#import <Foundation/Foundation.h>

@interface Person : NSObject
{
  NSString  *name;
  NSString  *address;
  NSInteger   personID;
}
@property(copy) NSString  *name;
@property(copy) NSString  *address;
@property NSInteger personID;
```

```objc
-(id)initWithName:(NSString*) theName
           andAddress:(NSString*) theAddress
           andID:(NSInteger) theID;
-(id)init;
- (NSComparisonResult)nameAscCompare:(Person *)aPerson;
@end

@implementation Person
@synthesize name;
@synthesize address;
@synthesize personID;

-(id)initWithName:(NSString*) theName
             andAddress:(NSString*) theAddress
             andID:(NSInteger) theID{
  self = [super init];
  if(self){
    self.name = theName;
    self.address  = theAddress;
    personID = theID;
  }
  return self;
}
-(id)init{
  return [self initWithName:@"" andAddress:@"" andID:0];
}
-(void)dealloc{
  [name    release];
  [address   release];
  [super   dealloc];
}

- (NSComparisonResult)nameAscCompare:(Person *)aPerson{
  return [name caseInsensitiveCompare:[aPerson name]];
}
@end
```

Suppose you want to sort an array containing Person objects in an ascending order of the personID. NSArray provides an instance method called: sortedArrayUsing-Function:context:. This method is declared as follows:

```objc
- (NSArray *)sortedArrayUsingFunction:
            (NSInteger (*)(id, id, void *))comparator
            context:(void *)context
```

The first parameter is a pointer to a function that takes two arbitrary objects as the first two parameters and a (**void**\*) as a third parameter. It returns an NSInteger. The second parameter is a generic C-pointer so that your implementation, if it wishes to, can use it as a context. This second pointer is actually the third pointer used in each call made to your implementation of comparator.

Your implementation of the comparator function should return:

1. NSOrderedAscending, if the first object is less than the second.

2. NSOrderedSame, if the two objects have the same ordering.

3. NSOrderedDescending, if the first object is greater than the second.

In Listing 2.8, we show the function intSort() that will be used as the comparator. The implementation of this function depends on the requirements of the application. Here, we just compare the personID of the two objects and return an appropriate comparison result.

In Listing 2.8, we send the following message to arr1:

sortedArrayUsingFunction:intSort context:NULL

and we store the new array reference in intSortedArray. Note that the new array is autoreleased and the objects in it are the same as objects in the original array, arr1.

The second approach for sorting an array is through equipping the object with a way to compare itself with other siblings. Listing 2.7 shows the addition of the new method: nameAscCompare:. This method simply compares the value of the instance variable name with the other object's name instance variable. It uses the caseInsensitiveCompare: method to do the actual comparison.

In Listing 2.8, we show how we can sort the array using this method. We use the sortedArrayUsingSelector: method. Notice that no context is needed as a parameter since you have the self and class object pointers.

Figure 2.6 shows the state of the three array objects and their elements. Notice how the retain count of the array elements is now 4 (1 for each array and 1 for the alloc).

**Listing 2.8**    Two different schemes for sorting an array.

```
NSInteger intSort(id p1, id p2, void *context)
{
    int v1 = [(Person *)p1 personID];
    int v2 = [(Person *)p2 personID];
    if (v1 < v2)
        return NSOrderedAscending;
    else if (v1 > v2)
        return NSOrderedDescending;
    else
        return NSOrderedSame;
}

int main(int argc, char *argv[])
{
```

```
NSAutoreleasePool *pool =
                  [[NSAutoreleasePool alloc] init];
Person   *a  = [[Person alloc]
                  initWithName:@"Kate Austen"
                  andAddress:@"" andID:5];
Person   *b  = [[Person alloc]
                  initWithName:@"Sayid Jarrah"
                  andAddress:@"" andID:4];
Person   *c  = [[Person alloc]
                  initWithName:@"Sun Kwon"
                  andAddress:@"" andID:1];
Person   *d  = [[Person alloc]
                  initWithName:@"Hurley Reyes"
                  andAddress:@"" andID:2];
Person   *e  = [[Person alloc]
                  initWithName:@"Jack Shephard"
                  andAddress:@"" andID:3];
NSArray *arr1 =
          [NSArray   arrayWithObjects: a,b,c,d,e,nil];
NSArray *intSortedArray =
          [arr1 sortedArrayUsingFunction:intSort
              context:NULL];
NSArray *strSortedArray =
          [arr1 sortedArrayUsingSelector:
                  @selector(nameAscCompare:)
          ];
// must release all objects
[a release];
[b release];
[c release];
[d release];
[e release];
[pool release];
return 0;
}
```

## 2.2   Sets

We saw in the previous section how we can store ordered objects in an array. Some scenarios, however, do not require object ordering, but are mostly concerned with maintaining unique objects and providing a fast verification mechanism on object membership.

The set collection provides such a behavior. As in the array case, sets come in two flavors: (1) static sets represented by the NSSet class, and (2) dynamic or mutable sets represented by the NSMutableSet class.

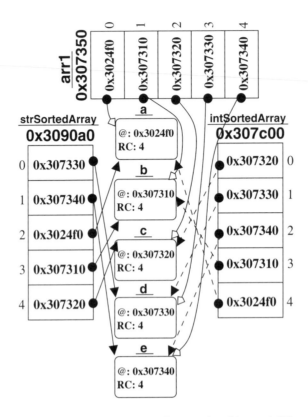

**Figure 2.6**   State of original array and two copies of it sorted differently.

## 2.2.1   Immutable sets

Listing 2.9 provides a sample code demonstrating the use of immutable sets.

To create an immutable set, you have to specify the members during the initialization phase. The method `initWithObjects:` does just that. This method is similar to the one in the `NSArray` class. The code below creates three sets.

**Listing 2.9**   Demonstration of immutable sets.

```
NSSet    *favoritShows = [[ NSSet  alloc ]
        initWithObjects:
        @"Everybody Loves Raymond",
        @"Lost",
        @"Nova",
        @"Late Show",
        @"Tom and Jerry",
        nil
        ];
```

```
NSSet    *reallyFavoritShows =
         [[NSSet alloc] initWithObjects:
             @"Everybody loves Raymond",
             @"Lost",
             nil
             ];
NSSet *hatedShows = [[NSSet alloc] initWithObjects:
             @"Heroes",
             @"60 minutes",
             @"The Tonight Show",
             @"Deal or no deal",
             nil
             ];
printf("Number of elements = %d\n", [favoritShows count]);

if( [favoritShows
     intersectsSet:hatedShows] == YES){
        printf("makes no sense!\n");
}
if( [reallyFavoritShows
     isSubsetOfSet:favoritShows] == YES){
        printf("makes sense!\n");
}

if( [reallyFavoritShows
     isEqualToSet:favoritShows] == YES){
        printf("makes some sense!\n");
}

NSString   *anyShow =[favoritShows anyObject];
if([hatedShows   containsObject:anyShow] == YES){
   printf("makes no sense!\n");
}
```

To find the number of elements in a set, use the `count` instance method. `NSSet` also provides methods that implement the mathematical operations defined on a set. For example, the code above demonstrates how you can find whether a set instance intersects (has common elements) with another set. The `intersectsSet:` method is declared as

– (BOOL) intersectsSet :( NSSet *)otherSet

It returns `YES` if there is at least one common element shared by the receiver and `otherSet`, and `NO`, otherwise.

You can also test if a set instance is a subset of another set using the `isSubsetOfSet:` declared as:

— (BOOL) i s S u b s e t O f S e t : ( NSSet ∗ ) o t h e r S e t

For this method to return YES, every element in the receiver must be present in otherSet.

If you want to see if all members of the receiver are present in another set and vice versa, use the method isEqualToSet:.

The method anyObject returns an arbitrary (not necessarily random) element in the set. The method containsObject: returns YES if a given element is present in a set and NO, otherwise. It is declared as:

— (BOOL) c o n t a i n s O b j e c t : ( **id** ) a n O b j e c t


## 2.2.2   *Mutable sets*

Listing 2.10 is a continuation of Listing 2.9. Here, we continue our example and demonstrate the dynamic version of the set collection: NSMutableSet.

To create a mutable set instance, you use alloc to set the initial capacity of the set. This initial capacity is not a limitation on the set size because it can grow and shrink dynamically. The statement [[NSMutableSet alloc] initWithCapacity:2] creates a new mutable set with an initial capacity of two elements.

To add an element to the set, use addObject:. As we saw in the array collection, the set does not copy the object you are adding, but it puts a claim on it by sending a retain message to it. If you add an element that is already in the set, the method has no effect on the set or the element. To remove an element from the set, use the removeObject: method. No side effect occurs if the element you are trying to remove is not found in the set.

After adding and removing objects from the set, we display the set using the description: method. The first printf statement produces:

```
dynamicSet = { (
    Heroes,
    Lost
) }
```

You can merge (make a union) of two sets using unionSet: declared as:

— ( **void** ) u n i o n S e t : ( NSSet ∗ ) o t h e r S e t

The unionSet: adds every object in otherSet that is not a member of the receiver to the receiver. After the union operation, the dynamicSet is displayed as:

```
dynamicSet = { (
    Everybody Loves Raymond,
    Heroes,
    Lost
) }
```

The method minusSet: is declared as:

$-$ (**void**) minusSet : (NSSet *) otherSet

It removes every member in otherSet from the receiver set. The contents of dynamicSet after executing the statement [dynamicSet minusSet:reallyFavoritShows] is:

```
dynamicSet = {(
    Heroes
)}
```

---

**Listing 2.10**   Demonstration of mutable sets.

```
NSMutableSet   *dynamicSet =
    [[NSMutableSet alloc] initWithCapacity:2];
[dynamicSet addObject:@"Lost"];
[dynamicSet addObject:@"Nova"];
[dynamicSet addObject:@"Heroes"];
[dynamicSet addObject:@"Lost"];
[dynamicSet removeObject:@"Everybody Loves Raymond"];
[dynamicSet removeObject:@"Nova"];
printf("dynamicSet = %s\n",
    [[dynamicSet description] cString]);
[dynamicSet unionSet:reallyFavoritShows];
printf("dynamicSet = %s\n",
    [[dynamicSet description] cString]);
[dynamicSet minusSet:reallyFavoritShows];
printf("dynamicSet = %s\n",
    [[dynamicSet description] cString]);
```

## 2.2.3   Additional important methods

To remove all elements of a set, you can use:

$-$ (**void**) removeAllObjects

To remove all elements of a set and then add all the elements in another set to it, use

$-$ (**void**) setSet : (NSSet *) otherSet

If you have an array of elements and you would like to add all its elements to a set, use:

$-$ (**void**) addObjectsFromArray : (NSArray *) anArray

To send every object in a set a message, use:

$-$ (**void**) makeObjectsPerformSelector : (SEL) aSelector

The method specified by the selector aSelector must not take any arguments.

   If you want to communicate with the members of the set using an object, you can use:

```
- (void)makeObjectsPerformSelector:(SEL)aSelector
     withObject:(id)anObject
```

This method will use a selector representing a method that takes exactly one argument of type id. In both methods above, the selector must not change the set instance itself.

## 2.3 Dictionaries

The immutable NSDictionary and its mutable subclass NSMutableDictionary give you the ability to store your objects and retrieve them using keys. Each entry of the dictionary consists of a key and a value. The key can be any object as long as it adopts the NSCopying protocol. Usually, instances of the NSString class are used as keys, but any class can be used.

In a dictionary, keys have to be unique. Keys and values cannot be nil. The framework, however, provides you with the class NSNull for storing null objects. When you add entries to the dictionary, the dictionary class makes a copy of the key and uses this copy as the key to store the value object. The storage follows a hash model, but the classes shield you from the implementation details. The value object is retained rather than copied.

As with the array collection classes, once the immutable dictionary is initialized, you cannot add or remove entries to/from it. You can get a mutable dictionary from an immutable one and vice versa. Listing 2.11 demonstrates working with dictionaries.

**Listing 2.11**    Working with dictionaries.

```
#import <Foundation/Foundation.h>

int main(int argc, char *argv[])
{
  NSAutoreleasePool * pool =
                     [[NSAutoreleasePool alloc] init];
  NSMutableArray  *kArr = [NSMutableArray arrayWithObjects:
                  @"1", @"2", @"3", @"4", nil];
  NSMutableArray  *aArr =
              [NSMutableArray arrayWithObjects:
                                    @"2", nil];
  NSDictionary  *guide =
              [NSDictionary dictionaryWithObjectsAndKeys:
              kArr, @"Kate", aArr, @"Ana-Lucia",  nil];

  NSEnumerator *enumerator = [guide keyEnumerator];
  id key;
  while ((key = [enumerator nextObject])) {
    if([[key  substringToIndex:1] isEqual:@"K"]){
      [[guide objectForKey:key]   addObject:@"5"];
    }
  }
```

```
NSMutableDictionary *dynaGuide = [guide mutableCopy];
for(key in dynaGuide){
  if([[key substringToIndex:1] isEqual:@"A"]){
    [[dynaGuide objectForKey:key] addObject:@"5"];
  }
}
NSArray *keys = [dynaGuide allKeys];
for(key in keys){
  if([[key substringToIndex:1] isEqual:@"A"]){
    [dynaGuide removeObjectForKey:key];
  }
}
[dynaGuide release];
[pool release];
return 0;
}
```

In the code above, we create an immutable dictionary whose keys are strings and whose values are mutable arrays. The creation of the dictionary is achieved using the method `dictionaryWithObjectsAndKeys:`. The method takes a list of alternating values and keys that is null-terminated.

To access the values stored in a dictionary, you can use an enumerator of the keys. The method `keyEnumerator` returns such an enumerator from a dictionary object. The code uses the enumerator to check for all objects whose key starts with an "A". For each such key, it updates the value stored in that entry. To retrieve the value of a given key, you use the `objectForKey:` method.

To generate a mutable copy of a dictionary, you use the `mutableCopy` method. This will create a new mutable dictionary initialized with the recipient dictionary's element. Since the method used has a "copy" in it, you own that object and you should release it when you're done with it.

Another way for traversing the dictionary is the use of fast enumeration. The line **for**(key **in** dynaGuide) enumerates the keys in the dictionary `dynaGuide`.

You can add/remove entries to/from a mutable dictionary. To remove a given entry, you use the `removeObjectForKey:` method. You should not, however, do that while enumerating a dictionary. You should, instead, make a snapshot of the keys and then update the dictionary. To get an `NSArray` instance of all the keys, use `allKeys` method. Once you have that, you can enumerate the keys and update the dictionary as you wish.

### 2.3.1 *Additional important methods*

- (BOOL)isEqualToDictionary:(NSDictionary *)otherDictionary

Returns YES if the receiver has the same number of entries, and for every key, the corresponding values in the two dictionaries are equal (i.e., isEqual: returns YES).

```
- (NSArray *)allValues
```

Creates a new array with the values contained in the dictionary entries.

```
- (NSArray *)keysSortedByValueUsingSelector:(SEL)comparator
```

Generates an array of keys ordered by sorting the values using comparator.

```
- (void)
addEntriesFromDictionary:(NSDictionary *)otherDictionary
```

The entries in `otherDictionary` are added to the receiver of the message. If the receiver already has an entry with the same key, that entry receives a `release` before being replaced.

## 2.4   Summary

In this chapter, we have covered the topic of collections. Collections are Cocoa objects that act as containers to other Cocoa objects. We introduced three types of collections defined in the Foundation framework. We first discussed the array collection in Section 2.1. Immutable arrays are instances of the `NSArray` class. `NSArray` allows for the creation of a static array that cannot be changed once initialized. The mutable version of `NSArray` is `NSMutableArray`. An instance of `NSMutableArray` can be modified by adding and removing elements during the lifetime of the program. The `NSArray` is more efficient than the `NSMutableArray` class. You should use instances of `NSArray` if the array is not required to change once initialized.

We discussed the concepts of shallow and deep copying. A shallow copy of an object is a new instance that shares the references (pointers) to other objects that the original object has. A deep copy, on the other hand, propagates the copying to the referenced objects. Collections implement a shallow copy regardless of what kind of objects they hold. For a class to implement a deep copy, it needs to adopt the `NSCopying` protocol and implement the `copyWithZone:` method. To produce a deep copy of a collection, you need to iterate through the objects contained in that collection, sending a `copy` message to each object, `autoreleaseing` each object, and adding it to the collection, in that order.

We also discussed sorting, and presented two schemes: (1) either using a function for comparing two instances, or (2) adding a method so that an instance can compare itself with another. The first scheme is employed in the array instance method `sortedArrayUsingFunction:context:`, while the second scheme is employed in the array instance method `sortedArrayUsing-Selector:`.

In Section 2.2, we covered the set collection. Immutable sets are instances of the `NSSet` class, while mutable sets are instances of `NSMutableSet`. We also presented several methods which implement mathematically inspired set operations.

In Section 2.3, we covered the dictionary collection. Dictionaries allow for the retrieval of objects using keys. Several examples were presented illustrating immutable and mutable dictionaries.

# 3

# Anatomy of an iPhone Application

In this chapter, we discuss the basic steps needed to build a simple iPhone application. First, we demonstrate the basic structure of a simple iPhone application, and then we show the steps needed to develop the application using XCode.

## 3.1 HelloWorld Application

In this section, we demonstrate the basic structure of a simple iPhone application. The application simply displays the message Hello World to the user. The following are the steps needed to write such an application.

1. Create a main.m function. As in any C program, the execution of Objective-C applications start from main(). You need to create the main() function in the main.m file as follows:

```
#import <UIKit/UIKit.h>

int main(int argc, char *argv[]) {
  NSAutoreleasePool * pool = [[NSAutoreleasePool alloc] init];
  int retVal = UIApplicationMain(argc, argv, nil,
                  @"HelloWorldAppDelegate");
  [pool release];
  return retVal;
}
```

The main() function starts by creating an autorelease pool and ends by releasing it. In between, it makes a call to the UIApplicationMain() function. UIApplicationMain() is declared as follows:

```
int
  UIApplicationMain(int argc, char *argv[],
    NSString *principalClassName,
    NSString *delegateClassName
)
```

*iPhone SDK Programming*   Maher Ali
© 2009 John Wiley & Sons, Ltd

This function takes four parameters. The first two parameters are the parameters passed in to the main() function. These parameters should be familiar to any C programmer. The third parameter is the name of the application class. If a nil is specified, the UIApplication class is used to instantiate the unique application object. The fourth and last parameter is the name of the application delegate class.

The UIApplicationMain() instantiates the application and the application delegate objects. After that, it sets the delegate property of the application object to the application delegate instance. The main run loop of the application is established. From this moment on, events, such as user touches, are queued by the system in a queue, and the application object dequeues these events and delivers them to the appropriate objects in your application (usually the main window).

2. Create the application delegate class. The instance of the application delegate class will receive important messages from the application object during the lifetime of the application. The following is a typical application delegate class:

```
#import <UIKit/UIKit.h>

@class MyView;
@interface HelloWorldAppDelegate :
        NSObject <UIApplicationDelegate> {
    UIWindow        *window;
    MyView          *view;
}
@end
```

Notice that the application delegate class adopts the UIApplicationDelegate protocol. In addition, references to the user-interface objects that will be created and presented to the user are stored in instance variables. Most of the time, you will have one window object and several views attached to it. In the example above, the variable window stores a reference to the main window object and view is used to store a reference to a custom view of type MyView.

One of the most important methods of the UIApplicationDelegate protocol is the applicationDidFinishLaunching: method. This method is invoked by the application object to inform the delegate that the application has finished launching. You usually implement this method to initialize the application and create the user interface. The following is a listing of the implementation of the application delegate class. In the applicationDidFinishLaunching: method, we first create the main window of the application.

Windows are instances of the class UIWindow. UIWindow is a subclass of the UIView class. UIView is the base class of user-interface objects. It provides access to handling user gestures as well as drawings. Like any other object, a UIWindow instance is allocated and then initialized. The initializer (as we shall see in Chapter 4) specifies the frame that the window object will occupy. After that, an instance of the MyView class is created and initialized with the frame that it will occupy. After configuring the MyView instance and setting its background color, we add it as a subview to the `window` and make the window object key and visible.

```
#import "HelloWorldAppDelegate.h"
#import "MyView.h"

@implementation HelloWorldAppDelegate

- (void)
applicationDidFinishLaunching:(UIApplication *)application {

    window = [[UIWindow alloc]
        initWithFrame:[[UIScreen mainScreen] bounds]];
    CGRect    frame = [UIScreen mainScreen].applicationFrame;
    view = [[MyView alloc] initWithFrame:frame];
    view.message = @"Hello World!";
    view.backgroundColor =[UIColor whiteColor];
    [window addSubview:view];
    [window makeKeyAndVisible];
}

- (void)dealloc {
    [view    release];
    [window  release];
    [super  dealloc];
}
@end
```

3. Create the user interface subclasses. To receive the user events (e.g., the touches) and draw in the view, you need to create a subclass of `UIView` and override its event-handling and drawing methods. The declaration of the `MyView` class used in our `HelloWorld` application is shown below:

```
#import <UIKit/UIKit.h>

@interface MyView : UIView {
    NSString *message;
}
@property(nonatomic, copy) NSString *message;
@end
```

The implementation of the `MyView` class is shown below. This class overrides the event-handling method for ending-of-touches (we will cover the multitouch interface in the next chapter) and the `drawRect:` for drawing in the view area. For drawing, we simply draw the contents of the `message` instance variable with a specific font. Whenever the user's finger is lifted from the screen, that event is stored in the application queue. The application object retrieves the event from the queue and sends it to the main window. The window searches its subviews for the view that should receive this event and delivers that event to it. In our example, since `MyView` instance spans the screen, all touch events will be delivered to it and the `touchesEnded:withEvent:` method will be invoked. You can put your code in this method in order to either update the state of the application or change its appearance or both.

```
#import "MyView.h"

@implementation MyView
@synthesize message;

- (void)
touchesEnded:(NSSet *)touches withEvent:(UIEvent *)event{
    if( [(UITouch *)[touches anyObject] tapCount] == 2){
      // handle a double-tap
    }
}

- (void)drawRect:(CGRect)rect{
    [message drawAtPoint:CGPointMake(100,100)
        withFont:[UIFont systemFontOfSize:32]];
}
@end
```

## 3.2   Building the `HelloWorld` Application

The following are the steps you need to take to realize the `HelloWorld` application.

1. Create a new project in XCode. In XCode, select `File->New Project` and select the `Window-Based Application` template (Fig. 3.1). Name the project `HelloWorld` and click `Save` as shown in Fig. 3.2.

2. Update the project for building the user interface programatically. You can create the user interface using either Interface Builder, programatically, or both. Interface Builder accelerates the development process, but it also hides important concepts. If you are a beginner, we suggest that you build the user interface programatically and do not rely on Interface Builder. This will help you understand what is going on. Once you have mastered this subject, you can use Interface Builder in your development.

   The project template assumes that you are using Interface Builder. You need to make some small changes to fully use the programatic approach. Select the `Info.plist` file in the `Groups&Files` window (Fig. 3.3) so that its content appears in the Editor. Right click on "Main nib file base name" and select Cut. Right click on the file `MainWindow.xib` in the `Groups&Files` window and select `Delete`. Click on `Also Move to Trash`.

**Figure 3.1**  Choosing a template for a new project.

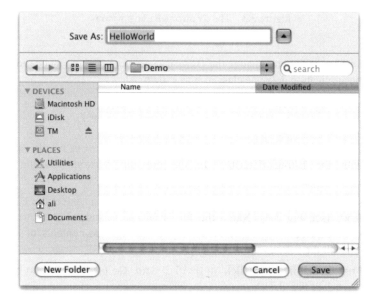

**Figure 3.2**  Naming a new project.

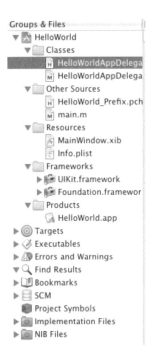

**Figure 3.3**    The Groups&Files window.

Select the main.m file and change the UIApplicationMain() invocation by adding the name of the application delegate class to it as shown below:

```
int retVal = UIApplicationMain(argc, argv, nil,
                    @"HelloWorldAppDelegate");
```

3. Write your code. Select the HelloWorldAppDelegate.h file and replace its content with the listing described in the previous section. Do the same for the HelloWorldAppDelegate.m file.

4. Create a subclass of UIView. Select File->New File and select the UIView subclass and hit Next (see Fig. 3.4). Name the file MyView.m and hit Finish (see Fig. 3.5). A subclass of UIView will be created for you. Change the contents of MyView.h and MyView.m with the listings shown in the previous section.

5. Build and run the application. Click on Build and Go (see Fig. 3.6) to build and launch the application (see Fig. 3.7).

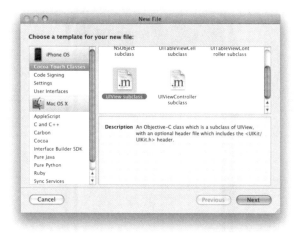

**Figure 3.4**     Choosing a template for a new file.

**Figure 3.5**     Naming the new UIView subclass.

**Figure 3.6**     XCode toolbar.

**Figure 3.7**     The HelloWorld application.

# 4

# The View

This chapter explains the main concepts behind views. You will learn about view geometry in Section 4.1. In Section 4.2, we cover the topic of view hierarchy. Next, Section 4.3 discusses, in great detail, the multitouch interface. In this section, you will learn how to recognize multitouch gestures. After that, we discuss several animation techniques in Section 4.4. Finally, Section 4.5 deals with how to use Quartz 2D functions for drawing inside a view.

## 4.1 View Geometry

There are three geometric properties of the UIView class that you need to understand. These properties are: frame, bounds, and center. Before explaining these properties, let's first look at some of the structures and functions used in specifying the values for these properties.

### 4.1.1 Useful geometric type definitions

The following types are used throughout the text:

- CGFloat represents a floating number and is defined as:

  **typedef float** CGFloat;

- CGPoint is a structure that represents a geometric point. It is defined as:

  **struct** CGPoint {
     CGFloat x;
     CGFloat y;
  };
  **typedef struct** CGPoint CGPoint;

  The x value represents the x-coordinate of the point and the y value represents its y-coordinate.

  You will use CGPoint a lot. CGPointMake() is a convenient function defined to make a CGPoint from a pair of x and y values, and is defined as follows:

```
CGPoint CGPointMake (
    CGFloat x,
    CGFloat y
);
```

- CGSize is a structure used to represent width and height values, and is declared as follows:

```
struct CGSize {
    CGFloat width;
    CGFloat height;
};
typedef struct CGSize CGSize;
```

where width is the width value and height is the height value.

To make a CGSize structure from a width and a height, use the utility function CGSizeMake(), declared as follows:

```
CGSize CGSizeMake (
    CGFloat width,
    CGFloat height
);
```

- CGRect is used to represent the location and dimension of a rectangle. It is declared as follows:

```
struct CGRect {
    CGPoint origin;
    CGSize size;
};
typedef struct CGRect CGRect;
```

The origin value represents the upper-left point of the rectangle, and size represents its dimension (i.e., its width and height).

To make a CGRect structure, you can use the utility function CGRectMake() declared as follows:

```
CGRect CGRectMake (
    CGFloat x,
    CGFloat y,
    CGFloat width,
    CGFloat height
);
```

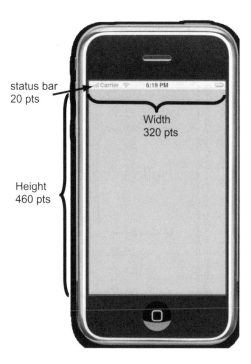

**Figure 4.1**   The dimensions of the device screen.

## 4.1.2   The UIScreen class

The UIScreen class is provided to you in order to obtain the dimensions of the device's screen. The device's screen is 320 × 480 points as shown in Fig. 4.1. The status bar takes 20 points from the total height, leaving 460 points for the application. You can turn off the status bar using the following statement:

```
[UIApplication sharedApplication].statusBarHidden = YES;
```

You can retrieve the size of the device's screen as follows:

```
[[UIScreen mainScreen] bounds].size
```

In the above statement, we first obtain the singleton UIScreen instance and then obtain the size of its bounding rectangle.

The application window resides just below the status bar. To retrieve the application's frame, use the following statement:

```
CGRect frame = [[UIScreen mainScreen] applicationFrame]
```

If there is a status bar, the application's frame is 320 × 460. Otherwise, it is equal to the screen's bounds.

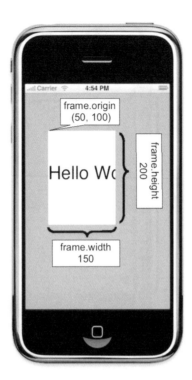

**Figure 4.2**    The frame and center geometric properties for a subview of a main window.

### 4.1.3   The frame and center properties

The UIView class declares the frame property which is used to locate and dimension the UIView instance inside another UIView instance. The property is declared as follows:

@property(nonatomic) CGRect frame

You usually specify the frame of a view during the initialization phase. For example, the following creates a UIView instance whose origin is located at (50, 100) in its super view's coordinates and whose width and height is 150 and 200, respectively.

```
CGRect   frame = CGRectMake(50, 100, 150, 200);
aView = [[UIView alloc] initWithFrame:frame];
[window addSubview:aView];
```

Figure 4.2 shows the result of adding the above UIView instance to a full-screen (minus the status bar) window. The figure shows the origin of this view as (50, 100) and its center as (125, 200), all in the parent view's (window) coordinates.

Changes to the center will result in changes to the origin of the frame. Similarly, changes to the origin or size of the frame will result in changes in the center. For the example above, if the

**Figure 4.3**   Moving the view location by changing its `center` property.

x-coordinate of the `center` property is increased by 80 points, the frame's origin will be equal to (130, 100) which would result in the view being shifted as a whole a distance of 80 points to the right as shown in Fig. 4.3.

## 4.1.4   The bounds property

The `bounds` property is used to specify the origin and size of the view in the view's own coordinate system. The property is declared as follows:

`@property(nonatomic) CGRect bounds`

When you initialize the view, the `bound's origin` is set to (0, 0) and its `size` to `frame.size`. Changes to the `bounds.origin` have no effect on the `frame` and the `center` properties. Changes to `bounds.size`, however, will result in a change in the `frame` and `center` properties.

As an example, consider Fig. 4.2. The `bound.origin` is equal to (0, 0). The view draws a string's value as shown below:

```
- (void)drawRect:(CGRect)rect {
    int x = 0;
```

**Figure 4.4** Changes to the bounds property's origin affect the content of the view not its dimension/location.

```
int y = self.bounds.size.height/3;
[@"Hello World!"
    drawAtPoint:CGPointMake(x,y)
    withFont:[UIFont systemFontOfSize:40]];
}
```

The x-axis of the point at which the string "Hello World!" is drawn is equal to 0. If we change the value of bounds.origin.x from 0 to 50, the string drawn will move 50 to the left as shown in Fig. 4.4.

## 4.2 The View Hierarchy

Most of the time, you will have one main window for the application and several views and controls with different sizes and locations. The main window (an instance of UIWindow which is a subclass of UIView) will act as a root of a tree. When you want to add a view to the application, you add that view to the window or to an existing view. Eventually, you end up with a tree structure rooted at that window. Every view will have exactly one parent view called *superview* and zero or more child views called *subviews*. To access the superview instance, use the property `superview` which is declared as follows:

@property(nonatomic, readonly) UIView *superview

To retrieve the children of a given view, use the property `subviews`, which is declared as follows:

@property(nonatomic, readonly, copy) NSArray *subviews

To add a view to an existing view, you first allocate it, initialize it, configure it, and then add it as a subview. The following two statements create a view that occupies the full-screen (minus the status bar).

CGRect frame = [UIScreen mainScreen].applicationFrame;
view1 = [[UIView alloc] initWithFrame:frame];

The initializer that is usually used is the `initWithFrame:` initializer.

To add a view as a subview, use the `addSubview:` method which is declared as follows:

− (**void**)addSubview:(UIView *)view

After invoking this method, the superview will `retain` the instance `view`.

To remove a view from the view hierarchy, you use the method `removeFromSuperview`. In addition to removing the view from the tree, this method will also `release` the view.

## 4.3   The Multitouch Interface

When the user touches the screen, he/she is requesting feedback from the application. Given that the application presents multiple views, subviews, and controls to the user at the same time, there is a need for the system to figure out which object is the intended recipient of the user's touches.

Every application has a single `UIApplication` object for handling users' touches. When the user touches the screen, the system packages the touches in an event object and puts that event object in the application's event queue. This event object is an instance of the class `UIEvent`.

The event object contains all the touches that are currently on the screen. Each finger on the screen has its own touch object, an instance of the class `UITouch`. As you will see later, each touch object can be in different phases, such as, has just touched the screen, moving, stationary, etc. Each time the user touches the screen, the event object and the touches objects get mutated to reflect the change.

The `UIApplication` unique instance picks up the event object from the queue and sends it to the key window object (an instance of `UIWindow` class). The window object, through a mechanism called *hit-testing*, figures out which subview should receive that event and dispatches the event to it. This object is referred to as the *first responder*. If that object is interested in handling the event, it does so and the event is considered as delivered. If, on the other hand, that object is not interested in handling the event, it passes it through a linked list of objects called the *responder chain*.

The responder chain of a given object starts from that object and ends in the application object. If any object on this chain accepts the event, then the event's propagation towards the application instance stops. If the application instance receives the event and does not know of a valid recipient of it, it throws that event away.

### 4.3.1  The *UITouch* class

Each finger touching the screen is encapsulated by an object of the UITouch class. The following are some of the important properties and methods of this class.

- phase. This property is used to retrieve the current phase of the touch. The property is declared as follows:

  @property(nonatomic, readonly) UITouchPhase    phase

  There are several UITouchPhase values available including:

  - UITouchPhaseBegan indicates that the finger touched the screen.
  - UITouchPhaseMoved indicates that the finger moved on the screen.
  - UITouchPhaseStationary indicates that the finger has not moved on the screen since the last event.
  - UITouchPhaseEnded indicates that the finger has left the screen.
  - UITouchPhaseCancelled indicates that the touch is being cancelled by the system.

- timestamp. The time when the touch changed its phase. The UITouch object keeps mutating during an event. This value refers to the last mutation.

- tapCount. The number of taps that the user made when he/she touched the screen. Successive tapping on the same place will result in a tap count greater than 1. The property is declared as follows:

  @property(nonatomic, readonly) NSUInteger    tapCount

- locationInView:. This method returns the location of the touch in a given view. The method is declared as follows:

  - (CGPoint)locationInView:(UIView *)view

  The returned value is in the coordinate system of view. If you pass nil, the returned value is in the window's coordinate system.

- previousLocationInView:. The previous location of the touch in a given view can be retrieved using this method. The method is declared as follows:

  - (CGPoint)previousLocationInView:(UIView *)view

### 4.3.2  The *UIEvent* class

A multitouch sequence is captured by an object of the class UIEvent. The application will receive the same UIEvent object throughout its lifetime. This object will be mutated during the execution of the application. You can retrieve the timestamp of this event using the timestamp property. To retrieve the touches that this event represents, use the allTouches method which is declared as follows:

- (NSSet *) allTouches

## 4.3.3   *The UIResponder class*

User interface objects receiving touches, such as instances of UIView, are subclasses of the UIResponder class. To understand the multitouch interface, we need to understand the UIResponder class and its four main multitouch-handling methods.

The following are the main methods which subclasses of UIResponder class (such as UIView subclasses) need to override in order to handle gestures.

1. touchesBegan:withEvent:. This method is invoked to tell the responder object that one or more fingers have just touched the screen. The method is declared as follows:

   − ( **void** )
   touchesBegan : ( NSSet *)touches withEvent : ( UIEvent *)event

   The first parameter is a set of UITouch objects that have just touched the screen. The second parameter is the event which these touches are associated with.

2. touchesMoved:withEvent:. This method is invoked to tell the responder object that one or more fingers have just moved on the screen. The method is declared as follows:

   − ( **void** )
   touchesMoved : ( NSSet *)touches withEvent : ( UIEvent *)event

   The first parameter is a set of UITouch objects that have just moved on the screen. The second parameter is the event which these touches are associated with.

3. touchesEnded:withEvent:. This method is invoked to tell the responder object that one or more fingers have just been lifted from the screen. The method is declared as follows:

   − ( **void** )
   touchesEnded : ( NSSet *)touches withEvent : ( UIEvent *)event

   The first parameter is a set of UITouch objects that have just been lifted from the screen. The second parameter is the event which these touches are associated with.

4. touchesCancelled:withEvent:. This method is invoked by the system to tell the responder object that the event has been cancelled. The method is declared as follows:

   − ( **void** )
   touchesCancelled : ( NSSet *)touches withEvent : ( UIEvent *)event

   The first parameter is a set containing a single UITouch object whose phase is UITouchPhaseCancel. The second parameter is the event which has been cancelled.

It is best to understand the multitouch mechanism through a detailed example. Let's imagine three fingers, F1, F2, and F3, touching the screen, moving on the screen, and ending at various times. We will show the invocation of the responder's methods as a result of these fingers. For each invocation, we show the content of the touches set as well as the allTouches set of the event object. Let's start with a screen that has no fingers.

1. Two fingers, `F1` and `F2`, touched the screen.
   `touchesBegan:withEvent:` is called.
   `touches`: a set of two elements:

   > Touch T1 representing F1:   `<UITouch: 0x14a360>`   phase: Began
   > Touch T2 representing F2:   `<UITouch: 0x14a0f0>`   phase: Began

   `event:` `<UIEvent: 0x143ae0>`. The `allTouches` set:

   > T1:   `<UITouch: 0x14a360>`     phase: Began
   > T2:   `<UITouch: 0x14a0f0>`     phase: Began

2. Fingers `F1` and `F2` moved.
   `touchesMoved:withEvent:` is called.
   `touches`: a set of two elements:

   > T1:   `<UITouch: 0x14a360>`   phase: Moved
   > T2:   `<UITouch: 0x14a0f0>`   phase: Moved

   `event:` `<UIEvent: 0x143ae0>`. The `allTouches` set:

   > T1:   `<UITouch: 0x14a360>`   phase: Moved
   > T2:   `<UITouch: 0x14a0f0>`   phase: Moved

3. Finger `F1` moved.
   `touchesMoved:withEvent:` is called.
   `touches`: a set of one element:

   > T1:   `<UITouch: 0x14a360>`   phase: Moved

   `event:` `<UIEvent: 0x143ae0>`. The `allTouches` set:

   > T1:   `<UITouch: 0x14a360>`   phase: Moved
   > T2:   `<UITouch: 0x14a0f0>`   phase: Stationary

4. Finger `F2` moved.
   `touchesMoved:withEvent:` is called.
   `touches`: a set of one element:

   > T2:   `<UITouch: 0x14a0f0>`   phase: Moved

   `event:` `<UIEvent: 0x143ae0>`. The `allTouches` set:

   > T1:   `<UITouch: 0x14a360>`   phase: Stationary
   > T2:   `<UITouch: 0x14a0f0>`   phase: Moved

5. Finger `F3` touched the screen, Finger `F2` moved.
   `touchesBegan:withEvent:` is called.
   `touches`: a set of one element:

T3:    <UITouch: 0x145a10> phase: Began

event: <UIEvent: 0x143ae0>. The allTouches set:

T1:    <UITouch: 0x14a360> phase: Stationary
T2:    <UITouch: 0x14a0f0> phase: Moved
T3:    <UITouch: 0x145a10> phase: Began

touchesMoved:withEvent: is called.
touches: a set of one element:

T2:    <UITouch: 0x14a0f0> phase: Moved

event: <UIEvent: 0x143ae0>. The allTouches set:

T1:    <UITouch: 0x14a360> phase: Stationary
T2:    <UITouch: 0x14a0f0> phase: Moved
T3:    <UITouch: 0x145a10> phase: Began

6. Fingers F2 and F3 moved.
   touchesMoved:withEvent: is called.
   touches: a set of two elements:

T2:    <UITouch: 0x14a0f0> phase: Moved
T3:    <UITouch: 0x145a10> phase: Moved

event: <UIEvent: 0x143ae0>. The allTouches set:

T1:    <UITouch: 0x14a360> phase: Stationary
T2:    <UITouch: 0x14a0f0> phase: Moved
T3:    <UITouch: 0x145a10> phase: Moved

7. Finger F2 moved, Finger F3 lifted.
   touchesMoved:withEvent: is called.
   touches: a set of one element:

T2:    <UITouch: 0x14a0f0> phase: Moved

event: <UIEvent: 0x143ae0>. The allTouches set:

T1:    <UITouch: 0x14a360> phase: Stationary
T2:    <UITouch: 0x14a0f0> phase: Moved
T3:    <UITouch: 0x145a10> phase: Ended

touchesEnded:withEvent: is called.
touches: a set of one element:

T3:    <UITouch: 0x145a10> phase: Ended

event: <UIEvent: 0x143ae0>. The allTouches set:

```
T1:   <UITouch: 0x14a360> phase: Stationary
T2:   <UITouch: 0x14a0f0> phase: Moved
T3:   <UITouch: 0x145a10> phase: Ended
```

8. Finger F2 moved.
   `touchesMoved:withEvent:` is called.
   `touches:` a set of one element:

   ```
   T2:   <UITouch: 0x14a0f0> phase: Moved
   ```

   event: `<UIEvent: 0x143ae0>`. The `allTouches` set:

   ```
   T1:   <UITouch: 0x14a360> phase: Stationary
   T2:   <UITouch: 0x14a0f0> phase: Moved
   ```

9. Finger F2 moved, Finger F1 lifted.
   `touchesMoved:withEvent:` is called.
   `touches:` a set of one element:

   ```
   T2:   <UITouch: 0x14a0f0> phase: Moved
   ```

   event: `<UIEvent: 0x143ae0>`. The `allTouches` set:

   ```
   T1:   <UITouch: 0x14a360> phase: Ended
   T2:   <UITouch: 0x14a0f0> phase: Moved
   ```

   `touchesEnded:withEvent:` is called.
   `touches:` a set of one element:

   ```
   T1:   <UITouch: 0x14a360> phase: Ended
   ```

   event: `<UIEvent: 0x143ae0>`. The `allTouches` set:

   ```
   T1:   <UITouch: 0x14a360> phase: Ended
   T2:   <UITouch: 0x14a0f0> phase: Moved
   ```

10. Finger F2 moved.
    `touchesMoved:withEvent:` is called.
    `touches:` a set of one element:

    ```
    T2:   <UITouch: 0x14a0f0> phase: Moved
    ```

    event: `<UIEvent: 0x143ae0>`. The `allTouches` set:

    ```
    T2:   <UITouch: 0x14a0f0> phase: Moved
    ```

11. Finger F2 lifted.
    `touchesEnded:withEvent:` is called.
    `touches:` a set of one element:

T2:        <UITouch:  0x14a0f0>  phase:  Ended

event:<UIEvent:  0x143ae0>. The allTouches set:

T2:        <UITouch:  0x14a0f0>  phase:  Ended

Listing 4.1 shows a UIView subclass that overrides three responder methods and logs the touches and events for all three phases. Use this in an application to test your understanding of the multitouch interface.

**Listing 4.1**   A UIView subclass that overrides three responder methods and logs the touches and events for all three phases.

```
@interface ViewOne : UIView {}
@end

@implementation ViewOne

- (void)touchesBegan:(NSSet *)touches withEvent:(UIEvent *)event{
    for(UITouch *t in touches)
        NSLog(@"B: touch: %@", t);
    NSLog(@"B: event:  %@", event);
}

- (void)touchesMoved:(NSSet *)touches withEvent:(UIEvent *)event{
    for(UITouch *t in touches)
        NSLog(@"M: touch: %@", t);
    NSLog(@"M: event:  %@", event);
}

- (void)touchesEnded:(NSSet *)touches withEvent:(UIEvent *)event{
    for(UITouch *t in touches)
        NSLog(@"E: touch: %@", t);
    NSLog(@"E: event:  %@", event);
}
@end
```

## 4.3.4   Handling a swipe

In this section, we demonstrate how you can intercept the phases of the user's touches in order to recognize a swipe gesture. The application that we are about to build will recognize a right/left swipe and present its speed (in points per second) in a view.

Listing 4.2 shows the declaration of the application delegate class. The SwipeAppDelegate application delegate uses the SwipeDemoView view as the main view for the application.

**Listing 4.2** The declaration of the application delegate class `SwipeAppDelegate`.

```
#import <UIKit/UIKit.h>
#import "SwipeDemoView.h"

@interface SwipeAppDelegate : NSObject <UIApplicationDelegate> {
    UIWindow            *window;
    SwipeDemoView       *viewOne;
}
@property (nonatomic, retain) UIWindow *window;
@end
```

Listing 4.3 shows the implementation of the application delegate class. The `application-DidFinishLaunching:` method creates an instance of the `SwipeDemoView` view class and enables it for multitouch by setting its `multipleTouchEnabled` property to YES. If you do not do that, the `touches` set in the four responder methods will always have the size of 1.

**Listing 4.3** The implementation of the application delegate class `SwipeAppDelegate`.

```
#import "SwipeAppDelegate.h"

@implementation SwipeAppDelegate
@synthesize window;

- (void)
applicationDidFinishLaunching:(UIApplication *)application {
    window = [[UIWindow alloc]
            initWithFrame:[[UIScreen mainScreen] bounds]];
    CGRect frame = [UIScreen mainScreen].applicationFrame;
    viewOne = [[SwipeDemoView alloc] initWithFrame:frame];
    viewOne.multipleTouchEnabled = YES;
    viewOne.backgroundColor = [UIColor whiteColor];
    [window addSubview:viewOne];
    [window makeKeyAndVisible];
}

- (void)dealloc {
    [viewOne release];
    [window release];
    [super dealloc];
}
@end
```

The view will keep track of the two touches' time and location. In addition, it uses a `state` variable to help in recognizing a swipe. If the view is in `state` S0, that means we haven't received any touch. If, however, it is in `state` S1, then that means that we have received exactly one touch and we are waiting for it to be lifted. Listing 4.4 shows the declaration of the `SwipeDemoView`

view class. Notice that we have two instance variables for the location and two instance variables for the time. The time is specified in NSTimeInterval (double) which is measured in seconds.

**Listing 4.4**    The declaration of the SwipeDemoView view class.

```
#import <UIKit/UIKit.h>
typedef enum  {
  S0,
  S1
} STATE;

@interface SwipeDemoView : UIView {
  CGPoint                startLocation, endLocation;
  NSTimeInterval         startTime, endTime;
  STATE                  state;
}
@end
```

Let's start analyzing the logic behind the recognition of a swipe gesture and displaying its speed. Listing 4.5 shows the touchesBegan:withEvent: method of the UIResponder class overridden by the SwipeDemoView class. What we would like to do in this method is to first make sure that we haven't received any touches before (i.e., we are in state S0). In addition, we would like to make sure that the number of touches in the event object and the number of elements in the touches object is the same and is equal to 1. After making sure that this condition holds, we record the start time and start location of the touch, and enter state S1.

**Listing 4.5**    The touchesBegan:withEvent: method used in the Swipe Determination application.

```
- (void)touchesBegan:(NSSet *)touches withEvent:(UIEvent *)event{
  int noTouchesInEvent = ((NSSet*)[event allTouches]).count;
  int noTouchesBegan = touches.count;
  NSLog(@"began %i, total %i",
       noTouchesBegan, noTouchesInEvent);
  if((state == S0) &&
    (noTouchesBegan== 1) &&
    (noTouchesInEvent==1)){
    startLocation =
        [(UITouch*)[touches anyObject]
                         locationInView:self];
    startTime = [(UITouch*)[touches anyObject] timestamp];
    state = S1;
  }
  else{
    state = S0;
    [self setNeedsDisplay];
  }
}
```

Listing 4.6 shows the `touchesEnded:withEvent:` method. In this method, we make sure that we are in state S1 (i.e., we have started with one touch and it is being lifted). We also make sure that the touch is the last one leaving the screen. We achieve that by ensuring that the number of touches in the `event` is equal to that in `touches` and is equal to 1. Once we have these conditions met, we record the location and time of the touch, and display the result to the user.

**Listing 4.6**    The `touchesEnded:withEvent:` method used in the Swipe Determination application.

```
- (void)touchesEnded:(NSSet *)touches withEvent:(UIEvent *)event{
    int noTouchesInEvent = ((NSSet *)[event allTouches]).count;
    int noTouchesEnded    = touches.count;
    NSLog(@"ended %i %i", touches.count,
        ((NSSet *)[event allTouches]).count);
    if( (state==S1) && (noTouchesEnded == 1) &&
    (noTouchesInEvent==1)){
        endLocation =
            [(UITouch *)[touches anyObject] locationInView:self];
        endTime    =
            [(UITouch *)[touches anyObject] timestamp];
        [self setNeedsDisplay];
    }
}
```

Listing 4.7 shows the remainder of the `SwipeDemoView` class definition. The `drawRect:` method presents the user with information about the swipe. If the state is S0, we clear the statistics from the previous swipe. If the state is S1, we check to see if the gesture was a swipe. The following statement checks to see whether: (1) the absolute difference in the y-coordinates of the beginning and ending touch is below or equal to the value Y_TOLERANCE, and (2) the absolute difference in the x-coordinates of the beginning and ending touch is above or equal to the value X_TOLERANCE.

```
if( (fabs(startLocation.y - endLocation.y) <= Y_TOLERANCE)  &&
    (fabs(startLocation.x - endLocation.x) >= X_TOLERANCE)
)
```

The tolerance values are defined as follows:

```
#define Y_TOLERANCE 20
#define X_TOLERANCE 100
```

You can specify the values that best fit your application.

Once we have determined that it is a swipe, we determine the direction of the swipe using the following statement:

```
direction = (endLocation.x > startLocation.x) ? "right" : "left";
```

Finally, we determine the speed of the swipe using the following statement:

```
fabs(endLocation.x - startLocation.x) /(endTime-startTime)
```

The result is displayed to the user as shown in Fig. 4.5.

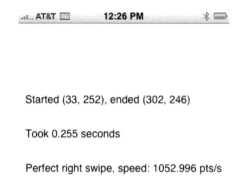

Started (33, 252), ended (302, 246)

Took 0.255 seconds

Perfect right swipe, speed: 1052.996 pts/s

**Figure 4.5**  A snapshot of the Swipe Determination application showing a perfect right swipe.

**Listing 4.7**  The remainder of the `SwipeDemoView` class definition.

```
- (id)initWithFrame:(CGRect)frame {
  if (self = [super initWithFrame:frame]) {
    state = S0;
  }
  return self;
}

- (void)drawRect:(CGRect)rect {
  NSString  *message;
  if(state==S0){
    [@"\t\t\t\t\t\t\t\t\t\t" drawAtPoint:CGPointMake(10,100)
        withFont:[UIFont systemFontOfSize:16]];
    [@"\t\t\t\t\t\t\t\t\t\t" drawAtPoint:CGPointMake(10,150)
        withFont:[UIFont systemFontOfSize:16]];
    [@"\t\t\t\t\t\t\t\t\t\t" drawAtPoint:CGPointMake(10,200)
        withFont:[UIFont systemFontOfSize:16]];
  }
  if(state == S1){
    message =
    [NSString
     stringWithFormat:
       @"Started (%.0f, %.0f), ended (%.0f, %.0f)",
     startLocation.x, startLocation.y,
     endLocation.x, endLocation.y
     ];
    [message drawAtPoint:CGPointMake(10,100)
        withFont:[UIFont systemFontOfSize:16]];
```

```
message =
[NSString
  stringWithFormat:
   @"Took %4.3f seconds", endTime-startTime
  ];
[message drawAtPoint:CGPointMake(10,150)
    withFont:[UIFont systemFontOfSize:16]];

if( (fabs(startLocation.y - endLocation.y) <= Y_TOLERANCE)
&&
   (fabs(startLocation.x - endLocation.x) >= X_TOLERANCE)
   ){
   char *direction;
   direction =
     (endLocation.x > startLocation.x) ? "right" : "left";
   message =
   [NSString
    stringWithFormat:
     @"Perfect %s swipe, speed: %4.3f pts/s", direction,
    (endTime-startTime) > 0 ?
        fabs(endLocation.x - startLocation.x) /
            (endTime-startTime) :
        0
    ];
   [message drawAtPoint:CGPointMake(10,200)
     withFont:[UIFont systemFontOfSize:16]];
}
else {
   [@"\t\t\t\t\t\t\t\t\t\t" drawAtPoint:CGPointMake(10,200)
     withFont:[UIFont systemFontOfSize:16]];
}
state = S0;
  }
}
```

It is worth noting that this gesture-recognition algorithm does not take into account the interme-diate movements of the touch. For that, you need to override the `touchesMoves:withEvent:` method and make sure that the `Y_TOLERANCE` value is not violated.

### 4.3.5  *More advanced gesture recognition*

In this section, we provide yet another application that deals with multitouch gestures. This application recognizes the following gesture: two fingers touch the screen together or at most within

2 seconds. The fingers move either together or separately. At the end, the two fingers are lifted from the screen together at the same time. The application will display the following statistics: (1) what is the percentage of the time that the two fingers moved together, and (2) the average distance (in points) between the two fingers.

The application delegate is identical to the one you saw in the previous section. The only difference is the custom view class `ResponderDemoView`. Listing 4.8 shows the declaration of the view class. We define three states: (1) S0, the initial state, (2) S1, the state where we have received two touches within a reasonable time and statistics can be collected, and (3) S2, where we have received only one touch and we are waiting for the second. We keep track of the current state in the instance variable `state`. The variables `movedTogether` and `movedSeperate` record the number of movements of the two fingers together and separately, respectively. The total distance between the two fingers is accumulated in the `accDistance` variable. In addition, the first touch's information (in the case of a delayed second touch) is cached in the two variables `firstTouchLocInView` and `firstTouchTimeStamp`.

**Listing 4.8**    The declaration of the view class `ResponderDemoView`.

```
#import <UIKit/UIKit.h>

typedef enum {
    S0,
    S1,
    S2
} STATE;

@interface ResponderDemoView : UIView {
    STATE               state;
    float               movedTogether, movedSeperate;
    float               accDistance;
    CGPoint             firstTouchLocInView;
    NSTimeInterval      firstTouchTimeStamp;
}
@end
```

Listing 4.9 shows the `touchesBegan:withEvent:` method for the advanced gesture tracking application. There are three major sections of this method. The first is checking to see if two simultaneous fingers have touched the screen. If that is the case, the method changes the state to S1 and initializes the variables for collecting the statistics. The initial distance is also calculated and used to initialize the accumulated distance variable. The distance, in points, is calculated using the `distance()` function shown below.

```
float distance(CGPoint a, CGPoint b){
    return sqrt( pow((a.x - b.x), 2) + pow((a.y - b.y), 2));
}
```

If the user did not use two fingers together at the same time, we check to see if this is a single touch and it is the first touch that is received. If that is the case, we enter state S2 (meaning that we have one touch and we are waiting for the second) and cache in the vital information about the touch.

If, on the other hand, we are in state S2 and the event object has two touches, we check to see if the second touch is received within an acceptable time. The following statement checks to see if the difference in arrival time of the two touches is below a threshold:

```
if ((aTouch.timestamp − firstTouchTimeStamp) <=
        MAX_ELAPSED_TIME)
```

If that is the case, we enter state S1; otherwise, the touch is considered the first touch and we wait for the next. The value for MAX_ELAPSED_TIME is defined to be equal to 2 seconds.

```
#define MAX_ELAPSED_TIME   2
```

**Listing 4.9**   The touchesBegan:withEvent: method for the advanced gesture tracking application.

```
− (void)touchesBegan:(NSSet *)touches withEvent:(UIEvent *)event{
  int noTouchesInEvent = ((NSSet*)[event allTouches]).count;
  int noTouchesBegan    = touches.count;
  NSLog(@"began %i, total %i",
      noTouchesBegan, noTouchesInEvent);
  if ((noTouchesBegan== 2) && (noTouchesInEvent==2)){
    NSArray *touchArray = [touches allObjects];
    state = S1;
    movedTogether = 1;
    movedSeperate = 0;
    accDistance =
        distance([[touchArray objectAtIndex:0]
                        locationInView:self],
                 [[touchArray objectAtIndex:1]
                        locationInView:self]
        );
  }
  else if ((state != S2) && ( (noTouchesBegan== 1) &&
    (noTouchesInEvent==1))){
    state = S2; // S2 means we got the first touch
    UITouch *aTouch = (UITouch*)[touches anyObject];
    firstTouchTimeStamp = aTouch.timestamp;
    firstTouchLocInView = [aTouch locationInView:self];
  }
  else if ((state == S2) && (noTouchesInEvent==2) ){
    UITouch *aTouch = (UITouch*)[touches anyObject];
    if ((aTouch.timestamp − firstTouchTimeStamp) <=
        MAX_ELAPSED_TIME){
// S1 means we got the second  touch within reasonable time
        state = S1;
```

```
        movedTogether = 1;
        movedSeperate = 0;
        accDistance = distance([aTouch      locationInView:self],
                      firstTouchLocInView
                      );
    }
    else {
      firstTouchTimeStamp = aTouch.timestamp;
      firstTouchLocInView = [aTouch locationInView:self];
    }
  }
  else state = S0;
}
```

Listing 4.10 shows the `touchesMoved:withEvent:` method. If the number of touches is two and we are in the state `S1` (collecting statistics), we increment the `movedTogether` counter and update the distance in `accDistance`. If, on the other hand, we receive just one movement, we increment the `movedSeperate` counter.

**Listing 4.10**    The `touchesMoved:withEvent:` method for the advanced gesture tracking application.

```
- (void)touchesMoved:(NSSet *)touches withEvent:(UIEvent *)event{
  NSLog(@"moved %i %i", touches.count,
      ((NSSet*)[event allTouches]).count);
  NSArray *allTouches = [touches allObjects];
  if((state == S1) && ([touches count] == 2) ){
    movedTogether++;
    accDistance +=
      distance([[allTouches objectAtIndex:0]
                    locationInView:self],
              [[allTouches objectAtIndex:1]
                    locationInView:self]
              );
  }
  else if((state == S1) && ([touches count] == 1) ){
    movedSeperate++;
  }
}
```

Listing 4.11 shows the `touchesEnded:withEvent:` method. The method makes sure that the two fingers have been lifted at the same time and requests the display of the statistics by sending the view instance a `setNeedsDisplay` message. This will eventually trigger the invocation of the `drawRect:` method in Listing 4.13.

**Listing 4.11**   The `touchesEnded:withEvent:` method for the Advanced Gesture Tracking application.

```
- (void)touchesEnded:(NSSet *)touches withEvent:(UIEvent *)event{
  NSLog(@"ended %i %i", touches.count,
          ((NSSet*)[event allTouches]).count);
  if((state == S1) && ([touches count] == 2) ){
    NSLog(@"started together and ended together,"
        "moved together %.0f%% "
        "of the time. AVG distance:%4.2f",
        (movedSeperate+movedTogether) ?
        100*(movedTogether/(movedTogether+movedSeperate)) :
        100.0,
        movedTogether ? accDistance/movedTogether : 0.0
    );
    [self setNeedsDisplay];
  }
  state = S0;
}
```

If the system is canceling the event, we reset the variables as shown in Listing 4.12.

**Listing 4.12**   The overridden method `touchesCancelled:withEvent:` for the Advanced Gesture Tracking application.

```
- (void)
touchesCancelled:(NSSet *)touches withEvent:(UIEvent *)event{
  state = S0;
  movedTogether = movedSeperate = 0;
  accDistance =0;
}
```

Listing 4.13 shows the remainder of the definition of the view class. The `initWithFrame:` initializer sets the statistics and state variables to their initial values. The `drawRect:` method, invoked when the view receives a `setNeedsDisplay` message, displays the percentage of the time that the two touches moved together and the average distance between them when they did move together.

Figure 4.6 shows a snapshot of the application.

**Listing 4.13**   The remainder of the implementation of the view class used in the Advanced Gesture Tracking application.

```
- (id)initWithFrame:(CGRect)frame {
  if (self = [super initWithFrame:frame]) {
    state = S0;
    movedTogether = movedSeperate = 0;
    accDistance =0;
  }
```

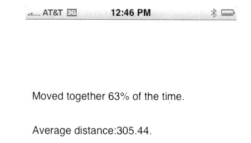

Moved together 63% of the time.

Average distance:305.44.

**Figure 4.6**    A snapshot of the Advanced Gesture Tracking application.

```
  return  self;
}

− (void)drawRect:(CGRect)rect {
  NSString  *message =
  [NSString
    stringWithFormat:@"Moved together %.0f%% of the time.",
   (movedSeperate+movedTogether) ?
     100*(movedTogether/(movedTogether+movedSeperate)) :
     100.0
   ];
  [message  drawAtPoint:CGPointMake(10,100)
      withFont:[UIFont systemFontOfSize:16]];
  message =
  [NSString
    stringWithFormat:@"Average distance:%4.2f.",
    movedTogether ? accDistance/movedTogether : 0.0
   ];
  [message  drawAtPoint:CGPointMake(10,150)
      withFont:[UIFont systemFontOfSize:16]];
}
```

## 4.4    Animation

Animation is a major feature of the iPhone OS. In this section, we will discuss basic examples that achieve animation. These examples do not require knowledge of image processing. We first start by discussing how you can use the `UIView` class to animate properties of views. After that, we give an example that performs view transitioning.

### 4.4.1    Using the `UIView` class animation support

The geometric properties of a view can be actually animated with ease. The `UIView` class provides several class methods that can be used to perform simple animations such as moving a view instance to a new position or enlarging it.

To animate views' properties, you must do that between two `UIView` class calls: `beginAnimations:context:` and `commitAnimations`. Inside this animation block, you specify the characteristics of the animation (e.g., its length, timing function, etc.) and change the view's properties (e.g., its `center`) to the final value. When you commit the animation, the view's properties are animated to the new values.

Let's start by building an application that enables the user to move a view around the screen by double-tapping on the new position. The move of the view is animated by changing its center. We will create a new subclass of `UIView` named `AnimView`. `AnimView` adds as a subview another child view and waits for the user's tapping. When the user double-taps a location in an `AnimView` instance, the child view's center property is animated and changed to the location where the user double-tapped.

Listing 4.14 shows the application delegate class for the application. The `applicationDid-FinishLaunching:` method creates a main window and adds to it an instance of the `AnimView` class. The `AnimView` instance occupies the full screen available to the user and has a gray background color.

**Listing 4.14**    The application delegate class for animating a view's `center` property.

```
#import <UIKit/UIKit.h>
#import "AnimView.h"

@interface AnimationApp1AppDelegate :
        NSObject <UIApplicationDelegate> {
    UIWindow *window;
}
@end

@implementation AnimationApp1AppDelegate
- (void)
applicationDidFinishLaunching:
(UIApplication *)application {
    window = [[UIWindow alloc]
        initWithFrame:[[UIScreen    mainScreen] bounds]];
    CGRect    frame =
        [UIScreen mainScreen].applicationFrame;
    AnimView *view = [[AnimView alloc]
                        initWithFrame:frame];
    view.backgroundColor = [UIColor grayColor];
    [window addSubview:view];
    [view release];
```

```
    [window makeKeyAndVisible];
}

- (void)dealloc {
    [window release];
    [super dealloc];
}
```
@**end**

Listing 4.15 shows the `AnimView` class. The class maintains a reference to a child view in the instance variable `childView`. The `initWithFrame:` initializer creates the child view instance, configures it with a white background color, and adds it as a subview.

The logic behind moving the child view to a new location is found in the `touches-Ended:withEvent:` method. The method first checks that we have a double-tap from the user. If that is the case, it starts the animation block by the following statement:

```
[UIView beginAnimations:nil context:NULL];
```

The class method is declared as follows:

```
+ (void)
beginAnimations:(NSString *)animationID
    context:(void *)context
```

The two parameters of this method can be NULL. The `animationID` and `context` can be used to communicate with animation delegates. Our example does not use an animation delegate, so we pass NULL values.

After starting the animation block, the method sets the optional animation curve. The following statement overrides the default animation curve and sets it to `UIViewAnimationCurve-EaseOut`:

```
[UIView setAnimationCurve:
            UIViewAnimationCurveEaseOut];
```

The `setAnimationCurve:` method is declared as follows:

```
+ (void)
setAnimationCurve:(UIViewAnimationCurve)curve
```

The following are some of the curves available:

- `UIViewAnimationCurveEaseInOut`. This curve specifies that the animation should be slow at the beginning and at the end. This curve is the default.

- `UIViewAnimationCurveEaseIn`. This curve specifies that the animation should be slow at the beginning only.

- `UIViewAnimationCurveEaseOut`. This curve specifies that the animation should be slow at the end only.

- `UIViewAnimationCurveLinear`. This curve specifies that the animation should be constant throughout.

The duration of the animation is set using the method setAnimationDuration: which is declared as follows:

```
+ (void)
setAnimationDuration:(NSTimeInterval)duration
```

The duration parameter is specified in seconds. The default is 0.2 seconds.

After the animation is set up, the method changes the properties of the views, which in our case is one property (center) and one view (childView), and commits the animation. The center property is changed in the following statement:

```
childView.center = [touch locationInView:self]
```

**Listing 4.15**    The AnimView class used in animating the center property of a child view.

```
#import <UIKit/UIKit.h>
#import <QuartzCore/QuartzCore.h>

@interface AnimView : UIView {
  UIView *childView;
}
@end

@implementation AnimView

- (id)initWithFrame:(CGRect)frame {
  if (self = [super initWithFrame:frame]) {
    childView = [[UIView alloc]
          initWithFrame:
            CGRectMake(100, 150, 100, 150)];
    childView.backgroundColor = [UIColor whiteColor];
    [self addSubview:childView];
  }
  return self;
}

- (void)touchesEnded:(NSSet *)touches
      withEvent:(UIEvent *)event{

  if( [(UITouch *)[touches anyObject] tapCount] == 2){
    UITouch *touch = [touches anyObject];
    [UIView beginAnimations:nil context:NULL];
    [UIView setAnimationCurve:
          UIViewAnimationCurveEaseOut];
    [UIView setAnimationDuration:1];
    childView.center = [touch locationInView:self];
```

```
      [UIView commitAnimations];
   }
}

- (void)dealloc {
   [childView release];
   [super dealloc];
}
@end
```

Sometimes you want to receive a message when the animation ends. You can set a delegate to the animation using the method `setAnimationDelegate:`. Calls are made to two methods in this delegate: `animationDidStart:` and `animationDidStop:finished:`. These methods are defined using a category on `NSObject`.

Let's update our animation application to change the color of the child view and animate its size. When the animation is finished, we revert back to the original size and color. The following is the updated `touchesEnded:withEvent:`.

```
- (void)
touchesEnded:(NSSet *)touches
withEvent:(UIEvent *)event{
   if( [(UITouch*)[touches anyObject] tapCount] == 2){
      childView.backgroundColor = [UIColor blueColor];
      [UIView beginAnimations:nil context:NULL];
      [UIView setAnimationCurve:UIViewAnimationCurveEaseOut];
      [UIView setAnimationDuration:0.5];
      [UIView setAnimationDelegate:self];
      childView.transform = CGAffineTransformMakeScale(1.5, 1.5);
      [UIView commitAnimations];
   }
}
```

In the code fragment above, on a double-tap, we change the color of the child view outside the animation block. This will result in an instantaneous color change rather than an animated change if it had been done inside the animation block. After that, the animation block is started, and the curve, duration, and delegate are set. To change the scale of the child view by increasing it by 50%, the method updates the `transform` property of the view. The property is declared as follows:

```
@property(nonatomic) CGAffineTransform transform
```

The transform is done using a $3 \times 3$ matrix that is used to rotate, scale, or translate the view. `CGAffineTransform` stores the first two columns of this matrix. The third column is always [0, 0, 1]. To scale the child view up by 50%, we use the following statement:

```
childView.transform =   CGAffineTransformMakeScale(1.5, 1.5)
```

In the above statement, we obtain an affine transform for scaling 50% using the `CGAffine-TransformMakeScale()` function, and set the value to the `transform` property.

After the animation ends, and the child view is enlarged 50%, a call is made to the method
animationDidStop:finished: defined in the AnimView class as follows:

```
- (void)
animationDidStop:(CAAnimation *)theAnimation
finished:(BOOL)flag {
  childView.transform = CGAffineTransformIdentity;
  childView.backgroundColor = [UIColor whiteColor];
}
```

The method above, changes the child view's background color to white and transforms
(instantaneously) the dimensions to no scaling.

## 4.4.2   Transition animation

The UIView class is actually a wrapper class that takes its event-handling capabilities from the
NSResponder class, through the inheritance chain, and its animation capabilities from its unique
CALayer instance variable. layer, an instance of CALayer, is the Core Animation object
that encapsulates information about the animation that should be rendered to the display.

When you make changes to a UIView instance by, for example, adding and removing subviews,
the changes happen instantaneously. To animate these changes, you create an animation object,
configure it, and add it to the layer property. In this section, we show how you can animate the
substitution of one view with another through transition animation. The application demonstrating
this will create two subviews of the main window and add one of them to the window. When the user
double-taps on the active view, the application will replace the view with the other inactive view and
animate the change by moving the new view from right to left.

The animation is performed in the application delegate class. Listing 4.16 shows the declaration
of the application delegate class. The class maintains two references to AnimView instances
representing the two views. The showOtherView: method is used to animate the replacement
of one view by the other.

**Listing 4.16**   The declaration of the application delegate class used in animating the transition of views.

```
#import <UIKit/UIKit.h>
@class AnimView;
@interface AnimationApp2AppDelegate :
      NSObject <UIApplicationDelegate> {
  UIWindow *window;
  AnimView    *view1, *view2;
}
-(void)showOtherView:(UIView*) oldView;
@end
```

Listing 4.17 shows the implementation of the application delegate class. The application-
DidFinishLaunching: method creates the main window as well as two subviews. It adds one
view to the window and makes the window key and visible.

When the current view asks the application delegate to switch to the other view, the showOtherView: is called with the reference to the active subview. The current view is removed from the window and the other view is added. To animate this change, we create an animation object and add it to the window's layer property.

Animation objects are instances of the class CAAnimation. The CATransition is a subclass of CAAnimation that makes it easy to animate transitions. We first obtain a new animation object by using the class method animation. Next, the type, duration, and timing of the animation are configured. The type of animation is move in from the right, and the duration chosen is 0.5 seconds. Also, an ease-in-ease-out timing function is used. To add the animation, we use the method addAnimation:forKey: which is declared as follows:

```
- (void)
addAnimation:(CAAnimation *)anim
forKey:(NSString *)key
```

The anim parameter is an instance of CAAnimation that represents the animation, and the key (can be nil) is to distinguish different animations on a given layer. Since the anim parameter is copied by the method, you need to invoke this method after you have configured the animation object.

**Listing 4.17**  The implementation of the application delegate class used in animating the transition of views.

```
#import <QuartzCore/QuartzCore.h>
#import "AnimationApp2AppDelegate.h"
#import "AnimView.h"


@implementation AnimationApp2AppDelegate


- (void)
applicationDidFinishLaunching:(UIApplication *)application {

   window = [[UIWindow alloc]
        initWithFrame:[[UIScreen mainScreen] bounds]];
   CGRect frame = [UIScreen mainScreen].applicationFrame;
   view1 = [[AnimView alloc] initWithFrame:frame];
   view1.message = @"View 1";
   view1.backgroundColor =[UIColor whiteColor];
   [window addSubview:view1];
   view2 = [[AnimView alloc] initWithFrame:frame];
   view2.message = @"View 2";
   view2.backgroundColor =[UIColor yellowColor];
    [window makeKeyAndVisible];
}

-(void)showOtherView:(UIView *) oldView{
  if(oldView == view1){
```

```
    [ view1    removeFromSuperview ];
    [ window  addSubview : view2 ];
  }
  else {
    [ view2    removeFromSuperview ];
    [ window  addSubview : view1 ];
  }
  CATransition *animation = [ CATransition  animation ];
  [ animation  setType : kCATransitionMoveIn ];
  [ animation  setSubtype : kCATransitionFromRight ];
  [ animation  setDuration : 0.5 ];
  [ animation  setTimingFunction :
      [ CAMediaTimingFunction
          functionWithName :
            kCAMediaTimingFunctionEaseInEaseOut ] ];
  [[ window  layer ]  addAnimation : animation  forKey : @"mykey" ];
}

– ( void ) dealloc  {
  [ view1    release ];
  [ view2    release ];
  [ window  release ];
  [ super  dealloc ];
}
@end
```

Listing 4.18 shows the `AnimView` class. The class maintains a message instance variable whose content is drawn to the screen. This will serve as a distinguishing mark between the two transitioning views.

**Listing 4.18**   The `AnimView` class used in the transition views application.

```
#import <UIKit / UIKit . h>
#import <QuartzCore / QuartzCore . h>

@interface AnimView  :  UIView  {
  NSString    *message ;
}
@property ( nonatomic ,  copy )  NSString  *message ;
@end

@implementation AnimView
@synthesize  message ;

– ( void )
touchesEnded : ( NSSet  *) touches  withEvent : ( UIEvent  *) event {
```

```
if (  [(UITouch*)[touches anyObject] tapCount] == 2){
    [[UIApplication sharedApplication].delegate
        showOtherView:self];
  }
}

- (void)drawRect:(CGRect)rect{
    [message drawAtPoint:CGPointMake(100,100)
        withFont:[UIFont systemFontOfSize:32]];
}
@end
```

## 4.5 Drawing

The drawRect: method is an ideal place for drawing in a view. The view will set up the environment for you, making it easy to draw. You use Quartz 2D functions for drawing simple and complex shapes. These functions require a graphics context as the first parameter. You can obtain a graphics context using the function UIGraphicsGetCurrentContext().

Once you have a graphics context, you can use it to draw paths. A path is a collection of one or more shapes. Once you construct the path, you can stroke it, fill it, or both.

Listing 4.19 shows a drawRect: that draws several shapes. The result of this drawing is shown in Fig. 4.7. After obtaining the graphics context, we set the line width of the path to 5 units (the default is 1). Then, we signal a new path location using the function CGContextMoveToPoint(). The function CGContextAddLineToPoint() is used to add a line to the path starting from (50, 100) and ending in (200, 100). At this stage, we have only one shape (a straight line) in this path. To draw it, we use the CGContextStrokePath() function. This function will draw the path and clear the current path.

To draw an ellipse, use the function CGContextAddEllipseInRect(). When you follow it up with the function call to CGContextStrokePath(), the ellipse is drawn. If you want to fill the ellipse, use the function CGContextFillPath().

You can set the stroke color using the function CGContextSetRGBStrokeColor(). In this function, you specify the RGB components and the alpha (opacity level). Similarly, the fill color can be set using the function CGContextSetRGBFillColor(). Similar to lines and ellipses, you can draw rectangles, curves, arcs, etc.

**Listing 4.19**    A drawRect: that draws several shapes.

```
- (void)drawRect:(CGRect)rect {
    CGContextRef  context = UIGraphicsGetCurrentContext ();

    CGContextSetLineWidth(context,  5.0);
    CGContextMoveToPoint(context,  50, 100);
    CGContextAddLineToPoint(context, 200, 100);
    CGContextStrokePath(context);
```

**Figure 4.7** Drawing several shapes using Quartz 2D.

```
CGContextAddEllipseInRect(context,
    CGRectMake(70.0, 170.0, 50.0, 50.0));
CGContextStrokePath(context);

CGContextAddEllipseInRect(context,
    CGRectMake(150.0, 170.0, 50.0, 50.0));
CGContextFillPath(context);

CGContextSetRGBStrokeColor(context, 0.0, 1.0, 0.0, 1.0);
CGContextSetRGBFillColor(context, 0.0, 0.0, 1.0, 1.0);
CGContextAddRect(context,
    CGRectMake(30.0, 30.0, 60.0, 60.0));
CGContextFillPath(context);

CGContextAddArc(context,
    260, 90, 40, 0.0*M_PI/180, 270*M_PI/180, 1);
CGContextAddLineToPoint(context, 280, 350);
CGContextStrokePath(context);
```

```
        CGContextMoveToPoint(context, 130, 300);
        CGContextAddLineToPoint(context, 80, 400);
        CGContextAddLineToPoint(context, 190, 400);
        CGContextAddLineToPoint(context, 130, 300);
        CGContextStrokePath(context);
}
```

# 5

# Controls

Controls are graphical objects used by the user of the application to express his/her objective. For example, a slider control can be used by the user as a way to fine tune a specific value. A switch control, on the other hand, can be used to turn on/off an option. In this chapter, we present several important graphical controls that can be used in building attractive iPhone applications.

We will cover the main graphical controls available, and their usage. Before we begin talking about specialized controls, let's understand the base class for all controls, UIControl, and the important *target-action* mechanism.

## 5.1 The Foundation of All Controls

Controls are subclasses of the UIControl class. The UIControl class position in the class hierarchy is shown in Fig. 5.1. The common behavior of controls is captured by this class. Therefore, understanding this class is essential to using its concrete subclasses such as UITextField, UISlider, UIDatePicker, etc.

### 5.1.1 UIControl attributes

As a superclass of controls, the UIControl class has several shared attributes that can be configured using accessor methods. These attributes include:

- enabled. This is a Boolean attribute that represents whether the control is enabled or not. The property is defined as:

  @property(nonatomic, getter=isEnabled) BOOL enabled

  If the value for enabled is NO, the user's touch events are ignored.

- highlighted. This Boolean value controls whether the control is highlighted or not. By default, the value is NO. When the user touches the control, the value of this attribute is YES, and the control is highlighted. When the user touch leaves the control, the value is NO, and the control is not highlighted. The property declaration of this attribute is:

  @property(nonatomic, getter=isHighlighted) BOOL highlighted

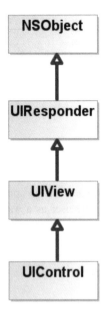

**Figure 5.1**    `UIControl` inheritance hierarchy.

- `selected`. This Boolean attribute indicates whether the control is selected or not. Most subclasses of `UIControl` do not use this. However, the `UISwitch` subclass might use it. The declaration of this property is as follows:

  `@property(nonatomic, getter=isSelected) BOOL selected`

- `state`. This is a read-only attribute of type `UIControlState`. `UIControlState` is defined as an unsigned integer (`NSUInteger`). `state` is a bit-mask representing more than one state. Examples of defined states are `UIControlStateHighlighted`, `UIControlStateDisabled`, and `UIControlStateNormal`.

  The property is defined as follows, but note that this attribute is read-only.

  `@property(nonatomic, readonly) UIControlState state`

### 5.1.2   *Target-action mechanism*

`UIControl` and its subclasses use the target-action mechanism to inform interested parties when changes to the control object occur. Basically, an object, which is usually a controller, sends a message to the control informing it that it is interested in monitoring some event related to the control. When such an event occurs, the control will inform the object (e.g., the controller).

An object registering itself using the target-action mechanism is required to include three pieces of information: (1) a pointer to the object (target) that should receive the message (usually itself), (2) the selector (action) representing the action method, and (3) the control event it is interested in.

When the control receives the registration message, it stores this information in an internal dispatch table. Note that the same target can register for different events with different selectors. Moreover, different targets can register for the same event.

When the event (such as a change in the value of the control) occurs, the control sends itself the sendActionsForControlEvents: message. This method will then consult the internal dispatch table (the same table built incrementally as a result of registration messages) to find all target-action entries for this event. The control then sends the singleton UIApplication instance a sendAction:to:from:forEvent: message for each such entry. The UIApplication instance is the one responsible for actually sending the action messages to the targets.

An object registers with a control using the following UIControl declared instance method:

– ( **void** ) addTarget : ( **id** ) target  action : ( SEL ) action
    forControlEvents : ( UIControlEvents ) controlEvents

The target is usually the instance registering for this event (e.g., a controller). The action is a selector that identifies the action message of the target (i.e., the method that gets called by the UIApplication instance when the event occurs). The selector takes any of the following three forms:

– ( **void** ) action
– ( **void** ) action : ( **id** ) sender
– ( **void** ) action : ( **id** ) sender  forEvent : ( UIEvent *) event

The controlEvents is a bit-mask specifying the control events that trigger the sending of an action message to the target. There are several of these control events defined in UIControl.h. Some examples include:

• UIControlEventValueChanged. Used to indicate that the value of the control has changed, for example, the slider moved.

• UIControlEventEditingDidBegin. The control (e.g., UITextfield) started editing.

• UIControlEventEditingDidEnd. A touch ending the editing of a field by leaving its bounds.

• UIControlEventTouchDown. A single tap touch inside the control's bounds.

Figure 5.2 shows a sequence diagram for a target-action scenario. Here, we have two controllers, ctrl1 and ctrl2, interested in the control event UIControlEventValueChanged. The diagram shows the role that the UIApplication singleton instance plays in delivering the action messages.

There are several other important methods available in the UIControl class that are related to the target-action mechanism.

• removeTarget:action:forControlEvents:. This method is used to remove a specific target and action entry from the dispatch table for a particular control events. The method is declared as:

  – ( **void** ) removeTarget : ( **id** ) target  action : ( SEL ) action
    forControlEvents : ( UIControlEvents ) controlEvents

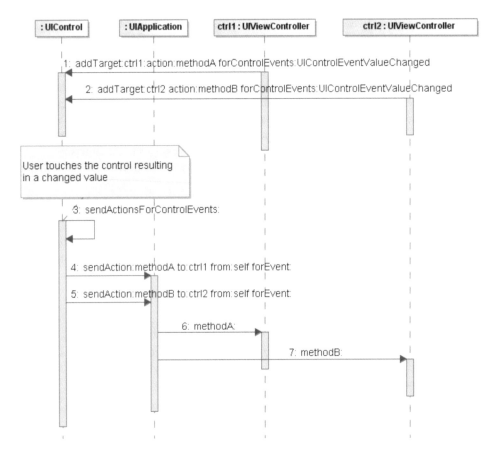

**Figure 5.2** Sequence diagram illustrating the target-action mechanism. Two controllers, `ctrl1` and `ctrl2`, add themselves as `targets` for control event `UIControlEventValueChanged`.

- `allTargets`. This method returns all target objects related to a control object. The method is declared as:

  − ( NSSet ∗ ) allTargets

- `allControlEvents`. This method returns all control events related to a control object. The method is declared as:

  − ( UIControlEvents ) allControlEvents

- `actionsForTarget:forControlEvent:`. This method return the actions associated with a specific target and a particular control event.

  − ( NSArray ∗ ) actionsForTarget : ( **id** ) target
    forControlEvent : ( UIControlEvents ) controlEvent

The return value is an `NSArray` of `NSString` objects of selector names. If there are no actions associated with the control events, the returned value is `nil`.

Now that we understand the `UIControl` class, let's look at some of its concrete implementations.

## 5.2   UITextField

`UITextField` (see Fig. 5.5) encapsulates a text editing control that allows the user to enter a small amount of information. This control provides an optional clear button on the right for clearing the text. `UITextField` uses the `UITextFieldDelegate` protocol for communicating with the delegate class (usually a controller). The `UITextField` itself adopts the `UITextInputTraits` protocol. This protocol must be implemented by any control which uses the keyboard. You create an instance of `UITextField` and add it to a view as a subview.

There are several important properties of this control:

- `text`. Using this property, you can obtain and set the text displayed by the control. The property is declared as:

  @property(nonatomic, copy) NSString *text

- `textAlignment`. This property is used to control the technique used to align the text inside the control. The property is declared as:

  @property(nonatomic) UITextAlignment textAlignment

  The `textAlignment` can be set to one of the following values: `UITextAlignmentLeft` (the default), `UITextAlignmentCenter`, and `UITextAlignmentRight`.

- `textColor`. The color of the text inside the control. The property is declared as:

  @property(nonatomic, retain) UIColor *textColor

  Having a value of `nil` (the default) results in a text that is an opaque black.

- `background`. An image that represents the background of the control. The property is declared as:

  @property(nonatomic, retain) UIImage *background

  The default value is `nil`.

- `clearButtonMode`. This property manages the appearance of the clear button. The property is declared as:

  @property(nonatomic) UITextFieldViewMode clearButtonMode

  You can set its value to one of the following: `UITextFieldViewModeNever` (clear button never appears), `UITextFieldViewModeWhileEditing` (appears only when the user is editing text), `UITextFieldViewModeUnlessEditing` (appears only when the user is not editing text), and `UITextFieldViewModeAlways` (always appear).

- borderStyle. This property is used to set the border style of the control. It is declared as:

  @property(nonatomic) UITextBorderStyle borderStyle

  The value can be one of the following border style values: UITextBorderStyleNone (default), UITextBorderStyleLine, UITextBorderStyleBezel, and UIText-BorderStyleRoundedRect.

- delegate. Use this property to assign the delegate of the control. The property declaration is as follows.

  @property(nonatomic, assign) **id**<UITextFieldDelegate> delegate

  If not nil, the control will send special messages to the delegate informing it of important editing changes, for example, the user tapping the return button on the keyboard. We will go over the UITextFieldDelegate protocol shortly.

- disabledBackground. If the value of this attribute is not nil, the disabled-Background value will be used as a background for the control when it is disabled. The property is declared as:

  @property(nonatomic, retain) UIImage *disabledBackground

- editing. This is a read-only attribute indicating whether the control is in edit mode. The property is declared as:

  @property(nonatomic, readonly, getter=isEditing)
          BOOL editing

- font. The value represents the font of the text. The property declaration is as follows:

  @property(nonatomic, retain) UIFont *font

  If this value is nil (the default), the font used is 12-point Helvetica plain.

- placeholder. The value used to show in the text control if there is no text in the field. The declaration of the property is as follows:

  @property(nonatomic, copy) NSString *placeholder

  The default value is nil (i.e., no placeholder string). If not nil, the string is drawn in a 70% grey color.

## 5.2.1   Interacting with the keyboard

We mentioned above that the UITextField control conforms to the UITextInputTraits protocol. This protocol must be implemented by any control that wishes to interact with the user using the keyboard. The protocol defines several properties:

- `keyboardType`. This property controls the style of the keyboard associated with the text field. The property is declared as:

  @property ( nonatomic ) UIKeyboardType keyboardType

  There are several types of keyboard. Examples include:

  - `UIKeyboardTypeDefault`. The default keyboard.
  - `UIKeyboardTypeAlphabet`. Represents the standard alphanumeric (Qwerty) keyboard.
  - `UIKeyboardTypeNumbersAndPunctuation`. A keyboard with numbers and punctuation.
  - `UIKeyboardTypeURL`. A keyboard style that makes it easy to enter a URL.
  - `UIKeyboardTypeNumberPad`. A numeric keyboard suitable for PIN entry.
  - `UIKeyboardTypePhonePad`. A keyboard designed for entering phone numbers.
  - `UIKeyboardTypeNamePhonePad`. A keyboard for entering a name and a phone number.
  - `UIKeyboardTypeEmailAddress`. A keyboard style for entering email addresses.

  Figures 5.3 and 5.4 show some of the available keyboard styles.

- `secureTextEntry`. This property is used to signal that the text entered should be hidden (e.g., each character replaced by a "*"). The property is declared as:

  @property ( nonatomic , getter=isSecureTextEntry )
           BOOL secureTextEntry

- `returnKeyType`. This property is used to define the title for the return key. The property is declared as:

  @property ( nonatomic ) UIReturnKeyType returnKeyType

  The attribute `returnKeyType` can hold any of the following values:
  `UIReturnKeyDefault`, `UIReturnKeyGo`, `UIReturnKeyGoogle`,
  `UIReturnKeyJoin`, `UIReturnKeyNext`, `UIReturnKeyRoute`,
  `UIReturnKeySearch`, `UIReturnKeySend`, `UIReturnKeyYahoo`,
  `UIReturnKeyDone`, and `UIReturnKeyEmergencyCall`.

- `keyboardAppearance`. This attribute is used to distinguish between text entry inside the application and text entry inside an alert panel. The property is declared as:

  @property ( nonatomic ) UIKeyboardAppearance
           keyboardAppearance

  The value can be either `UIKeyboardAppearanceDefault` (default) or `UIKeyboard-AppearanceAlert`.

UIKeyboardTypeDefault

UIKeyboardTypePhonePad

**Figure 5.3** Two keyboard types: `UIKeyboardTypeDefault` and `UIKeyboardTypePhonePad`.

- `enablesReturnKeyAutomatically`. If the value is `YES`, the keyboard's return key is disabled until the user enters some text. The default is `NO`. The property is declared as follows:

  `@property(nonatomic) BOOL enablesReturnKeyAutomatically`

- `autocorrectionType`. This property is used to manage the auto-correction of the user's input. The property is declared as:

  `@property(nonatomic) UITextAutocorrectionType`
  `autocorrectionType`

  The property can take one of the following values:
  `UITextAutocorrectionTypeDefault` (chooses the appropriate auto-correction),
  `UITextAutocorrectionTypeNo` (no auto-correction), and
  `UITextAutocorrectionTypeYes` (auto-correction is enabled).

- `autocapitalizationType`. Determines when the shift key is automatically pressed to produce capital letters. The property is declared as:

  `@property(nonatomic) UITextAutocapitalizationType`
  `autocapitalizationType`

UI KeyboardTypeEmailAddress

UI KeyboardTypeNumbersAndPunctuation

**Figure 5.4** Two keyboard types: `UIKeyboardTypeEmailAddress` and `UIKeyboardType-NumbersAndPunctuation`.

The property can take one of the following values:
`UITextAutocapitalizationTypeNone` (do not automatically capitalize),
`UITextAutocapitalizationTypeWords` (capitalize the first character of every word),
`UITextAutocapitalizationTypeSentences` (capitalize the first character of each sentence), and
`UITextAutocapitalizationTypeAllCharacters` (capitalize all characters automatically).

### 5.2.2  The delegate

We mentioned above that the control uses a delegate to communicate important editing events. The delegate protocol used is `UITextFieldDelegate`. It declares several optional methods.

- `textFieldShouldReturn:`. This delegate method is declared as follows:

  - (BOOL) t e x t F i e l d S h o u l d R e t u r n : ( U I T e x t F i e l d ∗ ) t e x t F i e l d

  It is called when the user presses the return key. Since this is a single-line text field, you can use this event as a signal to end editing of the text field. You should resign as the first responder.

Returning YES or NO has no effect on quitting the keyboard and has no meaning in the context of a single-line text field. See the sample code in Listing 5.2 for an example.

- textFieldShouldClear:. This method is called when the clear button is pressed. The method is declared as:

  - (BOOL) textFieldShouldClear:( UITextField *) textField

If you return YES, the text field content is cleared; otherwise, it is not.

- textFieldDidBeginEditing:. This method is called when the text field begins as the first responder ready for user input. The method is declared as:

  - (**void**) textFieldDidBeginEditing :( UITextField *) textField

- textField:shouldChangeCharactersInRange:replacementString:. This method is called asking the delegate's permission to change the specified text. The method is declared as:

  -(BOOL) textField :( UITextField *) textField
  shouldChangeCharactersInRange :( NSRange) range
  replacementString :( NSString *) string

range is the range of characters to be replaced, and string is the replacement string.

- textFieldDidEndEditing:. This method is called after the text field ends editing. The method is declared as:

  - (**void**) textFieldDidEndEditing :( UITextField *) textField

- textFieldShouldBeginEditing:. This method is called asking permission from the delegate so that the text field can start editing. The method declaration is as follows:

  - (BOOL) textFieldShouldBeginEditing :( UITextField *) textField

Return YES to start editing; NO, otherwise.

- textFieldDidBeginEditing:. This method is called when the text field starts editing. The method declaration is as follows:

  - (**void**) textFieldDidBeginEditing :( UITextField *) textField

### 5.2.3   *Creating of, and working with, a UITextField*

Let's demonstrate how one can create a UITextField instance and add it to a view. Listing 5.1 shows how to create a text field instance, configure it, and attach it to the view.

**Listing 5.1**    Creating and configuring a `UITextField` instance as a subview.

```
CGRect  rect  =  CGRectMake(10,10,  150,  30);
myTextField  =  [[ UITextField  alloc ]  initWithFrame : rect ];
myTextField . textColor  =  [ UIColor  blackColor ];
myTextField . font  =  [ UIFont  systemFontOfSize :17.0 ];
myTextField . placeholder  =  @"<enter text>";
myTextField . backgroundColor  =  [ UIColor  whiteColor ];
myTextField . borderStyle  =  UITextBorderStyleBezel ;
myTextField . keyboardType  =  UIKeyboardTypeDefault ;
myTextField . returnKeyType  =  UIReturnKeyDone ;
myTextField . clearButtonMode  =  UITextFieldViewModeAlways ;
myTextField . delegate  =  self ;
[ theView  addSubview : myTextField ];
```

You usually create these controls in the `loadView` method of the view controller. Here, we make `self` (i.e., the view controller) the delegate. You have a choice of which of the optional delegate methods you want to implement. Here, we implement the `textFieldShouldReturn:` method shown in Listing 5.2.

**Listing 5.2**    Implementation of the `textFieldShouldReturn:` method for a `UITextField` instance.

```
-  (BOOL) textFieldShouldReturn :( UITextField  *) textField {
  if ( myTextField  ==  textField ){
    if  (([[ myTextField  text]  isEqualToString :@"Hillary" ])  ==  NO){
      [ myTextField  resignFirstResponder ];  // hide KB
      return  NO;  // It 's  a  text  field ,  no  need  for  new  line
    }
    else  return  NO;  // It 's  a  text  field ,  no  need  for  new  line
  }
  return  NO;  // It 's  a  text  field ,  no  need  for  new  line
}
```

In the code above, we first test to see if the `textField` is the instance `myTextField`. If yes, we check the text entered. If it is "`Hillary`", we do not resign the first responder, and return NO. Otherwise, we send the text field control a `resignFirstResponder` message asking it to stop being the first responder. This will result in the disappearance of the keyboard. After that, we return NO. As we have mentioned above, the return value has no effect in a single-line text field.

## 5.3   Sliders

A `UISlider` control (see Fig. 5.5) is that familiar horizontal control used to select a single value from a continuous range of values. The following are the essential properties needed to set up a slider.

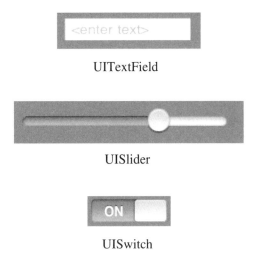

UITextField

UISlider

UISwitch

**Figure 5.5**   A `UITextField`, a `UISlider`, and a `UISwitch` instance.

- `value`. This attribute contains the current value indicated by the slider. The property is declared as:

  @property(nontatomic) **float** value

  You can read/write this value. If you set this value, the slider will redraw itself.

- `minimumValue`. Contains the minimum value of the slider control. The property is declared as:

  @property(nontatomic) **float** minimumValue

- `maximumValue`. Contains the maximum value of the slider control. The property is declared as:

  @property(nontatomic) **float** maximumValue

- `continuous`. A Boolean attribute controlling how frequently the slider sends updates with its current value to the associated target-action. If the value is YES (the default), the slider continuously sends updates of its current value as the user drags the slider's thumb. If the value is NO, it sends it only once: when the user releases the slider's thumb.

  @property(nonatomic, getter=isContinuous) BOOL continuous

Listing 5.3 shows how you can configure a slider instance and add it as a subview to a view.

**Listing 5.3**    Creating and configuring a `UISlider` instance.

```
CGRect rect = CGRectMake(10,60, 200, 30);
mySlider = [[UISlider alloc] initWithFrame:rect];
[mySlider addTarget:self
        action:@selector(sliderValueChaged:)
        forControlEvents:UIControlEventValueChanged];
mySlider.backgroundColor = [UIColor clearColor];
mySlider.minimumValue = 0.0;
mySlider.maximumValue = 10.0;
mySlider.continuous = YES;
mySlider.value = 5.0;
[theView addSubview: mySlider];
```

The slider's range is from 0.0 to 10.0. It continuously sends updates to the action method `sliderValueChaged:` as the user changes its value.

To receive updates of the current value of the slider, we use the target-action mechanism. We add the action method `sliderValueChaged:` (shown in Listing 5.4) for the control event `UIControlEventValueChanged`.

**Listing 5.4**    `sliderValueChaged:` action method.

```
- (void)sliderValueChaged:(id)sender
{
  UISlider *slider = sender;
  if(mySlider == slider){
    printf("Value of slider is %f\n", [mySlider value]);
  }
}
```

## 5.4   Switches

A `UISwitch` is a control that allows you to present an on/off switch to the user. The `UISwitch` class defines a property `on` for retrieving and setting the current state of the switch. The property is declared as:

```
@property(nonatomic, getter=isOn) BOOL on
```

You can also use the method `setOn:animated:` which allows you to set the switch state, optionally animating the change. The method is declared as:

```
- (void)setOn:(BOOL)on animated:(BOOL)animated
```

If `animated` is YES, the change in the state is animated.

As in any control, you can set up an action-target and associate it with an event. As a developer, you are mostly interested in the event when the user flips the switch. You can use the `UIControlEventValueChanged` event for this purpose. Listing 5.5 shows the creation and configuration of a `UISwitch` instance. Listing 5.6 shows the action method for the event `UIControlEventValueChanged`.

**Listing 5.5**   The creation and configuration of a `UISwitch` instance.

```
rect = CGRectMake(10,90,  100,  30);
mySwitch = [[UISwitch alloc] initWithFrame:rect];
[mySwitch addTarget:self
          action:@selector(switchValueChanged:)
          forControlEvents:UIControlEventValueChanged];
mySwitch.backgroundColor = [UIColor clearColor];
[theView addSubview: mySwitch];
```

**Listing 5.6**   The action method for the `UISwitch` instance example.

```
- (void)switchValueChanged:(id)sender
{
  UISwitch  *aSwitch = sender;
  if(mySwitch == aSwitch){
    if([mySwitch isOn] == YES){
      printf("The switch is on\n");
    }
    else
      printf("The switch is off\n");
  }
}
```

## 5.5  Buttons

A `UIButton` class is a control that encapsulates the behavior of buttons. You create a button using the `UIButton` class method `buttonWithType:`. After that, you set up a target-action in order to handle the user taping on the button.

The following are some of the available button types:

- `UIButtonTypeRoundedRect`. This style is used to produce a rounded-rectangle button.

- `UIButtonTypeDetailDisclosure`. This style is used to produce a detail disclosure button.

- `UIButtonTypeInfoLight`. This style produces an information button that has a light background.

- `UIButtonTypeInfoDark`. This style produces an information button that has a dark background.

- `UIButtonTypeContactAdd`. This style produces a contact add button.

Listing 5.7 shows the creation and configuration of a `UIButton` instance (see Fig. 5.6).

**Figure 5.6**   A button control example.

**Listing 5.7**   The creation and configuration of a `UIButton` instance.

```
myButton =
  [[ UIButton buttonWithType : UIButtonTypeRoundedRect] retain ];
myButton . frame = CGRectMake (40.0 , 100.0 , 100, 50);
[ myButton setTitle :@"Click Me" forState : UIControlStateNormal ];
[ myButton addTarget : self
               action : @selector ( buttonClicked :)
               forControlEvents : UIControlEventTouchUpInside ];
[ theView addSubview: myButton ];
```

The listing above configures a target-action for the tapping event. Listing 5.8 shows the action method that handles the tapping on the button. As you notice, this is a basic mechanism inherited from `UIControl` and no new mechanism is introduced.

**Listing 5.8**   The action method for the `UIButton` instance example.

```
−(void )buttonClicked :( id ) sender {
  UIButton ∗button = sender ;
  if ( myButton == sender ){
    printf ("The button was tapped\n" );
  }
}
```

## 5.6   Segmented Controls

A segmented control is a horizontal control that manages a set of button-like items. Each item can be either a text string or an image. A user taps on an item within a segmented control and that item is selected by being highlighted.

To create a segmented control, you need to instantiate a `UISegmentedControl` object. After allocating an instance, you initialize the control with an array of items. The array of items can consist of objects of `NSString` or objects of `UIImage`. You can mix and match text and images in the same segmented control.

After the creation and initialization of the segmented control, you need to add a target-action for the control event `UIControlEventValueChanged:`. The action method will be invoked

**Figure 5.7**    A segmented control of text items.

when the selected item has changed. To retrieve the index of the selected item, use the property
selectedSegmentIndex which is declared as:

@property(nonatomic) NSInteger selectedSegmentIndex

The default value for this property is UISegmentedControlNoSegment, indicating that no
item is selected. If you set the property to this value, no item is selected (i.e., highlighted).

After that, you need to specify the frame for the segmented control which specifies the location
and dimensions. Finally, the segmented control needs to be added to an existing view. Listing 5.9
shows the basic steps needed to display a functioning segmented control.

**Listing 5.9**    The creation and configuration of a UISegmentedControl instance.

```
NSArray  *textOptionsArray = [NSArray arrayWithObjects:
              @"Bart", @"Lisa", @"Maggie", nil];
segmentedCtrl = [[UISegmentedControl alloc]
                      initWithItems:textOptionsArray];
segmentedCtrl.frame = CGRectMake(20.0, 100.0, 280, 50);
[segmentedCtrl addTarget:self
                  action:@selector(segmentChanged:)
                  forControlEvents:UIControlEventValueChanged];
[theView addSubview:segmentedCtrl];
```

The control in the above listing has three items of text. The action invoked when the user taps on an
item is segmentChanged: and this is shown in Listing 5.10.

**Listing 5.10**    The segmentChanged: action method invoked when the segmented control changes the
selected item.

```
-(void)segmentChanged:(id)sender{
  if(segmentedCtrl == sender){
    printf("The segment was changed to %d\n",
            [segmentedCtrl selectedSegmentIndex]);
  }
}
```

Figures 5.7 shows the text-based segmented control and Fig. 5.8 shows it with the middle item
selected.

To create an image-based segmented control, follow the same procedure except for the
initialization phase. You can initialize the control by supplying an array of images as follows:

**Figure 5.8**    A segmented control of text items with a selected item.

**Figure 5.9**    A segmented control of image items.

**Figure 5.10**    A segmented control of image items with a selected item.

```
segmentedCtrl = [[UISegmentedControl alloc] initWithItems:
        [NSArray arrayWithObjects:
        [UIImage imageNamed:@"bart.png"],
        [UIImage imageNamed:@"lisa.png"],
        [UIImage imageNamed:@"maggie.png"],
        nil]];
```

Figures 5.9 shows the image-based segmented control and Fig. 5.10 shows it with the middle item selected.

In the previous examples, we accepted the default appearance of the segmented control. The property segmentedControlStyle allows you to select the style of the control. The property is declared as:

```
@property(nonatomic)
    UISegmentedControlStyle segmentedControlStyle
```

The available styles are:

- UISegmentedControlStylePlain. This is the default style which we have seen.
- UISegmentedControlStyleBordered. This a bordered style. Figure 5.11 shows an example of this style.
- UISegmentedControlStyleBar. This is a toolbar style. Figure 5.12 shows an example of this style.

**Figure 5.11**   A segmented control of image items with a style `UISegmentedControlStyleBordered`.

**Figure 5.12**   A segmented control of image items with a style `UISegmentedControlStyleBar`.

You can also dynamically change the items in a given segmented control. You can use `setTitle:forSegmentAtIndex:` to change a text item or `setImage:forSegment-AtIndex:` to change an item's image.

You can also add a new item to the control. If you would like to add a string item, use `insertSegmentWithTitle:atIndex:animated:` declared as:

− ( **void** ) insertSegmentWithTitle : ( NSString ∗ ) title
atIndex : ( NSUInteger ) segment  animated : ( BOOL ) animated

If you want to add an image item, use `insertSegmentWithImage:atIndex:animated:` declared as:

− ( **void** ) insertSegmentWithImage : ( UIImage ∗ ) image
atIndex : ( NSUInteger ) segment  animated : ( BOOL ) animated

You can also remove an item using `removeSegmentAtIndex:animated:` declared as:

− ( **void** ) removeSegmentAtIndex : ( NSUInteger ) segment
animated : ( BOOL ) animated

To remove all items, invoke `removeAllSegments`.

## 5.7   Page Controls

A page control (see Fig. 5.13) presents the user with a set of horizontal dots representing pages. The current page is presented as a white dot. The user can go from the current page to the next or previous page.

To present a page control to the user, allocate a new instance of `UIPageControl` and initialize it with the frame. After that, set the number of pages (maximum 20). To respond to the changes in the current page, add a target-action for the control event `UIControlEventValueChanged`. Finally, you add the page control to a view. Listing 5.11 shows the basic steps needed to present a page control to the user.

**Figure 5.13**   A page control with 15 pages.

**Listing 5.11**   The creation and configuration of a `UIPageControl` instance.

```
pageCtrl = [[ UIPageControl alloc ]
    initWithFrame :CGRectMake(20.0, 100.0, 280, 50)];
[ pageCtrl addTarget: self
            action :@selector( pageChanged : )
            forControlEvents : UIControlEventTouchUpInside ];
pageCtrl.numberOfPages = 15;
[ theView addSubview: pageCtrl ];
```

The action method is shown below. To retrieve the current page, use the property `currentPage`.

```
-( void )pageChanged :( id )sender {
  if ( pageCtrl == sender ){
    printf ("The page was changed to %d\n",
            [ pageCtrl currentPage ]);
  }
}
```

You can also change the current page programatically and update the visual page indicator by invoking `updateCurrentPageDisplay`.

## 5.8   Date Pickers

The `UIDatePicker` is a control that allows the user to select a time and a date using rotating wheels. Figure 5.14 shows four examples of a `UIDatePicker` instance.

Here are several important properties and methods declared by this class.

- `calendar`. The calendar used in the `UIDatePicker` instance. The property is declared as:

  `@property ( nonatomic , copy ) NSCalendar *calendar`

  If this value is `nil`, then the user's current calendar is used.

- `date`. This property represents the date used in the display of the date picker.

  `@property ( nonatomic , copy ) NSDate *date`

- `setDate : animated :`. This method is used to change the date. The method is declared as:

  — `( void ) setDate :( NSDate *) date  animated :( BOOL) animated`

  If `animated` is `YES`, the change is animated.

 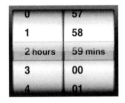

UIDatePickerModeTime    UIDatePickerModeCountDownTimer

UIDatePickerModeDateAndTime    UIDatePickerModeDate

**Figure 5.14**    Four examples of `UIDatePicker`.

• `datePickerMode`. Using this property you can select the date picker mode. The property is defined as:

@property(nonatomic) UIDatePickerMode datePickerMode

The `UIDatePicker` instance can be configured (see Fig. 5.14) to select a date, a time, a time and a date, or to act as countdown timer.

Listing 5.12 shows how you can configure a date picker instance and add it as a subview to a view.

**Listing 5.12**    Creating and configuring a `UIDatePicker` instance.

```
myDatePicker = [[ UIDatePicker alloc ] initWithFrame : CGRectZero ];
myDatePicker . autoresizingMask = UIViewAutoresizingFlexibleWidth ;
myDatePicker . datePickerMode = UIDatePickerModeDate ;
CGSize pickerSize = [ myDatePicker sizeThatFits : CGSizeZero ];
rect = CGRectMake(0 ,150 , pickerSize . width , pickerSize . height );
myDatePicker . frame = rect ;
[ myDatePicker addTarget : self
          action : @selector ( datePickerChanged : )
          forControlEvents : UIControlEventValueChanged ];
[ theView addSubview : myDatePicker ];
```

`UIDatePicker` instances differ from other controls in that they optimize their layout internally. You only need to specify the origin in the view; the size will be calculated automatically. The code above creates the instance, and sets up an action method for receiving value changes of the control.

When the user rotates the wheel, the control will call the action method as soon as the wheel finishes rotating. Listing 5.13 shows the action method `datePickerChanged:` that is triggered when the value is changed.

**Listing 5.13**   Action method for date picker value change.

```
- (void)datePickerChanged:(id)sender
{
  UIDatePicker  *datePicker = sender;
  if(myDatePicker == datePicker){
    printf("Value of picker is %s\n",
           [[[myDatePicker date] description] cString]);
  }
}
```

## 5.9   Summary

In this chapter, we have covered the topic of controls in the iPhone OS. We started by presenting the base class of all controls, `UIControl`, and its main features. We then talked about the important target-action mechanism used to communicate changes in the control to the clients. This chapter covered the text field, slider, switch, button, page control, date picker, and segmented controls.

# 6

# View Controllers

The model view controller (MVC) is a popular design pattern that is used in software construction to isolate the business logic from the graphical user interface. In MVC, a controller is used for the purpose of coordination between the model (where the business logic resides) and the view (where the user's interactions occur).

In this chapter, you will learn about the available view controllers that are provided to you in the iPhone SDK. Although you can build iPhone applications without the use of these view controllers, you shouldn't. As you will see in this chapter, view controllers greatly simplify your application.

The organization of this chapter is as follows. In Section 6.1, we provide a gentle introduction to view controllers by presenting a simple application with a single view controller. This application will demonstrate important view controller concepts. In Section 6.2, we talk about tab bar controllers and how they can be used in the construction of radio interfaces. In Section 6.3, we talk about navigation controllers used primarily for presenting hierarchical information to the user. After that, Section 6.4 talks about modal view controllers and provides a detailed example showing their appropriate usage. Finally, we summarize the chapter in Section 6.5.

## 6.1 The Simplest View Controller

In this section, we will demonstrate the simplest view controller. The application is composed of a view, a view controller, and a data model. The application simply displays a message that describes the orientation of the device. The view asks the controller for the message string, and the controller consults the device orientation and retrieves the appropriate text from the data model.

### 6.1.1  The view controller

Listing 6.1 shows the declaration of the view controller. The UIViewController is the base class for all view controllers. When creating a view controller, you either subclass this class or one of its subclasses. The data model is represented by three strings where each describes the orientation of the device. The method message is used by the view instance to retrieve the appropriate text describing the orientation of the device.

---

**Listing 6.1**   The declaration of a simple view controller CDAViewController in file CDAViewController.h.

```
#import <UIKit/UIKit.h>
@interface CDAViewController : UIViewController {
  NSString *strPortraitNormal, *strPortraitUpSideDown,
           *strLandscape;
}
-(NSString*)message;
@end
```

In Listing 6.2, we show the implementation of the view controller CDAViewController. We override the initialization method initWithNibName:bundle: in order to initialize the data model. The three strings are set according to their purpose.

Since we are creating the view programmatically, we need to override the method loadView. Our method creates a view instance of the class CDAUIView (discussed later) and configures it to have flexible height and width. This is achieved by setting the autoresizingMask property with the appropriate value. Since the view needs a reference to the controller, we also set the property myController of our custom view with the view controller's instance.

The method shouldAutorotateToInterfaceOrientation: is also overridden. This method is called whenever the device's orientation changes. If you return YES, then the device orientation is changed; otherwise, no change in the device orientation occurs. Since our application requires that the orientation be changed, we return YES. The message method is the method used by the view to retrieve the text that needs to be displayed. The method simply queries the current orientation of the device and returns the appropriate string using the simple data model. The UIViewController's property interfaceOrientation is used to retrieve the current orientation of the device. The property is declared as follows:

```
@property(nonatomic, readonly)
  UIInterfaceOrientation interfaceOrientation
```

There are four orientations of type UIInterfaceOrientation. These orientations are:

- UIInterfaceOrientationPortrait indicates that the iPhone is in portrait orientation where the home button is on the bottom.

- UIInterfaceOrientationPortraitUpSideDown indicates that the iPhone is in portrait orientation where the home button is on the top.

- UIInterfaceOrientationLandscapeLeft indicates that the iPhone is in landscape orientation where the home button is on the left.

- UIInterfaceOrientationLandscapeRight indicates that the iPhone is in landscape orientation where the home button is on the right.

**Listing 6.2**   The implementation of a simple view controller `CDAViewController` in file `CDAViewCon-`
`troller.m`.

```objc
#import "CDAViewController.h"
#import "CDAUIView.h"

@implementation CDAViewController
- (id)initWithNibName:(NSString *)nibNameOrNil
      bundle:(NSBundle *)nibBundleOrNil {
  if (self = [super initWithNibName:nibNameOrNil
          bundle:nibBundleOrNil]) {
    strPortraitNormal = @"Portrait";
    strPortraitUpSideDown = @"Portrait UpSideDown";
    strLandscape = @"Landscape";
  }
  return self;
}
- (void)loadView {
  CGRect rectFrame = [UIScreen mainScreen].applicationFrame;
  // Create the main view
  CDAUIView *theView =
    [[CDAUIView alloc] initWithFrame:rectFrame];
  theView.backgroundColor = [UIColor whiteColor];
  theView.myController = self;
  theView.autoresizingMask =
          UIViewAutoresizingFlexibleHeight |
          UIViewAutoresizingFlexibleWidth;
  self.view = theView;
  [theView autorelease];
}
- (BOOL)shouldAutorotateToInterfaceOrientation:
      (UIInterfaceOrientation)interfaceOrientation {
  return YES;
}
- (NSString *)message {
  switch (self.interfaceOrientation) {
    case UIInterfaceOrientationPortrait:
      return strPortraitNormal;
    case UIInterfaceOrientationPortraitUpsideDown:
      return strPortraitNormal;
    default:
      return strLandscape;
  }
}
@end
```

## 6.1.2   The view

The view managed by the view controller is an instance of the class CDAUIView declared in Listing 6.3. The view has a property used to assign the view controller that is managing the view.

**Listing 6.3**   The declaration of the view CDAUIView in CDAUIView.h used to demonstrate the simplest view controller.

```
#import <UIKit/UIKit.h>
@class CDAViewController;
@interface CDAUIView : UIView {
  CDAViewController *myController;
}
@property(nonatomic, assign) CDAViewController* myController;
@end
```

Listing 6.4 shows the implementation of the view class. The class overrides the drawRect: method. The method simply asks the controller for a text message and draws that message on the view.

**Listing 6.4**   The implementation of the view CDAUIView in CDAUIView.m used to demonstrate the simplest view controller.

```
#import "CDAUIView.h"
@implementation CDAUIView
@synthesize myController;
- (void)drawRect:(CGRect)rect {
  [[myController message]   drawAtPoint:CGPointMake(80, 30)
      withFont:[UIFont systemFontOfSize:50]];
}
@end
```

## 6.1.3   The application delegate

Listing 6.5 shows the declaration of the application delegate. It holds two instance variables: a window instance and a view controller instance.

**Listing 6.5**   The declaration of the application delegate CDAAppDelegate in CDAAppDelegate.h demonstrating the simplest view controller.

```
@class CDAViewController;
@interface CDAAppDelegate : NSObject {
  UIWindow          *window;
  CDAViewController *viewController;
}
@end
```

In Listing 6.6, we show the implementation of the application delegate class. As usual, we initialize the user interface objects in the method applicationDidFinishLaunching:. First,

we create the application window. Next, the view controller instance is created and initialized using
`initWithNibName:bundle:`. Since we are creating the controller programatically, we pass
`nil` for both parameters. The controller's view is then added to the window as a subview, and the
window is made key and visible.

The `UIViewController` declares a `view` property as follows:

```
@property(nonatomic, retain) UIView *view
```

The `view` property is initially `nil`. When the property is accessed (as in the statement
`viewController.view`), the controller checks to see if it is `nil`. If it is `nil`, it sends itself
a `loadView` message. As we saw before, we create the view in the `loadView` method and set the
property `view` with the instance created. Therefore, when the controller's view is eventually added
to the window, our `CDAUIView` instance is actually added as a subview to the window.

**Listing 6.6**   The implementation of the application delegate `CDAAppDelegate` in `CDAAppDelegate.m`
demonstrating the simplest view controller.

```
#import "CDAAppDelegate.h"
#import "CDAViewController.h"
@implementation CDAAppDelegate
- (void)applicationDidFinishLaunching:
    (UIApplication *)application {
  window = [[UIWindow alloc]
      initWithFrame:[[UIScreen mainScreen] bounds]] ;
  viewController = [[CDAViewController alloc]
      initWithNibName:nil bundle:nil];
  [window addSubview:viewController.view];
  [window makeKeyAndVisible];
}
- (void)dealloc {
  [window release];
  [viewController release];
  [super dealloc];
}
@end
```

Figures 6.1 and 6.2 show the application in portrait and landscape orientations, respectively.

### 6.1.4  Summary

To summarize the process of creating a simple MVC application, let's look at the major steps we
have performed:

1. Create a subclass of `UIViewController`. Create the subclass and override the following
   methods:

   (a) `initWithNibName:bundle:`. This is the initializer of the view controller. You can
       perform initialization of the data model and the controller instance.

**Figure 6.1**    The application demonstrating the simplest view controller in portrait orientation.

**Figure 6.2**    The application demonstrating the simplest view controller in landscape orientation.

(b) `loadView`. This method is used to load the view managed by the controller. You should create the view instance, configure it, and set its reference to the `view` property of the controller.

(c) `shouldAutorotateToInterfaceOrientation:`. If your application allows for the orientation to change, you should override this method and return `YES` for the acceptable orientations.

2. Create a subclass of `UIView`. If your application requires a specialized view, you should subclass the `UIView` class. Optionally, add a property for the controller so that the controller can set this property in order for the view to communicate with the controller concerning changes in the data model. Otherwise, the view can communicate with the application delegate.

3. Create an application delegate class. In the `applicationDidFinishLaunching:` method, you should create the main window and the view controller, and add the `view` property of the view controller as a subview to the main window.

## 6.2    Radio Interfaces

Often you need to design an application that has several functionalities or operates in parallel modes. The interface of such an application is sometimes referred to as a *radio interface*. Each functionality or mode will be managed by a view controller, and the set of these controllers defines the application. You can use a tab bar controller to manage several view controllers similar to the one you saw in the previous section. Each controller is represented by a button, and the set of buttons is available at the bottom of the screen on a tab bar managed by the tab bar controller. When the user taps a button, the view of the corresponding controller becomes the visible view, and the button changes to indicate that it is the active mode. Adding a tab bar to your application is simple: you simply create a tab bar controller, add the set of view controllers to it, and add its view to an existing view. In the next section, we will present a simple application that demonstrates the basic steps needed in developing radio-based interface applications.

### 6.2.1    A detailed example

In this section, we will create a simple application that utilizes a tab bar. The application snapshot is shown in Fig. 6.3.

The application presents to the user a number of geometric shapes to select from. Each item is represented by a view controller that, when its item is selected, displays the name of the shape in its view.

The first step is writing the classes for the view controllers of each item. In this example, we use a single view controller class to represent every item. Each controller instance will be configured to output a different message. Note that it is usually the case that every item (or mode) has its own view controller class. The view controller class is `CDBViewController`, and it is declared in Listing 6.7.

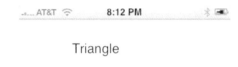

**Figure 6.3**    A snapshot of a simple tab bar application.

**Listing 6.7**    The declaration of the view controller representing each item in the tab bar application.

```
#import <UIKit/UIKit.h>
@interface CDBViewController : UIViewController {
  NSString *message;
}
@property (nonatomic, retain) NSString *message;
- (id)initWithMessage:(NSString *)theMessage
    andImage:(UIImage*) image;
@end
```

The view controller uses a custom initializer, initWithMessage:andImage:, that initializes the view controller with the custom message that will be displayed when it becomes active, and an image used to represent its item in the item list on the tab bar.

The implementation of the view controller class is shown in Listing 6.8. The initializer first calls the super's initializer, initWithNibName:bundle:. Since we are going to build our graphical interface programatically, we pass nil values for both parameters. The initializer then stores the custom message in the message property for later use by its managed view, and stores the image representing this controller in the image property of the tabBarItem property of the view controller instance.

The tabBarItem property is declared in the UIViewController class as follows:

```
@property(nonatomic, readonly, retain)
   UITabBarItem *tabBarItem
```

The value for this property is an object (possibly `nil`) of the class `UITabBarItem` representing the view controller on the tab bar. The `UITabBarItem` class is a subclass of `UIBarItem`. It inherits from its superclass the `image` and `title` properties. The default value for the image is `nil`. However, the `title` value, if not set, is set to the value of the view controller's `title` property. The `UITabBarItem` class adds an additional property: `badgeValue` which is an instance of `NSString` and its value is shown inside a red oval to the right of the corresponding tab bar item. More on this later.

The controller, as usual, overrides the `loadView` method for setting up its managed view. This method is similar to what we saw in the previous section. The view class is a custom view class `CDBUIView` that we will see shortly. Since we plan to add the view controller to a tab bar controller, the view managed by the view controller needs to be able to resize so that it fits above the tab bar. Therefore, it is important to set the `autoresizingMask` property of the managed view as shown in the method.

**Listing 6.8**    The implementation of the view controller used in the tab bar application.

```objc
#import "CDBViewController.h"
#import "CDBUIView.h"

@implementation CDBViewController
@synthesize message;
- (id)initWithMessage:(NSString *)theMessage
    andImage:(UIImage*) image {
  if (self = [super initWithNibName:nil bundle:nil]) {
    self.message = theMessage;
    self.tabBarItem.image = image;
  }
  return self;
}
- (void)loadView {
  CGRect rectFrame =
      [UIScreen mainScreen].applicationFrame;
  CDBUIView *theView =
      [[CDBUIView alloc] initWithFrame:rectFrame];
  theView.backgroundColor = [UIColor whiteColor];
  theView.myController = self;
  theView.autoresizingMask =
          UIViewAutoresizingFlexibleHeight |
          UIViewAutoresizingFlexibleWidth;
  self.view = theView;
  [theView release];
}
@end
```

The CDBUIView view class is declared in Listing 6.9. It simply maintains a myController property to hold a reference to its controller. This reference is needed so that the view can retrieve the proper message to be drawn in the view.

**Listing 6.9**    The view class declaration used in the tab bar application.

```
#import <UIKit/UIKit.h>
@class CDBViewController;
@interface CDBUIView : UIView {
  CDBViewController *myController;
}
@property(nonatomic, assign) CDBViewController* myController;
@end
```

The implementation of the CDBUIView class is shown in Listing 6.10. The class overrides the drawRect: method of its superclass to draw the message obtained from the controller.

**Listing 6.10**    The implementation of the view class used in the tab bar application.

```
#import "CDBUIView.h"
@implementation CDBUIView
@synthesize myController;
- (void)drawRect:(CGRect)rect {
  [[myController message] drawAtPoint:CGPointMake(80, 30)
    withFont:[UIFont systemFontOfSize:20]];
}
@end
```

Now that we have constructed the view controller and its required view class, we can use the application delegate to present the application window to the user. The application delegate class declaration is shown in Listing 6.11. In addition to maintaining a reference to the main window, it has six references to view controllers, all of type CDBViewController. These controllers will be added to a tab bar controller of type UITabBarController whose reference is in the instance variable tabBarController.

**Listing 6.11**    The application delegate class declaration used to present the main window in the tab bar application.

```
#import <UIKit/UIKit.h>
@class CDBViewController;
@interface CDBAppDelegate : NSObject {
  UIWindow          *window;
  CDBViewController *viewController1, *viewController2,
              *viewController3, *viewController4,
              *viewController5, *viewController6;
  UITabBarController    *tabBarController;
}
@end
```

Listing 6.12 shows the implementation of the application delegate class. The application delegate overrides the `applicationDidFinishLaunching:` method for setting up the main window. First, we create six instances of the `CDBViewController` view controller class. Each of these instances is initialized with the message that will be displayed in their view and the image that will be displayed as their representation on the tab bar. In addition, the view controller's title is set, which also has the side effect of setting the tab bar item's title to the same value.

The image files are stored in the application's bundle. Using the class method `imageNamed:`, we retrieve the image encapsulated by a `UIImage` class. See Chapter 9 for more information.

After creating the view controllers, we create the tab bar controller that will manage them. This class is of type `UITabBarController`. To add the view controllers, we set its `viewControllers` property. This property is declared as:

`@property(nonatomic, copy) NSArray *viewControllers`

Therefore, all we have to do is create an instance of `NSArray` with the six view controller instances as its elements and use it as the value for the `viewControllers` property.

Finally, we have to add the tab bar's view as a subview to the main window. When the window appears, the tab bar's view appears and it will consist of the tab bar (at the bottom) and the currently selected view controller's view above it. Initially, the first controller is selected.

**Listing 6.12** The application delegate class implementation used to present the main window in the tab bar application.

```
#import "CDBAppDelegate.h"
#import "CDBViewController.h"
@implementation CDBAppDelegate

- (void)applicationDidFinishLaunching:(UIApplication *)
      application {
  window = [[UIWindow alloc]
        initWithFrame:[[UIScreen mainScreen] bounds]] ;
  viewController1 = [[CDBViewController alloc]
          initWithMessage:@"Triangle"
            andImage:[UIImage imageNamed:@"tri.png"]];
  viewController1.title = @"Tri";
  viewController2 = [[CDBViewController alloc]
          initWithMessage:@"Rectangle"
            andImage:[UIImage imageNamed:@"rect.png"]];
  viewController2.title = @"Rect";
  viewController3 = [[CDBViewController alloc]
          initWithMessage:@"Ellipse"
            andImage:[UIImage imageNamed:@"ellipse.png"]];
  viewController3.title = @"Elli";
  viewController4 = [[CDBViewController alloc]
          initWithMessage:@"Rectangle+Ellipse"
            andImage:[UIImage imageNamed:@"rect-elli.png"]];
```

```
viewController4.title = @"R&E";
viewController5 = [[CDBViewController alloc]
            initWithMessage:@"Rectangle+Triangle"
            andImage:[UIImage imageNamed:
                @"rect-tri.png"]];
viewController5.title = @"R&T";
viewController6 = [[CDBViewController alloc]
            initWithMessage:@"Rectangle+Rectangle"
            andImage:[UIImage imageNamed:
                @"two-tri.png"]];
viewController6.title = @"R&R";
tabBarController = [[UITabBarController alloc] init];
tabBarController.viewControllers =
                [NSArray arrayWithObjects:
                    viewController1,
                    viewController2,
                    viewController3,
                    viewController4,
                    viewController5,
                    viewController6,
                    nil];
[window addSubview:tabBarController.view];
[window makeKeyAndVisible];
}

- (void)dealloc {
    [window release];
    [viewController1 release];
    [viewController2 release];
    [viewController3 release];
    [viewController4 release];
    [viewController5 release];
    [viewController6 release];
    [tabBarController release];
    [super dealloc];
}
@end
```

### 6.2.2   Some comments on tab bar controllers

There are several additional aspects of the tab bar controller that need to be highlighted.

- The More List. If there are more than five view controllers to be managed, the tab bar will show the first four controllers and an additional More item is added as the fifth controller.

**Figure 6.4** Showing the additional items on the tab bar by tapping on the More item.

Tapping on the More item will present a list of the rest of the view controllers. Figure 6.4 shows how the view changes when the More item is tapped.

The user can then tap on any of the items to activate the corresponding view controller. Figure 6.5 shows what happens when the user taps on the R&T item. The user can tap on the More button to go back to the list of More items.

The More item is managed by a navigation controller which can be accessed using the tab bar controller's property moreNavigationController which is declared as:

```
@property(nonatomic, readonly) UINavigationController *
    moreNavigationController
```

We will talk more about navigational controllers in the section to come. For now, note that a navigational controller allows the application developer to present to the user hierarchical information in a natural way.

- Badge. Every item on the tab bar can have an optional value displayed in its upper-right corner surrounded by a red oval. The property that controls this is badgeValue which is declared as:

```
@property(nonatomic, copy) NSString *badgeValue
```

Rectangle+Triangle

**Figure 6.5**    Showing an item on the More list. Tapping on "More" shows the More list.

The default value for this property is nil. You can assign any string value to it, but usually it is a short message (e.g., a number). For example, to add a badge value to the third controller, we can write:

```
viewController3.tabBarItem.badgeValue = @"3";
```

Figure 6.6 shows the effect of this line on the appearance of the tab bar.

- Selected Controller. You can retrieve or change the selected controller by manipulating the selectedViewController property. The property is declared as:

```
@property(nonatomic, assign) UIViewController
    *selectedViewController
```

Note that if the "More" item is selected, the view controller for the "More" list is returned. Also note that you can change the selected view controller for the items that are displayed on the tab bar. In our example, writing something like this will result in an NSRangeException exception:

```
tabBarController.selectedViewController = viewController5;
```

You can also retrieve/change the selected view controller using the selectedIndex property which is declared as:

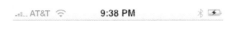

Rectangle+Ellipse

**Figure 6.6**    Showing a badge value for a view controller on a tab bar.

@property(nonatomic) NSUInteger selectedIndex

Where the index 0 (first controller selected) is the default value. Note that, again, an NSRangeException will result if you try to select a view controller whose item is not present on the tab bar. The selectedViewController and selectedIndex properties are connected; changing one will result in a change to the other.

- Customization. If you have more than five items managed by the tab bar controller, you can give the user the ability to rearrange the position of these controllers. Since only the first four controllers will appear on the main screen, and the rest will be displayed in a table, the user may want to move some of the controllers in the table to the main window.

You can specify that a view controller can be customized by putting its reference in the customizableViewControllers array which is declared as follows:

@property(nonatomic, copy) NSArray
    *customizableViewControllers

To change the position of a specific controller, the user taps on the More list and then on the Edit button. He/she can then tap the image of that controller and drag it to its new position. Figure 6.7 shows R&R while it is in the process of being moved to the first position. Figure 6.8 shows the state just after the move.

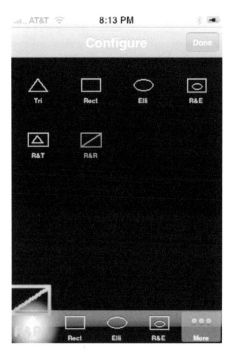

**Figure 6.7**  Rearranging the items on the tab bar by moving the R&R item to the first place.

A controller that has lost its position (in our example the Tri controller), will be moved to the table display as shown in Fig. 6.9.

By default, when you set the viewControllers property, the same object references go to the customizableViewControllers property. That means that all view controllers are customizable. If you would like to pin down one or more view controllers, you need to change this property. For example, to make the only customizable view controllers to be the first, second, and fifth controllers, you can write something like the following:

```
tabBarController.customizableViewControllers =
        [NSArray arrayWithObjects:
        viewController1, viewController2,
        viewController5, nil];
```

## 6.3   Navigation Controllers

Often, you would like to present hierarchical information to the user. The user starts at the top level of the information hierarchy. He/she then taps on a specific item and the next level of hierarchy is displayed. The process of drilling-down continues until the user reaches his/her desired level.

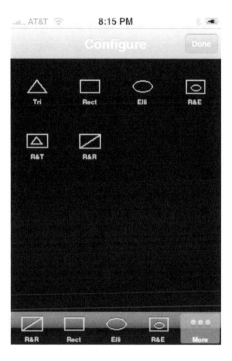

**Figure 6.8**    The state of the tab bar after moving the R&R item to the beginning, but while still being in editing mode.

The class UINavigationController is provided to you for managing hierarchical views to the user. As we saw in the previous section, the controller rather manages view controllers and each view controller manages the actual view for a given level. This class presents to the user a navigation bar and the view of the current level of hierarchy. In Section 8.8, we shall see how table views are ideal for such data presentation. In that section, we will use a navigation controller with table views to present hierarchal information in a user-friendly manner. In this section, however, we would like to look at the basic mechanisms behind the UINavigationController class. We first present a detailed example showing the default behavior of this class and then discuss some of the customization options available to you.

## 6.3.1   A detailed example

In this section, we will present a detailed example that utilizes a navigation controller. The application has three levels of hierarchy: Level I, Level II, and Level III. To keep the example simple and to the point, the user moves to the next level of hierarchy by just tapping on the view of the previous level. Also, all view controllers managed by the navigation controller are instances of the same class; it's the message displayed inside each view that distinguishes these levels of hierarchy. Figure 6.10 shows the first level of hierarchy.

**Figure 6.9**  The state of the tab bar after moving the R&R item to the beginning and exiting the editing mode.

The figure shows the navigation bar and the view of the controller that is shown below it. The navigation bar has a title in the middle. By default, the title in the middle of the navigation bar is the same as the title property of the top most view controller. Figure 6.11 shows the application snapshot when the user taps on the view of the first level. A new view appears that shows the second level of hierarchy. The second view appears by *pushing* a new view controller on the stack of navigation managed by the navigation controller. Notice that, by default, a back button appears on the left that has the title of the previous level. Tapping on the back button will result in the current view controller being *popped* from the stack and the view of the previous view controller appearing. Figure 6.12 shows the third and final level of hierarchy.

### The view controller

Let's start by building the view controller classes whose instances will be pushed/popped on/off the navigation stack. To simplify things, we assume that all view controllers are instances of one view controller, CDCViewController. Listing 6.13 shows the declaration of this class. It declares the showNextLevel method used by the view to show the next level of the view hierarchy.

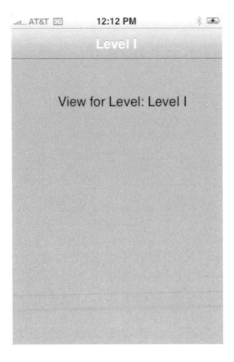

**Figure 6.10**   The navigation controller application showing the first level of hierarchy.

**Listing 6.13**   The declaration of the view controller used in the navigation controller example.

```
#define    LEVELI @"Level I"
#define    LEVELII @"Level II"
#define    LEVELIII @"Level III"

@interface CDCViewController : UIViewController {
}
-(void)showNextLevel;
@end
```

Listing 6.14 shows the implementation of the view controller. The showNextLevel uses the application delegate to push the view controller of the next level on the stack of the navigation controller (which itself is managed by the application delegate). To retrieve a reference to the single application delegate, use the class method sharedApplication of the UIApplication class. The loadView method is similar to what we saw before. It uses the CDCUIView class for the view.

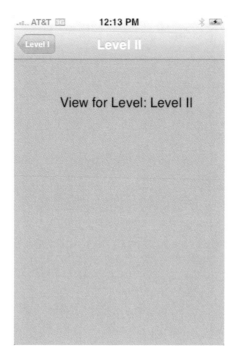

**Figure 6.11** The navigation controller application showing the second level of hierarchy.

**Listing 6.14** The implementation of the view controller used in the navigation controller example.

```
#import "CDCViewController.h"
#import "CDCUIView.h"

@implementation CDCViewController

-(void)showNextLevel{
  [[[UIApplication sharedApplication] delegate]
      showNextLevel:self.title];
}

- (void)loadView {
  CGRect rectFrame =
      [UIScreen mainScreen].applicationFrame;
  CDCUIView *theView =
      [[CDCUIView alloc] initWithFrame:rectFrame];
  theView.backgroundColor = [UIColor grayColor];
  theView.myController = self;
  theView.autoresizingMask =
```

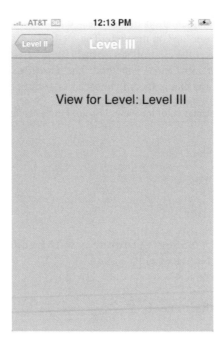

**Figure 6.12**    The navigation controller application showing the third (and last) level of hierarchy.

```
            UIViewAutoresizingFlexibleHeight |
            UIViewAutoresizingFlexibleWidth;
    self.view = theView;
    [theView release];
}
@end
```

### The view

Listing 6.15 shows the declaration of the view class CDCUIView used by the view controller. The view has a reference to its controller in the property myController. We will see how this reference is used in the method intercepting the user's tapping in order to navigate to the next level.

**Listing 6.15**    The declaration of the view class used in the navigation controller example.

```
@class CDCViewController;

@interface CDCUIView : UIView {
    CDCViewController *myController;
}
@property(nonatomic, assign) CDCViewController* myController;
@end
```

Listing 6.16 shows the implementation of the view class. As we have mentioned before, to navigate to the next level, the user taps on the view. The method `touchesBegan:withEvent:` intercepts the tapping and invokes the controller's `showNextLevel` method which in turn invokes the application delegate `showNextLevel:` method. The `drawRect:` method is used to display a unique message in the view area that is specific to each of the three navigation levels.

**Listing 6.16**    The implementation of the view class used in the navigation controller example.

```
#import "CDCUIView.h"
#import "CDCViewController.h"

@implementation CDCUIView

@synthesize myController;

- (void)touchesBegan:(NSSet *)touches withEvent:(UIEvent *)event{
  [myController showNextLevel];
}

- (void)drawRect:(CGRect)rect {
  NSString *message;
  message =
    [NSString stringWithFormat:@"View for Level: %@",
        [myController title]];
  [message
    drawAtPoint:CGPointMake(70, 50)
    withFont:[UIFont systemFontOfSize:20]];
}
@end
```

**The application delegate**

Listing 6.17 shows the declaration of the application delegate class. It keeps track of the window and the three view controllers. In addition, it maintains a reference to the navigation controller. The application delegate also declares the method `showNextLevel:` that will be invoked by the view controller to go to the next level.

**Listing 6.17**    The declaration of the application delegate class of the navigation controller example.

```
@class CDCViewController;

@interface CDCAppDelegate : NSObject {
  UIWindow          *window;
  CDCViewController *levelI, *levelII, *levelIII;
  UINavigationController *navController;
}
```

−(**void**)showNextLevel:(NSString∗) level;
**@end**

Listing 6.18 shows the implementation of the application delegate class. The `application-DidFinishLaunching:` method is used to initialize the application GUI. It starts by creating a window and then the view controller for the first level of hierarchy. After that the navigation controller is created and initialized. A navigation controller is an instance of the class `UINavigationController` which is a subclass of the `UIViewController` class. The instance of the navigation controller is initialized by the `initWithRootViewController:` method which is declared as follows:

− (**id**)initWithRootViewController:(UIViewController ∗)
        rootViewController

The initializer has a single parameter: the view controller instance that will become the first level (root) of the hierarchy. This controller is pushed on the (empty) stack without animation. After creating and initializing the navigation controller, we add its view as a subview to the window. This will result in having the navigation bar added below the status bar and the view of the root controller below it.

The `showNextLevel:` method takes as a parameter the current level's name. It pushes the second level controller if the current level is the root and the third level controller if it is the second level. To push a new view controller on the stack, you need to first create it and then use the `pushViewController:animated:` method to put it on the stack. This method is declared as follows:

− (**void**)pushViewController:(UIViewController ∗)viewController
            animated :(BOOL)animated

If `animated` is `YES`, the transition to the next level is animated. By default, when a view controller is pushed on the stack, the title of the current view controller becomes the title of the left button. The title in the middle will be changed to reflect the title of the newly pushed view controller. When the user taps on the left button, the current view controller is popped from the stack, the view of the previous controller replaces the view below the navigation bar, the title in the middle of the navigation bar is replaced with the title of the previous view controller, and the back button's title is changed accordingly. The method for popping the top view controller is `popViewControllerAnimated:` and it is declared as follows:

− (UIViewController ∗)popViewControllerAnimated :
            (BOOL)animated

If animated is `YES`, the popping is animated, otherwise it is not. Notice that the method also returns a reference to the popped view controller. It is worth noting that if there is only one view controller on the stack (root), the method will not be able to pop it, but will gracefully return without generating an exception.

**Listing 6.18**    The implementation of the application delegate class of the navigation controller example.

```
#import "CDCAppDelegate.h"
#import "CDCViewController.h"
```

```objc
@implementation CDCAppDelegate

-(void)showNextLevel:(NSString *) level{
    if([level isEqualToString:LEVELI]){
        levelII = [[CDCViewController alloc]
            initWithNibName:nil bundle:nil];
        levelII.title = LEVELII;
        [navController pushViewController:levelII
            animated:YES];
    }
    else if([level isEqualToString:LEVELII]){
        levelIII = [[CDCViewController alloc]
            initWithNibName:nil bundle:nil];
        levelIII.title = LEVELIII;
        [navController pushViewController:levelIII
            animated:YES];
    }
}

- (void)
applicationDidFinishLaunching:(UIApplication *)application {
    window = [[UIWindow alloc]
        initWithFrame:[[UIScreen mainScreen] bounds]];
    levelI = [[CDCViewController alloc]
            initWithNibName:nil
            bundle:nil];
    levelI.title = LEVELI;
    navController =
    [[UINavigationController alloc]
        initWithRootViewController:levelI];
    [window addSubview:navController.view];
    [window makeKeyAndVisible];
}

- (void)dealloc {
    [window release];
    [levelI release];
    [levelII release];
    [levelIII release];
    [navController release];
    [super dealloc];
}
@end
```

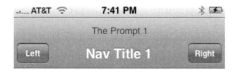

**Figure 6.13**   Customizing a navigation bar to show custom right/left buttons, prompt, and title.

## 6.3.2  Customization

In the previous section, we showed the default behavior of navigation controllers. In this section, we will look at ways to customize the appearance and behavior of navigation bars.

**Navigation item**

Every view controller is represented on the navigation bar by a navigation item. A navigation item is an instance of the UINavigationItem class. This class declares several properties that define the appearance of the view controller when it is pushed onto the stack or when another view controller is pushed on top of it (i.e., it becomes the immediate child controller). By default, when a view controller is pushed onto the stack, the title in the middle of the navigation bar becomes the same as the view controller's title. When another view controller is pushed onto the stack, the title for the back button becomes the title of the currently active view controller (the controller about to become a child). To change this behavior, you can access the navigation item of each view controller instance and set its various properties instead of them being taken from the default values. To obtain the instance of the navigation item, use the property navigationItem which is declared in the UIViewController class as follows:

```
@property(nonatomic, readonly, retain)
      UINavigationItem *navigationItem
```

In the following, we will look at important properties of the navigation item.

- The title. To specify the title of the navigation bar when the view controller is the topmost on the stack, set the title property of its navigation item. The title property is declared as:

  ```
  @property(nonatomic, copy)    NSString    *title
  ```

  For example, to set the title of the navigation item for the view controller, ctrl1, change the title property as follows:

  ```
  ctrl1.navigationItem.title = @"Nav Title 1";
  ```

  Every time ctrl1 is the topmost controller on the stack, the title of the navigation bar is "Nav Title 1".

- The prompt. There is an optional text that can be displayed above the navigation bar buttons. To take advantage of this option, set the prompt property of the navigation item which is declared as:

```
@property(nonatomic, copy)    NSString *prompt
```

For example, the following code will result in the prompt in Fig. 6.13.

```
ctrl1.navigationItem.prompt = @"The Prompt 1";
```

- Right/left buttons. You can add a right and/or a left button to the navigation bar. To add a right button that will appear when the view controller becomes the topmost on the stack, set the property `rightBarButtonItem` which is declared as follows:

```
@property(nonatomic, retain)
    UIBarButtonItem *rightBarButtonItem
```

To add a left button to the navigation bar, set the `leftBarButtonItem` property which is declared as:

```
@property(nonatomic, retain)
    UIBarButtonItem *leftBarButtonItem
```

Note that this custom left button will replace the regular back button on the bar if one exists.

For example, to create a right button, you can write something like the following in the view controller's initializer:

```
UIBarButtonItem * rightButton =
    [[ UIBarButtonItem alloc] initWithTitle:@"Right"
        style: UIBarButtonItemStyleDone
        target: self
        action: @selector(rightButtonTapped:)
    ];
self.navigationItem.rightBarButtonItem = rightButton;
[rightButton release];
```

In the above code, we are creating an instance of a `UIBarButtonItem` and initializing it with the title, the style, and the method that will be invoked when the button is tapped. You might want to review Section 5.1.2 and come back here for a better understanding of the target-action mechanism.

Figure 6.13 shows a navigation bar with right and left custom buttons. The right button is the one created by the code above having a style of `UIBarButtonItemStyleDone`. The left button is created using the style `UIBarButtonItemStylePlain`. You do have another style that can be used: `UIBarButtonItemStyleBordered`.

- Title view. You have the option of displaying a view instead of the title of the navigation bar. To specify a view, set the `titleView` property which is declared as follows:

```
@property(nonatomic, retain) UIView *titleView
```

To demonstrate this, let's consider the view class `MyBarView` shown in Listing 6.19. This class simply implements a view that has a white background and draws a `"Hello"` text inside.

**Figure 6.14**    A navigation bar with custom view title.

**Listing 6.19**    A custom view that will replace the title in a navigation bar.

```
@interface MyBarView : UIView {}
@end

@implementation MyBarView

- (id)initWithFrame:(CGRect)frame {
    if (self = [super initWithFrame:frame]) {
        self.backgroundColor = [UIColor whiteColor];
    }
    return self;
}

- (void)drawRect:(CGRect)rect {
    [@"Hello" drawAtPoint:CGPointMake(55, 5)
        withFont:[UIFont systemFontOfSize:20]];
}
@end
```

To replace the title text with a view (see Fig. 6.14) for controller `ctrl1`, you write something like the following:

```
MyBarView *titleView = [[[MyBarView alloc]
    initWithFrame:CGRectMake(0, 0, 150, 30)] autorelease];
ctrl1.navigationItem.titleView = titleView;
```

• Editing support. Some subclasses of `UIViewController`, such as `UITableView-Controller`, support editing a view. When the view managed by a controllers can be edited, it is customary to have an "Edit" button on the right-hand side. When this "Edit" button is tapped by the user, the view is supposed to enter editing mode and the button's title be changed to "Done". Once the user finishes his/her editing, he/she taps on the "Done" button and the view controller is supposed to save the changes made.

It turns out that such a mechanism is already built-in, and using it requires little effort. First, the `UIViewController` class has a method to communicate that change in its editing mode. This method is `setEditing:animated:` which is declared as:

```
- (void)setEditing:(BOOL)editing animated:(BOOL)animated
```

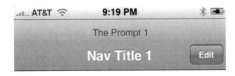

**Figure 6.15**   An Edit button on a navigation bar.

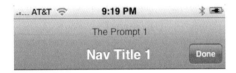

**Figure 6.16**   An Done button on a navigation bar.

Subclasses of UIViewController override this method in order to respond appropriately.

Furthermore, the UIViewController declares a property editing that can be set to change the editing mode of the view controller. This property is declared as:

@property(nonatomic, getter=isEditing) BOOL editing

When you change the value of this property, the setEditing:animated: is invoked with the corresponding change. Furthermore, when the user taps on the Edit/Done button, the property's value is changed accordingly.

To add an Edit/Done button to the right-hand side when ctrl1 is the topmost view controller, you can write something like the following:

```
ctrl1.navigationItem.rightBarButtonItem =
    [ctrl1 editButtonItem];
ctrl1.editing = NO;
```

Notice how we have obtained the button using the view controller's instance method editButtonItem which is declared as:

```
- (UIBarButtonItem *)editButtonItem
```

Figures 6.15 and 6.16 show the Edit/Done buttons on a navigation bar, respectively.

## 6.4   Modal View Controllers

A modal view controller allows you to overlay another view controller on top of an existing one. When the modal view controller is presented to the user, it occupies the whole space below the status bar. Just as navigation levels appear animated from left to right, modal view controllers appear animated from bottom to top.

Every view controller can present at most one modal view controller at a time. The modalViewController property holds the reference to the modal view controller. This property is declared as:

@property ( nonatomic ,  readonly )  UIViewController
                  ∗modalViewController ;

Likewise, the view controller, if presented as a modal view controller by another view controller, has a reference to its parent view controller using the parentViewController property which is declared as:

@property ( nonatomic , readonly )  UIViewController
            ∗parentViewController

To display a modal view controller, the view controller invokes the instance method presentModalViewController:animated: which is declared as:

− ( **void** ) presentModalViewController :
( UIViewController ∗) modalViewController
animated : ( BOOL ) animated

After the view of the modal view controller appears and the user finishes interacting with it, a mechanism (usually a button on the navigation bar) is used to dismiss the modal view controller. To dismiss the modal view controller, the parent view controller needs to invoke the method dismissModalViewControllerAnimated: which is declared as:

− ( **void** ) dismissModalViewControllerAnimated : ( BOOL ) animated

### 6.4.1  A detailed example

Let's illustrate modal view controllers using a detailed example. In the following example, we will build an application that first presents a view controller managed by a navigation controller. When the user taps on the view (Fig. 6.17), another navigation controller is presented modally (Fig. 6.18). The modal controller has a "Dismiss" button on the navigation bar which, when tapped, will dismiss the modal controller and show the view of the hidden parent controller (Fig. 6.17).

The parent view controller class is MainViewController which is declared in Listing 6.20.

**Listing 6.20**   The declaration of MainViewController that presents a modal view controller.

```
@class SecondaryViewController ;

@interface MainViewController : UIViewController {
  SecondaryViewController ∗secondaryCtrl1 ;
  UINavigationController ∗secondaryNavigationCtrl ;
}
−(void) showModalController ;
−(void) dismissModelController ;
@end
```

**Figure 6.17**    The view of the `MainViewController` and the navigation bar.

The controller has a reference to the modal view controller as it will create it when the user taps on its view. A reference to the navigation controller which will also be created at that time is also maintained. As we will see shortly, the `showModalController` method will be invoked from its view and the `dismissModelController` is the action method of the "Dismiss" navigation bar button found on the modal controller. Listing 6.21 shows the implementation of the class.

**Listing 6.21**    The implementation of `MainViewController` that presents a modal view controller.

```
#import "MainViewController.h"
#import "SecondaryViewController.h"
#import "MainView.h"

@implementation MainViewController

- (void)loadView {
    CGRect    rectFrame =
            [UIScreen mainScreen].applicationFrame;
    MainView *theView    =
            [[MainView alloc] initWithFrame:rectFrame];
    theView.myController = self;
```

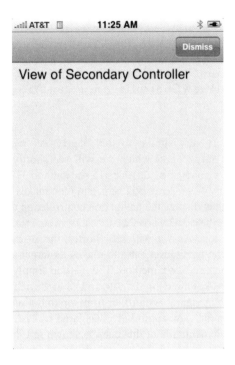

**Figure 6.18**   The view of the modal view controller and the navigation bar with the "Dismiss" button.

```
theView . backgroundColor = [ UIColor grayColor ];
theView . autoresizingMask =
       UIViewAutoresizingFlexibleHeight |
       UIViewAutoresizingFlexibleWidth ;
self . view = theView ;
[ theView release ];
}

-(void) showModalController{
  secondaryCtrl1 =
  [[ SecondaryViewController alloc ]
     initWithNibName : nil
     bundle : nil parent : self ];
  secondaryNavigationCtrl =
  [[ UINavigationController alloc ]
     initWithRootViewController : secondaryCtrl1 ];
  [ self presentModalViewController : secondaryNavigationCtrl
     animated : YES ];
}
```

```
−(void) dismissModelController {
   [secondaryCtrl1 release];
   [secondaryNavigationCtrl release];
   [self dismissModalViewControllerAnimated:YES];
}
@end
```

The `loadView` method is very similar to the `loadView` methods we have seen so far. The view created is of type `MainView` which we will see shortly. When the user taps on the view, the view invokes the `showModalController` method. This method creates the view controller of type `SecondaryViewController`, and then makes it the root controller of a new navigation controller. It will then display the navigation controller on top of itself and the navigation bar by invoking the `presentModalViewController:animated:` method animating the appearance from bottom to top. As we will see shortly, the `SecondaryViewController` adds a "Dismiss" button to the navigation bar and makes its target-action this controller instance and the `dismissModelController` method. The method simply deallocates the view and the navigation controllers, and invokes the `dismissModalViewControllerAnimated:` method animating the dismissal of the navigation controller from top to bottom.

The view class for the parent view controller is declared in Listing 6.22. It is similar to what we have seen so far. The implementation of this class is shown in Listing 6.23. The view overrides the `touchesBegan:withEvent:` method to ask the view controller to show the modal view controller.

**Listing 6.22**  The declaration of the `MainView` class used as the view for the controller presenting a modal view controller.

```
@class MainViewController;
@interface MainView : UIView {
   MainViewController *myController;
}
@property(nonatomic, assign) MainViewController* myController;
@end
```

**Listing 6.23**  The implementation of the `MainView` class used as the view for the controller presenting a modal view controller.

```
#import "MainView.h"
#import "MainViewController.h"

@implementation MainView
@synthesize myController;
− (void)
touchesBegan:(NSSet *)touches withEvent:(UIEvent *)event{
   [myController showModalController];
}
@end
```

Listing 6.24 shows the declaration of the `SecondaryViewController` class. The initializer has a reference parameter to the parent view controller which will become the target of the "Dismiss" button.

**Listing 6.24**   The declaration of `SecondaryViewController` class.

```
@class MainViewController;

@interface SecondaryViewController : UIViewController {
}
- (id)
initWithNibName:(NSString *)nibNameOrNil
bundle:(NSBundle *)nibBundleOrNil
parent:(MainViewController*) myParent;
@end
```

Listing 6.25 shows the implementation of the `SecondaryViewController` class. The initializer adds a "Dismiss" right button on the navigation bar.

**Listing 6.25**   The implementation of `SecondaryViewController` class.

```
#import "SecondaryViewController.h"
#import "SecondaryView.h"
#import "MainViewController.h"

@implementation SecondaryViewController

- (id)
initWithNibName:(NSString *)nibNameOrNil
bundle:(NSBundle *)nibBundleOrNil
parent:(MainViewController*) myParent{
  if (self = [super initWithNibName:nibNameOrNil
      bundle:nibBundleOrNil]) {
    UIBarButtonItem *rightButton =
    [[UIBarButtonItem alloc]
       initWithTitle:@"Dismiss"
       style:UIBarButtonItemStyleDone
       target:myParent
       action:@selector(dismissModelController)
     ];
    self.navigationItem.rightBarButtonItem = rightButton;
    [rightButton release];

  }
  return self;
}
```

```
– (void)loadView {
  CGRect   rectFrame = [UIScreen mainScreen].applicationFrame;
  SecondaryView *theView   =
    [[SecondaryView alloc] initWithFrame:rectFrame];
  theView.backgroundColor = [UIColor yellowColor];
  theView.autoresizingMask =
      UIViewAutoresizingFlexibleHeight |
      UIViewAutoresizingFlexibleWidth;
  self.view = theView;
  [theView release];

}
@end
```

Listing 6.26 shows the `SecondaryView` class used by the `SecondaryViewController` view controller.

Listing 6.26    The `SecondaryView` class.

```
@interface SecondaryView : UIView {
}
@end

@implementation SecondaryView
– (void)drawRect:(CGRect)rect {
  [@"View of Secondary Controller"
        drawAtPoint:CGPointMake(10, 5)
        withFont:[UIFont systemFontOfSize:20]];
}
@end
```

To put all the previous pieces together, the application delegate class is shown in Listings 6.27 and 6.28. The application delegate has reference to the navigation controller and its lone view controller. It creates the navigation controller, initializes it with the view controller, and displays it to the user.

Listing 6.27    The declaration of the application delegate class for the modal view controller application.

```
@class MainViewController;

@interface CDEAppDelegate : NSObject <UIApplicationDelegate> {
  UIWindow *window;
  MainViewController *ctrl1;
  UINavigationController *navCtrl1;
}
@property (nonatomic, retain) UIWindow *window;
@end
```

**Listing 6.28**    The implementation of the application delegate class for the modal view controller application.

```
#import "CDEAppDelegate.h"
#import "MainViewController.h"

@implementation CDEAppDelegate
@synthesize window;

- (void)applicationDidFinishLaunching:(UIApplication *)
      application {
  window = [[UIWindow alloc]
      initWithFrame:[[UIScreen mainScreen] bounds]];
  ctrl1 = [[MainViewController alloc]
      initWithNibName:nil bundle:nil];
  navCtrl1 =
  [[UINavigationController alloc]
      initWithRootViewController:ctrl1];
  [window addSubview:navCtrl1.view];
  [window makeKeyAndVisible];
}

- (void)dealloc {
  [window release];
  [ctrl1 release];
  [navCtrl1 release];
  [super dealloc];
}
@end
```

## 6.5   Summary

In this chapter, we have covered the topic of view controllers. In Section 6.1, we provided a gentle introduction to view controllers by presenting a simple application with a single view controller. This application demonstrated important view controller concepts. In Section 6.2, we talked about tab bar controllers and how they can be used in the construction of radio interfaces. In Section 6.3, we talked about navigation controllers used primarily for presenting hierarchical information to the user. After that, Section 6.4 talked about modal view controllers and provided a detailed example showing their appropriate usage.

# 7

# Special-Purpose Views

In this chapter, we present several important subclasses of the `UIView` class. In Section 7.1, we discuss picker views and show how they can be used for item selection. In Section 7.2, we discuss progress views and also talk about activity indicator views. Section 7.3 presents text views used in displaying multiline text. In Section 7.4 we show how to use alert views for the display of alert messages to the user. Similar to alert views are action sheets which are discussed in Section 7.5. In Section 7.6, we discuss several aspects of web views.

## 7.1  Picker View

The `UIPickerView` class can be used for giving the user a fancy way to select an item from a set of values. The class allows you to have multiple sets of values where each set is represented by a wheel. The user spins the wheel in order to select a specific value from a given set. The values in a given set can be views (such as instances of `UILabel`, `UIImageView`, etc.) or strings.

Each wheel is a graphical representation of a *component*. Components are numbered starting from 0. Each component contains *rows* (i.e., the set of values). Rows are also numbered starting from 0.

You can dynamically change the contents of any component. To force a change in the contents of a specific component, change the underlying data model (e.g., the array) representing the values of the component and call the `UIPickerView`'s method `reloadComponent:` passing in the component index. If you would like to change all the components, call the method `reloadAllComponents`.

### 7.1.1  The delegate

To use an instance of a `UIPickerView`, you need to set up a delegate for it. This delegate must adopt the protocol `UIPickerViewDelegate` and implement specific methods defined by this protocol.

To actually construct the view contents, the `UIPickerView` instance needs the value for each (component, row) pair. The delegate has to implement either a method which returns an `NSString` instance, or a `UIView` instance. The method which returns an `NSString` instance is declared as:

```
- (NSString *)pickerView:(UIPickerView *)pickerView
          titleForRow:(NSInteger)row
          forComponent:(NSInteger)component
```

Where `pickerView` is the picker view requesting the title value, and `row` is the row number inside `component`.

The method which returns an instance of a `UIView` is declared as:

```
- (UIView *)pickerView:(UIPickerView *)pickerView
          viewForRow:(NSInteger)row
          forComponent:(NSInteger)component
          reusingView:(UIView *)view
```

where `view` is a previously used view for this (`component`, `row`) pair. If this is adequate, you can just return this value. Otherwise, return a new view instance.

In addition, the delegate must implement the following two methods:

```
- (NSInteger)numberOfComponentsInPickerView:
          (UIPickerView *)pickerView
```

This method provides the number of components (wheels) that the picker view instance should construct.

```
- (NSInteger)pickerView:(UIPickerView *)pickerView
      numberOfRowsInComponent:(NSInteger)component
```

This method provides the number of rows that the `component` contains.

In addition to these required methods, you can implement the following methods if you choose to:

- `pickerView:rowHeightForComponent:` is used to provide the view with the height (in points) of a given component. The method is declared as:

  ```
  - (CGFloat)pickerView:(UIPickerView *)
      pickerViewrowHeightForComponent:
      (NSInteger)component
  ```

- `pickerView:widthForComponent:` is used to provide the view with the width (in points) of a given component. The method is declared as:

  ```
  - (CGFloat)pickerView:(UIPickerView *)
      pickerViewwidthForComponent:
      (NSInteger)component
  ```

- `pickerView:didSelectRow:inComponent:` is used by the picker view to inform the delegate that a given row in a specific component was selected. The method is called once the wheel settles on a specific row. The method is declared as:

  ```
  - (void)pickerView:(UIPickerView *)
      pickerView didSelectRow:(NSInteger)
      row inComponent:(NSInteger)component
  ```

## 7.1.2   An example

Let's illustrate the concepts behind the `UIPickerView` class through a concrete example. We would like to construct a view in which the user chooses a street name and the direction on that street. The example utilizes two classes: the application delegate, `PVAppDelegate`, and the view controller, `PVViewController`.

Listings 7.1 and 7.2 show the declaration and definition of the application delegate class, respectively.

**Listing 7.1**    The file `PVAppDelegate.h` declaring the application delegate.

```
#import <UIKit/UIKit.h>
#import <Foundation/Foundation.h>

@class PVViewController;

@interface PVAppDelegate : NSObject {
  UIWindow *window;
  PVViewController  *viewController;
}
@end
```

The application delegate creates the view controller and initializes it with the array of street names.

**Listing 7.2**    The file `PVAppDelegate.m` defining the application delegate.

```
#import "PVAppDelegate.h"
#import "PVViewController.h"

@implementation PVAppDelegate

- (void)applicationDidFinishLaunching:
    (UIApplication *)application {
  window = [[UIWindow alloc] initWithFrame:
              [[UIScreen  mainScreen] bounds]] ;
  NSArray *arr = [NSArray arrayWithObjects:
                    @"Plano PKWY", @"Coit Road",
                    @"Preston Road", @"Legacy",
                    @"Independence", nil];
  viewController = [[PVViewController alloc]
                      initWithStreetNames:arr];
  [window addSubview:viewController.view];
  [window makeKeyAndVisible];
}

- (void)dealloc {
```

```
    [window release];
    [viewController release];
    [super dealloc];
}
@end
```

Listings 7.3 and 7.4 show the view controller declaration and definition, respectively.

**Listing 7.3**    The file `PVViewController.h` declaring the view controller.

```
#import <UIKit/UIKit.h>
#import <Foundation/Foundation.h>

@interface PVViewController :
    UIViewController <UIPickerViewDelegate> {
  UIPickerView *pickerView;
  NSArray *streetNames;
  NSMutableArray *directions;
}
-(id) initWithStreetNames:(NSArray*) streets;
@end
```

**Listing 7.4**    The file `PVViewController.m` defining the view controller.

```
#import "PVViewController.h"

@implementation PVViewController
-(id)initWithStreetNames:(NSArray*) streets{
  if (self = [super init]) {
    directions = [[NSMutableArray arrayWithObjects:
            @"East",
            @"West",
             nil] retain];
    streetNames = [streets copy];
  }
  return self;
}
- (id)init{
  return [self initWithStreetNames:
            [NSArray arrayWithObjects:
            @"Street Name", nil]];
}
- (void)loadView {
  // Create the main view
  UIView *theView    = [[UIView alloc]
```

```
            initWithFrame:
            [UIScreen mainScreen].applicationFrame];
    theView.autoresizingMask =
            UIViewAutoresizingFlexibleHeight|
            UIViewAutoresizingFlexibleWidth;
    // Create the picker view
    pickerView =
        [[UIPickerView alloc] initWithFrame:CGRectZero];
    CGSize pickerSize =
        [pickerView sizeThatFits:CGSizeZero];
    pickerView.frame =
        CGRectMake(0,0, pickerSize.width, pickerSize.height);
    pickerView.autoresizingMask =
        UIViewAutoresizingFlexibleWidth;
    pickerView.delegate = self;
    pickerView.showsSelectionIndicator = YES;

    [theView addSubview:pickerView];
    self.view = theView;
}
- (void)dealloc {
    [pickerView release];
    [directions release];
    [streetNames release];
    [super dealloc];
}
// Delegate methods
- (void)pickerView:(UIPickerView *)pickerView
    didSelectRow:(NSInteger)row
    inComponent:(NSInteger)component
{
    NSString *street, *direction;
    street = [streetNames objectAtIndex:
        [pickerView selectedRowInComponent:0]];
    direction = [directions objectAtIndex:
        [pickerView selectedRowInComponent:1]];
    if(component ==0){
        if(  ([street isEqual:@"Coit Road"] == YES) ||
            ([street isEqual:@"Preston Road"] == YES) ||
            ([street isEqual:@"Independence"] == YES)){
            [directions removeAllObjects];
            [directions addObject:@"North"];
            [directions addObject:@"South"];
            [pickerView reloadComponent:1];
```

```
    }
    else {
      [directions removeAllObjects];
      [directions addObject:@"East"];
      [directions addObject:@"West"];
      [pickerView reloadComponent:1];
    }
    printf("Selected row in Component 0 is now %s.
           Selected row in Component 1 remains %s\n",
        [street cStringUsingEncoding:
         NSUTF8StringEncoding],
        [direction cStringUsingEncoding:
         NSUTF8StringEncoding]);
  }
  else {
    printf("Selected row in Component 1 is now %s.
        Selected row in Component 0 remains %s\n",
        [direction cStringUsingEncoding:
         NSUTF8StringEncoding],
        [street cStringUsingEncoding:
         NSUTF8StringEncoding]);
  }
}
- (NSString *)pickerView:(UIPickerView *)pickerView
              titleForRow:(NSInteger)row
              forComponent:(NSInteger)component
{
  if (component == 0)
  {
    return [streetNames objectAtIndex:row];
  }
  else
  {
    return [directions objectAtIndex:row];
  }
}
- (CGFloat)pickerView:(UIPickerView *)pickerView
        widthForComponent:(NSInteger)component
{
  if (component == 0)
    return 200.0;
  else
    return 100.0;
}
```

```
— ( CGFloat ) pickerView :( UIPickerView * ) pickerView
        rowHeightForComponent :( NSInteger ) component
{
  return 40.0;
}
— ( NSInteger ) pickerView :( UIPickerView * ) pickerView
        numberOfRowsInComponent :( NSInteger ) component
{
  if ( component == 0 ){
    return [ streetNames count ];
  }
  else
  {
    return [ directions count ];
  }
}
— ( NSInteger ) numberOfComponentsInPickerView :
                ( UIPickerView * ) pickerView
{
  return 2;
}
@end
```

The controller uses two arrays as the underlying data model for the picker view. The streetNames array holds the names of the streets. The directions mutable array is a dynamic array that contains the directions available on the currently selected street. Initialization of the data model is done in the method initWithStreetNames:.

The creation of the picker view is done in the controller's loadView method. The UIPickerView object is special in that it calculates the optimal size of itself internally. Therefore, you should use CGRectZero in the initialization. To fit the view using the internally calculated frame, use the UIPickerView instance method sizeThatFits: and pass a CGRectZero.

Once you have the optimal width and height of the view, you should update the picker view's frame. To finish the setup, set the property showsSelectionIndicator to YES, make the controller the delegate, and add the picker view to the main view.

Since the second component, the street directions, is a function of the selected street, we need to change its underlying data model when the currently selected street changes. The method pickerView:didSelectRow:inComponent: is a delegate method that is called whenever the selected row of a component changes. This is a good place to put the logic that will change the data model of the street directions component.

The method starts by retrieving the two selected rows. To retrieve a selected value from a component, use the method selectedRowInComponent:. If the selected row is in the first component (the streets wheel), the method determines the street directions, and updates the second wheel. To update a component, you should update the data model (the array directions), and call the picker view's method reloadComponent: passing in the component number.

**Figure 7.1**   A picker view allowing the user to choose a street name and a direction.

Figure 7.1 shows the application main window.

## 7.2   Progress Views

Progress views (see Fig. 7.2) are visual indicators to the user showing that a task is being executed. If you can quantify the progress of a task, an instance of `UIProgressView` is used. If, on the other hand, you do not know how long the task will take, an instance of `UIActivityIndicatorView` is more suitable.

There is only one main attribute of a `UIProgressView` instance: `progress`. The property declaration of `progress` is as follows:

```
@property(nonatomic) float progress
```

The value taken by `progress` ranges from `0.0` to `1.0`. Whenever `progress` value is changed, the view updates itself.

To make an instance of `UIActivityIndicatorView` start spinning, invoke the method `startAnimating`. To make it stop, send the message `stopAnimating`. If the Boolean attribute `hidesWhenStopped` is `YES` (the default), the activity indicator view hides itself

**Figure 7.2**    Providing visual clues to the user regarding the progress of a given task.

when you send the `stopAnimating` message. There are several `UIActivityIndicator-Style` values that you can use to set the `activityIndicatorViewStyle` property. Examples include: `UIActivityIndicatorViewStyleGray`, `UIActivityIndicator-ViewStyleBlueSmall`, and `UIActivityIndicatorViewStyleWhiteLarge`.

## 7.2.1   An example

Let's illustrate the concepts behind the two classes through a concrete example. The example utilizes two classes: the application delegate, `PVAppDelegate`, and the view controller, `PVViewController`.

Listings 7.5 and 7.6 show the declaration and definition of the application delegate class, respectively.

**Listing 7.5**    The file `PVAppDelegate.h` declaring the application delegate.

```
#import <UIKit/UIKit.h>
#import <Foundation/Foundation.h>
@class PVViewController;
@interface PVAppDelegate : NSObject {
```

```
   UIWindow *window;
   PVViewController *viewController;
}
@end
```

**Listing 7.6**   The file `PVAppDelegate.m` defining the application delegate.

```
#import "PVAppDelegate.h"
#import "PVViewController.h"
@implementation PVAppDelegate
- (void)applicationDidFinishLaunching:
   (UIApplication *)application {
   window =
      [[UIWindow alloc] initWithFrame:
         [[UIScreen mainScreen] bounds]] ;
   viewController = [[PVViewController alloc] init];
   [window addSubview:viewController.view];
   // make the window key and visible
   [window makeKeyAndVisible];
}
- (void)dealloc {
   [window release];
   [viewController release];
   [super dealloc];
}
@end
```

Listings 7.7 and 7.8 show the declaration and definition of the view controller class. The main view, `theView`, houses two subviews: an instance of a `UIProgressView` and an instance of a `UIActivityIndicatorView`.

We first create the progress bar and set the initial progress to 0. After that, the activity indicator is created and animation is started. Next, we create, for demonstration purposes, an instance of `NSTimer`. The timer is set up to invoke our method `updateProgress:` every second.

Inside the `updateProgress:` method, we update the value for `progress`; thus advancing the indicator of the progress bar by $1/10^{th}$. If the task is finished (i.e., 10 seconds have passed), we send a `stopAnimating` to the activity indicator and stop the timer.

**Listing 7.7**   The file `PVViewController.h` declaring the view controller.

```
#import <UIKit/UIKit.h>
#import <Foundation/Foundation.h>
@interface PVViewController : UIViewController {
   UIProgressView *progressBar;
   UIActivityIndicatorView *activityIndicator;
}
@end
```

**Listing 7.8**   The file `PVViewController.m` defining the view controller.

```objc
#import "PVViewController.h"
@implementation PVViewController
- (void)loadView {
  // Create the main view
  UIView *theView =
      [[UIView alloc] initWithFrame:
        [UIScreen mainScreen].applicationFrame];
  theView.autoresizingMask =
      UIViewAutoresizingFlexibleHeight |
      UIViewAutoresizingFlexibleWidth;
  [theView setBackgroundColor:[UIColor grayColor]];
  // Create the progress bar
  CGRect frame = CGRectMake(50.0, 100.0, 200, 40);
  progressBar =
    [[UIProgressView alloc] initWithFrame:frame];
  progressBar.progressViewStyle =
     UIProgressViewStyleDefault;
  progressBar.progress = 0.0;
  [theView addSubview:progressBar];
  // Create the activity indicator
  frame = CGRectMake(150.0, 200.0, 40, 40);
  activityIndicator = [[UIActivityIndicatorView alloc]
         initWithFrame:frame];
  activityIndicator.activityIndicatorViewStyle =
     UIActivityIndicatorViewStyleWhite;
  [activityIndicator startAnimating];
  [theView addSubview:activityIndicator];
  // Create a timer for demo purposes
  [NSTimer scheduledTimerWithTimeInterval:1
             target:self
             selector:@selector(updateProgress:)
             userInfo:nil repeats:YES];
  self.view = theView;
}
- (void)updateProgress:(NSTimer *)theTimer {
  progressBar.progress += 0.1;
  if (progressBar.progress >= 1.0){
    [theTimer invalidate];
    [activityIndicator stopAnimating];
  }
}
- (void)dealloc {
  [progressBar release];
```

```
    [ activityIndicator  release ];
    [ super  dealloc ];
}
@end
```

## 7.3   Text View

The class `UITextView` is a subclass of `UIScrollView` (which extends `UIView`). You can use this class to display multiline text with a given color, font, and text alignment.

The following are the main properties of this class.

- `text`. The value of this property is the text displayed inside this view. The property is declared as:

  ```
  @property(nonatomic,  copy)  NSString  *text
  ```

- `font`. This represents the font of the text. Note that you can only have one font for the whole text. The property is declared as:

  ```
  @property(nonatomic,  retain)  UIFont  *font
  ```

- `textColor`. This represents the color of the text. As in the font's case, only one color can be used. The property is declared as:

  ```
  @property(nonatomic,  retain)  UIColor  *textColor
  ```

- `textAlignment`. The value dictates the alignment of the text in the view. The property is declared as:

  ```
  @property(nonatomic)  UITextAlignment  textAlignment
  ```

  The alignment can be left (`UITextAlignmentLeft`), right (`UITextAlignment-Right`), or center (`UITextAlignmentCenter`). The default is left alignment.

- `editable`. This value determines whether the text can be edited or not. The property is declared as:

  ```
  @property(nonatomic,  getter=isEditable)  BOOL  editable
  ```

### 7.3.1   The delegate

The delegate of this class should adopt the `UITextViewDelegate` protocol. All methods in this protocol are optional. The delegate will receive messages related to the editing of the text. These message are the following:

- `textViewShouldBeginEditing:`. The delegate is queried whether the text view should begin editing. This is triggered by the user touching inside the text area. You return `YES`, if you want editing to begin, and `NO`, otherwise.

- `textViewDidBeginEditing:`. This is received immediately after editing starts, but before the text is actually changed.

- `textViewShouldEndEditing:`. This is received when the text view resigns as the first responder. You return YES to end editing, and NO, otherwise.

- `textViewDidEndEditing:`. This is received to inform the delegate that the text view has ended the editing.

### 7.3.2   An example

To illustrate the concepts behind the `UITextView` class, let's look at an example. We will create a multiline text area and allow the user to edit it. The user will be able to signal the end of the editing by pressing a Done button.

The example uses two classes: the application delegate shown in Listings 7.9 and 7.10, and the view controller shown in Listings 7.11 and 7.12.

Listing 7.9   The file `TVAppDelegate.h` declaring the application delegate.

```
#import <UIKit/UIKit.h>
#import <Foundation/Foundation.h>
@class TVViewController;
@interface TVAppDelegate : NSObject {
  UIWindow *window;
  TVViewController *viewController;
}
@end
```

Listing 7.10   The file `TVAppDelegate.m` defining the application delegate.

```
#import "TVAppDelegate.h"
#import "TVViewController.h"
@implementation TVAppDelegate
- (void)applicationDidFinishLaunching:
    (UIApplication *)application {
  window = [[UIWindow alloc] initWithFrame:
        [[UIScreen mainScreen] bounds]] ;
  viewController = [[TVViewController alloc] init];
  [window addSubview:viewController.view];
  // make the window key and visible
  [window makeKeyAndVisible];
}
- (void)dealloc {
  [window release];
  [viewController release];
  [super dealloc];
}
@end
```

Inside the loadView method of the view controller, we allocate an instance of UITextView, initialize it with a size of (320, 200) and position it at (0, 50). The text color, font, and background color of the text area are then configured.

An initial text can be added to the view. Notice how the "\n" is used to form a new line. The return key type used is UIReturnKeyDefault. The keyboard type is assigned a value of UIKeyboardTypeDefault.

After creating the text view area and adding it to the view, theView, the method continues and creates and configures a Done button. When pushed, the Done button will resign the text view instance as the first responder, thus hiding the keyboard.

**Listing 7.11**    The file TVViewController.h declaring the view controller.

```
#import <UIKit/UIKit.h>
#import <Foundation/Foundation.h>
@interface TVViewController :
    UIViewController <UITextViewDelegate>{
  UITextView *textView;
  UIButton *doneButton;
}
@end
```

**Listing 7.12**    The file TVViewController.m defining the view controller.

```
#import "TVViewController.h"
@implementation TVViewController
-(void)loadView {
  //Create the main view
  UIView *theView    = [[UIView alloc] initWithFrame:
        [UIScreen mainScreen].applicationFrame];
  theView.autoresizingMask =
      UIViewAutoresizingFlexibleHeight|
      UIViewAutoresizingFlexibleWidth;
  CGRect frame = CGRectMake(0.0, 50.0, 320, 200.0);
  textView = [[UITextView alloc] initWithFrame:frame];
  textView.textColor = [UIColor blackColor];
  textView.font = [UIFont fontWithName:@"Arial" size:20];
  textView.delegate = self;
  textView.backgroundColor = [UIColor whiteColor];
  textView.text = @"Dear Sir/Madam, \n I would like ";
  textView.returnKeyType = UIReturnKeyDefault;
  textView.keyboardType = UIKeyboardTypeDefault;
  [theView addSubview: textView];

  doneButton = [[UIButton
     buttonWithType:UIButtonTypeRoundedRect] retain];
  doneButton.frame = CGRectMake(210.0, 5.0, 100, 40);
```

```
    [doneButton setTitle:@"Done"
      forState:UIControlStateNormal];
    [doneButton addTarget:self action:
      @selector(doneAction:)
      forControlEvents:UIControlEventTouchUpInside];
    doneButton.enabled = NO;
    [theView addSubview: doneButton];

    self.view = theView;
}
- (void)doneAction:(id)sender{
    [textView resignFirstResponder];
    doneButton.enabled = NO;
}
// UITextView delegate methods
- (BOOL)textViewShouldBeginEditing:
      (UITextView *)textView{
    printf("textViewShouldBeginEditing\n");
    return YES;
}
- (void)textViewDidBeginEditing:
    (UITextView *)textView
{
    printf("textViewDidBeginEditing\n");
    doneButton.enabled = YES;
}
- (BOOL)textViewShouldEndEditing:(UITextView *)textView{
    printf("textViewShouldEndEditing\n");
    return YES;
}
- (void)textViewDidEndEditing:(UITextView *)textView{
    printf("textViewDidEndEditing\n");

}
- (void)dealloc {
    [textView release];
    [doneButton release];
    [super dealloc];
}
@end
```

As we mentioned earlier, all the delegate methods are optional. Of those, we implement four methods. When the editing of the text view starts, the method `textViewDidBeginEditing:` is called. In this method, we enable the Done button, thus allowing the user to quit editing when

**Figure 7.3**    Editing a multiline text area.

he/she is finished. The other three methods are for demo purposes and achieve the default behavior. Figure 7.3 shows a snapshot of the application.

## 7.4   Alert View

Alert views are used to display an alert message to the user. This alert message consists of a title and one or more buttons. The class used for an alert view is UIAlertView which is a subclass of UIView. To initialize an alert view, you use the convenient initializer initWithTitle:message:delegate:cancelButtonTitle: otherButtonTitles: declared as:

− (**id**)initWithTitle :(NSString ∗)title  message :(NSString ∗)message
      delegate :(**id**<UIAlertViewDelegate >)delegate
      cancelButtonTitle :(NSString ∗)cancelButtonTitle
      otherButtonTitles :(NSString ∗)otherButtonTitles ,  ...

The title is a string used as the title for the alert view. The message is a descriptive text providing more details about the purpose of the alert view. The delegate is an object that adopts the UIAlertViewDelegate that will receive messages from the UIAlertView instance. The `cancelButtonTitle` is the title of the cancel button used to dismiss the alert view. You need at least one button in order for the user to have the ability to dismiss the alert view. You can add one or more other buttons in `otherButtonTitles` by listing their titles in a comma-separated `nil`-terminated list. After initializing the alert view instance, you send it a show message to make it appear. The following shows the basic steps described above:

```
UIAlertView *alert = [[ UIAlertView alloc ]
            initWithTitle :@"Host Unreachable"
            message :@"Please check the host address"
            delegate : self  cancelButtonTitle :@"OK"
            otherButtonTitles :  nil ];
[ alert show ];
```

The `UIAlertViewDelegate` has several declared methods. You mostly need the `alertView:clickedButtonAtIndex:` method. This method will be invoked by the alert informing the delegate of the index of the button used to dismiss the alert view. The method is declared as:

```
– ( void ) alertView :( UIAlertView *) alertView
    clickedButtonAtIndex :( NSInteger) buttonIndex
```

where `alertView` is the instance of the alert view that originated the call, and `buttonIndex` is the index of the button used to dismiss the alert view. The index of the first button is 0. Our implementation for this example simply logs the index used to dismiss the alert view as shown below:

```
– ( void ) alertView :( UIAlertView *) alertView
        clickedButtonAtIndex :( NSInteger) buttonIndex
{
  NSLog(@"The index of the alert button clicked is %d",
            buttonIndex );
}
```

In our example, the index logged will always be 0 as we have only one button. Figure 7.4 shows the alert view example.

As we mentioned above, you can have more than one button in an alert view. The following statement adds two buttons in addition to the cancel button.

```
UIAlertView *alert = [[ UIAlertView alloc ]
            initWithTitle :@"Disk Error"
            message :@"Error reading sector 18"
            delegate : self  cancelButtonTitle :@"Abort"
            otherButtonTitles :@"Retry", @"Fail", nil ];
```

The index of the "Abort" button remains 0. The indices of the "Retry" and "Fail" buttons are 1 and 2, respectively. Figure 7.5 shows the alert view with the three buttons.

The delegate defines the method `alertViewCancel:`. This method will be called when the user taps the home button of the iPhone. If the delegate does not implement this method, tapping of the cancel key is simulated and the alert view is dismissed.

**Figure 7.4**    An alert view with one button.

## 7.5    Action Sheet

Action sheets are similar to alert views in that they present a message to the user and one or more buttons. Action sheets, however, differ in how they look and in how they are presented to the user. To present an action sheet to the user, allocate a new instance of the class `UIActionSheet` and initialize it using the `initWithTitle:delegate:cancelButton-Title:destructiveButtonTitle:otherButtonTitles:` initializer. The initializer is declared as:

```
- (id)initWithTitle:(NSString *)title
    delegate:(id <UIActionSheetDelegate>)delegate
    cancelButtonTitle:(NSString *)cancelButtonTitle
    destructiveButtonTitle:(NSString *)destructiveButtonTitle
    otherButtonTitles:(NSString *)otherButtonTitles, ...
```

The `title` is used to specify the title of the action sheet. You specify a delegate using the `delegate` parameter. A cancel button title is specified in the `cancelButtonTitle` parameter. A destructive button (shown in red) title is specified in `destructiveButtonTitle`. Additional buttons can be specified in a comma-separated `nil`-terminated list using the

**Figure 7.5**    An alert view with three buttons.

`otherButtonTitles` parameter. After the creation and initialization of the action sheet, you show it within a view using the `showInView:` method passing in the parent view instance. A simple action sheet is presented to the user as follows:

```
UIActionSheet *
actionSheet = [[ UIActionSheet alloc ]
      initWithTitle :@"Are you sure you want to erase all data?"
      delegate: self cancelButtonTitle :@"Cancel"
      destructiveButtonTitle :@"ERASE" otherButtonTitles : nil ];
[ actionSheet showInView: self . view ];
```

Figure 7.6 shows the action sheet created by the above code.

The delegate `UIActionSheetDelegate` defines several optional methods. If you want to know which button was tapped by the user, you need to implement the method `actionSheet:clickedButtonAtIndex:`. The indices start at 0. In the example above, "Cancel" has an index of 0 and "ERASE" has an index of 1.

**Figure 7.6** An action sheet with two buttons.

## 7.6 Web View

In this section, we will introduce the UIWebView class. UIWebView is a subclass of UIView that allows you to present rich content to the user. We begin by first showing a simple web view application.

### 7.6.1 A simple web view application

Let's start by looking at a simple application that utilizes a web view. The application will present an array of personal records in the form of an HTML table.

Listing 7.13 shows the declaration of the application delegate class. The class keeps a reference to the records, to be presented in the form of a table, in the records NSArray instance. The allRecordsInHTML method is used by the application delegate to produce an HTML representation of the personal records found in the array as we shall see later.

**Listing 7.13**   The declaration of the application delegate class used in the simple web view application.

```
#import <UIKit/UIKit.h>

@interface DWebViewAppDelegate :
 NSObject <UIApplicationDelegate> {
   UIWindow *window;
   NSArray  *records;
}
@property (nonatomic, retain) UIWindow *window;
-(NSString*) allRecordsInHTML;
@end
```

Listing 7.15 shows the implementation of the application delegate class. The `application-DidFinishLaunching:` method builds the data model by invoking the method `loadData`. For demonstration purposes, two `Person` instances are initialized and added to the `records` array. After that, the `applicationDidFinishLaunching:` creates and initializes a `UIWebView` instance similar to other `UIView` subclasses. To make the content fit the screen and allow the user zooming in/out, the `scalesPageToFit` property should be set to `YES`.

To load a web view instance with HTML content for display, the application uses the `loadHTMLString:baseURL:` method. This method is declared as follows:

```
- (void)
loadHTMLString:(NSString *)string
baseURL:(NSURL *)baseURL
```

The first parameter is the HTML to be displayed and the second parameter is the base URL for the content. Our application builds the HTML content (as we shall see shortly) and uses `nil` as the base URL. The HTML content is composed of a static part and a dynamic part. The static part consists of the HTML tags and the formatting needed to display the HTML table. The dynamic part is the portion produced by concatenating the output of every personal record, as we shall see later. Listing 7.14 shows the HTML page that is finally loaded and visualized by the web view.

If you would like the have the text of the page appear with reasonable size, you should use the meta tag `viewport` and specify 320 for the width of the page content as shown below:

```
<meta name="viewport" content="width=320"/>
```

The static part of the HTML also includes the table tag and the first row specifying the columns' headings.

**Listing 7.14**   The HTML page that is finally loaded and visualized by the web view for the simple web view application.

```
<html>
  <meta name="viewport" content="width=320"/>
  <body>
    <h4> Records Found: </h4>
    <table border="6">
```

```
<caption>Database</caption>
<tr>
  <td>Name</td> <td>Address</td> <td>Phone</td>
</tr>
<tr>
  <td>John Doe</td> <td>1234 Fake st</td>
   <td>(555) 555-1234</td>
</tr>
<tr>
  <td>Jane Doe</td> <td>4321 Fake st</td>
  <td>(555) 555-7898</td>
</tr>
    </table>
  </body>
</html>
```

**Listing 7.15**    The implementation of the application delegate class used in the simple web view application.

```
#import "DWebViewAppDelegate.h"
#import "Person.h"

@implementation DWebViewAppDelegate
@synthesize window;

-(void)loadData{
  Person *a, *b;
  a = [[Person alloc] autorelease];
  a.name = @"John Doe";
  a.address = @"1234 Fake st";
  a.phone = @"(555) 555-1234";
  b = [[Person alloc] autorelease];
  b.name = @"Jane Doe";
  b.address = @"4321 Fake st";
  b.phone = @"(555) 555-7898";
  records = [NSArray arrayWithObjects:a, b, nil];
}

- (void)
applicationDidFinishLaunching:(UIApplication *)application {
  [self loadData];
  CGRect   rectFrame =
    [UIScreen mainScreen].applicationFrame;
  window = [[UIWindow alloc] initWithFrame:rectFrame];
  UIWebView *webView =
```

```
       [[ UIWebView  alloc ]  initWithFrame : rectFrame ];
    webView. scalesPageToFit  =  YES;

    NSMutableString  *html  =
        [[ NSMutableString  alloc ]  initWithCapacity :200];
    [ html  appendString :
     @"<html>"
      " <meta name=\"viewport\" content=\"width=320\"/>"
      " <body>"
      " <h4>"
      " Records Found:"
      " </h4>"
      " <table border=\"6\">"
      " <caption>Database</caption>"
      " <tr>"
      " <td>Name</td>"
      " <td>Address</td>"
      " <td>Phone</td>"
      " </tr>"];
    [ html  appendString :[ self  allRecordsInHTML ]];
    [ html  appendString :
     @"</table>"
      " </body>"
      " </html>"
      ];
    [ webView  loadHTMLString : html  baseURL : nil ];
    [ window  addSubview : webView ];
    [ webView  release ];
    [ html  release ];
    [ window  makeKeyAndVisible ];
}

-(NSString *)  allRecordsInHTML {
    NSMutableString  *myRecords  =
        [[[ NSMutableString  alloc ]  initWithCapacity :200]
          autorelease ];
    for  (Person  *p  in  records) {
      [ myRecords  appendString :[ p  html ]];
    }
    return  myRecords ;
}

-  (void ) dealloc {
    [ window  release ];
```

```
    [super dealloc];
}
@end
```

The dynamic part of the HTML page is produced in the `allRecordsInHTML` method. This method simply iterates over all the elements in the `records` array and appends each item's HTML content representation. Items in the `records` array are instances of the `Person` class shown in Listings 7.16 and 7.17.

Each `Person` instance contains references to the strings `name`, `address`, and `phone` of the individual represented. The `html` method is used to produce an HTML code for a row in the table with the values of these three strings as the columns.

Listing 7.16   The declaration of the `Person` class used in the simple web view application.

```
#import <Foundation/Foundation.h>

@interface Person : NSObject {
  NSString *name, *address, *phone;
}
@property(nonatomic, assign) NSString* name;
@property(nonatomic, assign) NSString* address;
@property(nonatomic, assign) NSString* phone;
-(NSString*)html;
@end
```

Listing 7.17   The implementation of the `Person` class used in the simple web view application.

```
#import "Person.h"

@implementation Person
@synthesize name, address, phone;
-(NSString*)html{
  NSMutableString *output =
    [[[NSMutableString alloc] initWithCapacity:50]
      autorelease];
  [output appendString:@"<tr> <td>"];
  [output appendString:name];
  [output appendString:@"</td> <td>"];
  [output appendString:address];
  [output appendString:@"</td> <td>"];
  [output appendString:phone];
  [output appendString:@"</td> </tr>"];
  return output;
}
@end
```

Figure 7.7 shows a snapshot of the simple web view application that we have built in this section.

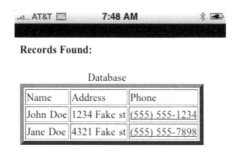

**Figure 7.7**    A snapshot of the simple web view application showing the data in the form of an HTML table.

## 7.6.2    Viewing local files

In this section, you will learn how to embed images stored in your Home directory in a web page and present the page to the user in a web view. Listings 7.18 and 7.19 show the application delegate class declaration and implementation, respectively. The application delegate simply creates a view controller of type MyWebViewController and adds its view as a subview to the main window.

**Listing 7.18**    The declaration of the application delegate class used in viewing images in a web view.

```
#import <UIKit/UIKit.h>

@class MyWebViewController;
@interface BWebViewAppDelegate :
 NSObject <UIApplicationDelegate> {
  UIWindow           *window;
  MyWebViewController *ctrl;
}
@property (nonatomic, retain) UIWindow *window;
@end
```

**Listing 7.19**    The implementation of the application delegate class used in viewing images in a web view.

```
#import "BWebViewAppDelegate.h"
#import "MyWebViewController.h"

@implementation BWebViewAppDelegate
@synthesize window;

- (void)
applicationDidFinishLaunching:(UIApplication *)application {
  window = [[UIWindow alloc]
        initWithFrame:[[UIScreen mainScreen] bounds]
        ];
```

```
ctrl = [[ MyWebViewController alloc ]
        initWithNibName : nil  bundle : nil ];
[ window  addSubview : ctrl . view ];
[ window  makeKeyAndVisible ];
}

- ( void ) dealloc {
[ ctrl  release ];
[ window  release ];
[ super  dealloc ];
}
@end
```

Listing 7.20 shows the declaration of the view controller used by the application delegate. The view controller maintains a reference to a UIWebView instance. In addition, the produceImageReference:withType: method, as we shall see shortly, is used internally to generate an IMG HTML tag for a given local image file.

**Listing 7.20**    The declaration of the view controller used by the application delegate of the application showing local image files in a web view.

```
#import <UIKit / UIKit . h>

@interface MyWebViewController : UIViewController {
UIWebView    *webView;
}
-( NSString *)
produceImageReference : ( NSString *)  imgFileName
  withType : ( NSString *)  imgType ;
@end
```

Listing 7.22 shows the implementation of the view controller class. The loadView method starts by creating the GUI objects (as we have seen in the previous section). It then proceeds to produce the web page containing image references.

To embed an image in a web page, you can use an IMG element. The IMG element has two required attributes: (1) the src, which is a URL specifying the location of the image, and (2) the alt, defining a short description of the image.

In our example, the image is stored in the application bundle (see Fig. 7.8 and Chapter 9). To specify the URL of the local image, you simply use the file protocol with the full path of the image file. For example, the following HTML is dynamically generated on the device:

```
<IMG  SRC="file:///var/mobile/Applications/
     8884F8E2-E466-4500-8FFF-6263C99016DB/web view 2.app/
     hurley.jpg" ALT="hurley"
>
```

You do not need to know how we obtained the path for the image as you will learn about that in Chapter 9. The htmlContents mutable string is incrementally constructed to contain the full web page source. For simplicity, we embed the same image three times with different headings. The full web page that is loaded on the device is shown in Listing 7.21.

**Listing 7.21** The HTML page that is finally loaded and visualized by the web view for the web view application with a page containing embedded local images.

```
<meta name="viewport" content="width=320"/>
<html>
  <body>
    <H2>Hurley</H2>
    <IMG SRC="file:///var/mobile/Applications/
      8884F8E2-E466-4500-8FFF-6263C99016DB/web view 2.app/
      hurley.jpg" ALT="hurley">
    <H1>Hugo</H1>
    <IMG SRC="file:///var/mobile/Applications/
      8884F8E2-E466-4500-8FFF-6263C99016DB/web view 2.app/
      hurley.jpg" ALT="hurley">
    <H3>Jorge Garcia</H3>
    <IMG SRC="file:///var/mobile/Applications/
      8884F8E2-E466-4500-8FFF-6263C99016DB/web view 2.app/
      hurley.jpg" ALT="hurley">
  </body>
</html>
```

**Listing 7.22** The implementation of the view controller used by the application delegate of the application showing local image files in a web view.

```
#import "MyWebViewController.h"

@implementation MyWebViewController

- (void)loadView {
  CGRect   rectFrame = [UIScreen mainScreen].applicationFrame;
  UIView  *view = [[UIView alloc] initWithFrame:rectFrame];
  view.autoresizingMask = UIViewAutoresizingFlexibleHeight |
                          UIViewAutoresizingFlexibleWidth;
  webView = [[UIWebView alloc] initWithFrame:rectFrame];
  webView.scalesPageToFit = YES;

  NSMutableString *htmlContents =
      [[NSMutableString alloc] initWithCapacity:100]; ;
  [htmlContents appendString:
   @"<meta name=\"viewport\" content=\"width=320\"/>"
   "<html>"
   "<body>"
   ];
```

```
[htmlContents appendString:@"<H2>Hurley</H2>"];
[htmlContents
  appendString:[self produceImageReference:
      @"hurley" withType:@"jpg"]];
[htmlContents appendString:@"<H1>Hugo</H1>"];
[htmlContents
  appendString:[self produceImageReference:
      @"hurley" withType:@"jpg"]];
[htmlContents appendString:@"<H3>Jorge Garcia</H3>"];
[htmlContents
  appendString:[self produceImageReference:
      @"hurley" withType:@"jpg"]];
[htmlContents appendString:@
 "</body>"
 "</html>"];

[webView loadHTMLString:htmlContents baseURL:nil];
[view addSubview:webView];
self.view = view;
[view release];
[htmlContents release];
}

-(NSString*)
produceImageReference:(NSString*) imgFileName
withType:(NSString*) imgType{
  NSMutableString *returnString =
     [[[NSMutableString alloc] initWithCapacity:100]
      autorelease];
  NSString *filePath =
    [[NSBundle mainBundle]
      pathForResource:imgFileName
      ofType:imgType];
  if(filePath){
    [returnString appendString:@"<IMG SRC=\"file://"];
    [returnString appendString:filePath];
    [returnString appendString:@"\" ALT=\""];
    [returnString appendString:imgFileName];
    [returnString appendString:@"\">"];
    return returnString;
  }
  else return @"";
}
- (void)dealloc {
```

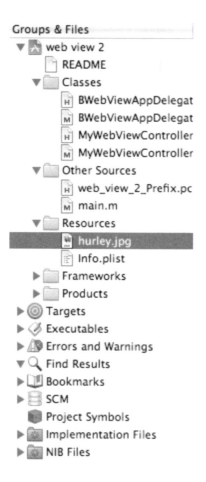

**Figure 7.8**  The Groups & Files content showing hurley.jpg image in Resources group.

```
    [webView release];
    [super dealloc];
}
@end
```

## 7.6.3  Evaluating Javascript

In this section, we would like to build an application that performs the following: it presents the user with a web page with a form and one text field (Fig. 7.10). The user enters text in the field and taps on the "Process" button on the navigation bar. If the text entered is "forbidden" (we will define the meaning of forbidden shortly), the application presents an alert view informing the user that he/she

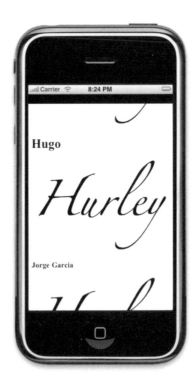

**Figure 7.9**    A snapshot of the application showing local image files in a web view.

needs to re-enter the text (Fig. 7.11). The text field is cleared and the user is given the opportunity to re-enter the text. If the text entered is not "forbidden", the application will retrieve the text value of the field, and update the web page to have a link to a Google query of the word entered (Fig 7.12). When the user taps on the generated link, the search result is displayed (Fig. 7.13). That is what the application is supposed to do. Let's start constructing it.

Listing 7.23 shows the declaration of the application delegate. It maintains both a navigation and a view controller.

**Listing 7.23**    The declaration of the application delegate class used to demonstrate the execution of Javascript code in a web view.

```
#import <UIKit/UIKit.h>

@class MyViewController;
@interface AWebViewDelegate :
  NSObject <UIApplicationDelegate> {
  UIWindow            *window;
  MyViewController       *ctrl;
```

```
    UINavigationController      *navCtrl;
}
@property (nonatomic, retain) UIWindow *window;
@end
```

Listing 7.24 shows the implementation of the application delegate class. The `application-DidFinishLaunching:` method creates a navigation controller, adds a `MyViewController` instance to it and then adds the navigation controller's view as a subview to the main window.

**Listing 7.24** The implementation of the application delegate class used to demonstrate the execution of Javascript code in a web view.

```
#import "AWebViewDelegate.h"
#import "MyViewController.h"

@implementation AWebViewDelegate
@synthesize window;

- (void)
applicationDidFinishLaunching:(UIApplication *)application {
  window =
     [[UIWindow alloc]
        initWithFrame:[[UIScreen mainScreen] bounds]];
  ctrl = [[MyViewController alloc]
       initWithNibName:nil bundle:nil];
  navCtrl = [[UINavigationController alloc]
     initWithRootViewController:ctrl];
  [window addSubview:navCtrl.view];
  [window makeKeyAndVisible];
}

- (void)dealloc {
  [ctrl release];
  [navCtrl release];
  [window release];
  [super dealloc];
}
@end
```

Listing 7.26 shows the declaration of the view controller class. The controller maintains a reference to the web view instance and a right button implementing the "Process" navigation bar button. Listing 7.27 shows the implementation of this class. The `initWithNibName:bundle:` initializes the view controller's instance and adds a "Process" navigation button. The action method for this button is `processJavaScript` which we will cover shortly.

The `loadView` method creates and initializes a `UIWebView` instance and adds it to the main window. The web view is loaded with the `loadHTMLString` string. The HTML in this string is all

static and is shown in Listing 7.25. The HTML contains a form with one text field. It also declares
the following three functions:

- getQuery(): retrieves the text value of the field in the form.
- clearQuery(): clears the contents of the text field.
- loseFocusOfField(): makes the text field lose focus so that the keyboard disappears.

**Listing 7.25**    A static HTML specifying the main page for the application demonstrating the execution of
Javascript in a web view from within Objective-C code.

```html
<html>
  <head>
    <title>Query Assistant</title>
    <meta name="viewport" content="width=320"/>
    <script>
      function getQuery(){
        return document.queryform.query.value;
      }
      function clearQuery(){
        return document.queryform.query.value="";
      }
      function loseFocusOfField(){
        return document.queryform.query.blur();
      }
    </script>
  </head>
  <body>Please enter your query:
    <form name="queryform">
      <input name="Query" type="text" value="" id="query" />
      <br/>
      <br/>
      <br/>
      <a id="anchor" href=""></a>
    </form>
  </body>
</html>
```

The UIWebView class allows you to evaluate Javascript code on demand. To execute a Javascript
code, you use the stringByEvaluatingJavaScriptFromString: method. This method
is declared as follows:

```
- (NSString *)
stringByEvaluatingJavaScriptFromString:(NSString *)script;
```

The script parameter is an NSString instance containing the Javascript code that you wish to
execute. The result value of the executed Javascript code, if any, is returned as an NSString object.

When the user taps on the "Process" navigation bar right button, the `processJavaScript` method is executed. In this method, we start by retrieving the text value of the field. The `getQuery()` Javascript statement is executed and the result is returned to us. After retrieving the value, we check to see if it is equal to the text `"dissent"`. If that is the case, we show an alert view to the user (see Fig. 7.11) and clear the text field by invoking the `clearQuery()` Javascript function.

If the text value is valid, we update the web page by changing the `href` of the element whose ID is `anchor` to the Google search query. Below, we show the code generated for the search term `"iPhone"`.

```
document.getElementById('anchor').href=
    "http://www.google.com/search?q=iPhone";
```

We also update the `innerHTML` as shown in the example below:

```
document.getElementById('anchor').innerHTML="Google iPhone";
```

Both updates of the web page are then executed. In addition, we invoke the `loseFocus-OfField()` Javascript function in order to lose the keyboard.

**Listing 7.26**    The declaration of the view controller class used in demonstrating evaluation of Javascript code in a web view.

```
#import <UIKit/UIKit.h>

@interface MyViewController : UIViewController {
  UIWebView        *webView;
  UIBarButtonItem *rightButton;
}
@end
```

**Listing 7.27**    The implementation of the view controller class used in demonstrating evaluation of Javascript code in a web view.

```
#import "MyViewController.h"

@implementation MyViewController

- (id)initWithNibName:(NSString *)nibNameOrNil
  bundle:(NSBundle *)nibBundleOrNil {
  if (self = [super initWithNibName:nibNameOrNil
          bundle:nibBundleOrNil]) {
    rightButton =
    [[UIBarButtonItem alloc]
     initWithTitle:@"Process"
     style:UIBarButtonItemStyleDone
     target:self
     action:@selector(processJavaScript)
     ];
```

```
      self.navigationItem.rightBarButtonItem = rightButton;
      [rightButton release];
   }
   return self;
}

-(void)processJavaScript{
   NSString* var =
      [webView stringByEvaluatingJavaScriptFromString:
       @"getQuery()"];
   if([var isEqualToString:@"dissent"] == YES){
      UIAlertView *alert =
      [[UIAlertView alloc]
       initWithTitle:@"Forbidden!"
       message:@"Please enter a valid query."
       delegate:nil
       cancelButtonTitle:@"OK"
       otherButtonTitles:nil
       ];
      [alert show];
      [webView stringByEvaluatingJavaScriptFromString:
                @"clearQuery()"];
      return;
   }
   NSMutableString *query =
      [[NSMutableString alloc] initWithCapacity:200];
   [query appendString:
    @"document.getElementById('anchor').href"
       "=\"http://www.google.com/search?q="];
   [query appendString:var];
   [query appendString:@"\";"];

   NSMutableString *innerHTML =
      [[NSMutableString alloc] initWithCapacity:200];
   [innerHTML appendString:
    @"document.getElementById('anchor').innerHTML=\"Google "];
   [innerHTML appendString:var];
   [innerHTML appendString:@"\";"];

   [webView
     stringByEvaluatingJavaScriptFromString:
       @"loseFocusOfField()"];
   [webView stringByEvaluatingJavaScriptFromString:innerHTML];
   [webView stringByEvaluatingJavaScriptFromString:query];
```

```objc
    rightButton.enabled = NO;
    [query release];
    [innerHTML release];
}

- (void)loadView {
    CGRect  rectFrame = [UIScreen mainScreen].applicationFrame;
    UIView  *view = [[UIView alloc] initWithFrame:rectFrame];
    view.autoresizingMask = UIViewAutoresizingFlexibleHeight|
                UIViewAutoresizingFlexibleWidth;
    webView = [[UIWebView alloc] initWithFrame:rectFrame];
    webView.scalesPageToFit = YES;
    [webView loadHTMLString:
     @"<html><head><title>Query Assistant</title>\n"
     "<meta name=\"viewport\" content=\"width=320\"/>"
     "<script>"
     "function getQuery(){"
     "return document.queryform.query.value;}"
     "function clearQuery(){"
     "return document.queryform.query.value=\"\";}"
     "function loseFocusOfField(){"
     "return document.queryform.query.blur();}"
     "</script>"
     "</head><body>Please enter your query: "
     "<form name=\"queryform\">"
     "<input name=\"Query\" type=\"text\" "
     "value=\"\" id=\"query\" />"
     "<br/>"
     "<br/>"
     "<br/>"
     "<a id=\"anchor\" href=\"\"></a>"
     "</form></body></html>" baseURL:nil];
    [view addSubview:webView];
    self.view = view;
    [view release];

}

- (void)dealloc {
    [webView release];
    [rightButton release];
    [super dealloc];
}
@end
```

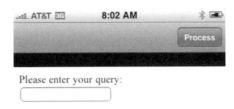

**Figure 7.10** A snapshot of the application demonstrating the Javascript–Objective-C interaction. An HTML form is provided to the user for inputting a search term.

**Figure 7.11** A snapshot of the application that demonstrates Javascript execution from within Objective-C code. The snapshot shows an alert view when a forbidden query is used.

## 7.6.4    The web view delegate

In this section, we will build an application that intercepts the user's navigation. If the user taps on a link for a PDF file, the user is asked whether he/she wants to download a copy for later use. We do not implement the actual downloading/storage management as this has been demonstrated in other chapters. What this section provides is an illustration of how you can intercept important changes to the web view instance due to user's interaction.

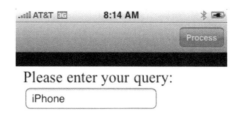

**Figure 7.12**   The application responding to a valid search term by updating the web page in the web view.

The UIWebView class has an important property, delegate, that allows you to intercept important calls. The delegate property is declared as follows:

@property(nonatomic , assign )  **id** <UIWebViewDelegate>  delegate

The UIWebViewDelegate protocol declares the following four optional methods:

1. webView:shouldStartLoadWithRequest:navigationType:. This method is invoked just before loading the content of the web page. The method is declared as follows:

   – (BOOL )
   webView:(UIWebView *)webView
   shouldStartLoadWithRequest:(NSURLRequest *)request
   navigationType:(UIWebViewNavigationType)navigationType

   You return YES if you want the web view to perform the loading of this request and NO otherwise. The first parameter is the web view instance. The second parameter is an instance of NSURLRequest representing the request, and the third is the navigation type that has led to loading the content.

   The NSURLRequest class defines the URL method for obtaining an instance of the NSURL class. The NSURL class defines the absoluteString for obtaining an NSString instance representing the URL of the request. As you will see later, we will look into this string in order to decide whether to trigger actions or not.

   There are several predefined navigation type values. The values are as follows:

   - UIWebViewNavigationTypeLinkClicked indicates that the user tapped on a link on the page.
   - UIWebViewNavigationTypeFormSubmitted indicates that the user submitted a form.
   - UIWebViewNavigationTypeBackForward indicates that the user tapped on forward/backward button.

**Figure 7.13**    The search result of a valid search term viewed in the web view.

- `UIWebViewNavigationTypeReload` indicates that the user tapped on the reload button.
- `UIWebViewNavigationTypeFormResubmitted` indicates that the user resubmitted the form.
- `UIWebViewNavigationTypeOther` indicates some other navigation trigger.

This method will be implemented in our application. If the URL is a request to a PDF file, we ask the user if he/she wants to download a copy of the file for later use.

2. `webViewDidStartLoad:`. This method is used to communicate that the web view has started loading content. The method is declared as follows:

    − ( **void** ) web View Did Start Load : ( UIWebView  ∗ ) webView

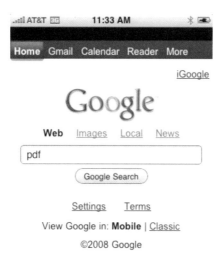

**Figure 7.14**  A snapshot of the application allowing additional local caching of PDF files.

3. `webViewDidFinishLoad:`. This method is used to communicate that the web view has finished loading the content. The method is declared as follows:

   − ( **void** ) webViewDidFinishLoad : ( UIWebView ∗ ) webView

4. `webView:didFailLoadWithError:`. This method is used to communicate that the web view encountered an error in loading content. The method is declared as follows:

   − ( **void** )
   webView : ( UIWebView ∗ ) webView
   didFailLoadWithError : ( NSError ∗ ) error

Listings 7.28 and 7.29 show the declaration and implementation, respectively, of the application delegate class. The delegate creates an instance of the `MyViewController` view controller and adds its view as a subview to the main window.

**Listing 7.28**  The declaration of the application delegate class of the application, demonstrating interception of web view user interactions.

```
#import <UIKit/UIKit.h>

@class MyViewController;
@interface EWebViewAppDelegate :
NSObject <UIApplicationDelegate> {
    UIWindow *window;
    MyViewController *ctrl;
}
@property (nonatomic, retain) UIWindow *window;
@end
```

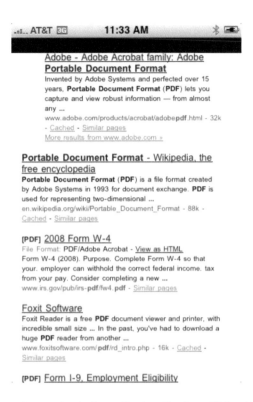

**Figure 7.15**    Result of a search operation in the application allowing additional local caching of PDF files.

**Listing 7.29**    The implementation of the application delegate class of the application, demonstrating interception of web view user interactions.

```
#import "EWebViewAppDelegate.h"
#import "MyViewController.h"

@implementation EWebViewAppDelegate
@synthesize window;

- (void)
applicationDidFinishLaunching:(UIApplication *)application {
  window = [[UIWindow alloc]
     initWithFrame:[[UIScreen mainScreen] bounds]];
  ctrl = [[MyViewController alloc]
     initWithNibName:nil bundle:nil];
  [window addSubview:ctrl.view];
  [window makeKeyAndVisible];
}
```

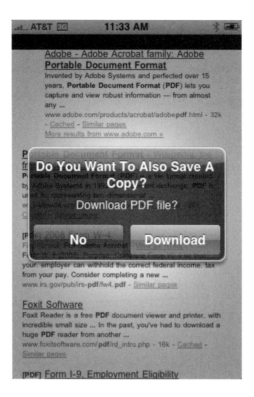

**Figure 7.16**   A snapshot of the application that allows additional downloading of PDF files. The alert view asks the user to decide whether to download a PDF file or not.

```
- (void)dealloc {
  [ctrl release];
  [window release];
  [super dealloc];
}
@end
```

Listings 7.30 and 7.31 show the declaration and implementation, respectively, of the view controller class. The class maintains a reference to the web view that is created in the `loadView` method. The web view is made to allow scaling and the `delegate` property is set to the view controller instance. The web view is made to start with the Google search page (Fig. 7.14). The view controller only implements the `webView:shouldStartLoadWith-Request:navigationType:` method of the `UIWebViewDelegate` protocol.

The `webView:shouldStartLoadWithRequest:navigationType:` method first retrieves the URL string of the request. It checks to see if it is for a PDF file by using the `NSString`'s method `hasSuffix:`. If it is for a PDF file, an alert view is displayed to the user asking for the opportunity to download it into a local directory (Fig. 7.16). The PDF file is always downloaded into the web view.

**Listing 7.30**   The declaration of the view controller class used in the application, demonstrating interception of web view user interactions.

```
#import <UIKit/UIKit.h>

@interface MyViewController :
UIViewController <UIWebViewDelegate> {
  UIWebView      *webView;
  NSString       *url;
}
@end
```

**Listing 7.31**   The implementation of the view controller class used in the application, demonstrating interception of web view user interactions.

```
#import "MyViewController.h"

@implementation MyViewController

- (void)loadView {
  CGRect   rectFrame = [UIScreen mainScreen].applicationFrame;
  UIView   *view = [[UIView alloc] initWithFrame:rectFrame];
  view.autoresizingMask = UIViewAutoresizingFlexibleHeight |
                 UIViewAutoresizingFlexibleWidth;
  webView = [[UIWebView alloc] initWithFrame:rectFrame];
  webView.scalesPageToFit = YES;
  webView.delegate = self;
  [webView  loadRequest:
          [NSURLRequest requestWithURL:
            [NSURL URLWithString:
              @"http://www.google.com"]]];
  [view addSubview:webView];
  self.view = view;
  [view release];
}

- (void)dealloc {
  [webView release];
  [super dealloc];
}

- (BOOL)webView:(UIWebView *)webView
shouldStartLoadWithRequest:(NSURLRequest *)request
```

```objc
navigationType :( UIWebViewNavigationType ) navigationType {
  url = [[ request URL] absoluteString ];
  NSLog( url );
  if ([ url hasSuffix :@".pdf"] == YES ){
    UIAlertView *alert =
    [[[ UIAlertView alloc ]
      initWithTitle :
        @"Do You Want To Also Save A Copy?"
      message :@"Download PDF file?"
      delegate : self
      cancelButtonTitle :@"No"
      otherButtonTitles :@"Download", nil ]
     autorelease ];
    [ alert show ];
  }
  return YES;
}

- ( void )
alertView :( UIAlertView *) alertView
clickedButtonAtIndex :( NSInteger ) buttonIndex {
  if ( buttonIndex == 1 ){ // download?
    NSLog(@"Downloading %@ ...", url );
  }
}

@end
```

# 8

# Table View

A table view is an important and widely used graphical user interface object in the iPhone OS. Understanding table views is essential to writing iPhone applications. Fortunately, programming table views could not be easier.

This chapter will take you through a step-by-step journey to the world of table views. We start by presenting an overview of the main concepts behind table views in Section 8.1. After that, we present in Section 8.2 a simple table view application and discuss the mandatory methods you need to implement in order to populate and respond to user's interaction with the table view.

In Section 8.3, we show how easy it is to add images to table rows. Section 8.4 introduces the concept of sections and provides a table view application that has sections with section headers and footers.

In Section 8.5, we introduce the concept of editing a table view. An application that allows the user to delete rows is presented and the main ideas are clarified. In Section 8.6, we address the insertion of new rows in a table view. An application that presents a data entry view to the user and adds that new data to the table's rows is discussed. In Section 8.7, we continue our discussion of the editing mode and present an application for re-ordering table entries. The main concepts of reordering rows are presented.

In Section 8.8, we discuss the mechanism for presenting hierarchical information to the user, and an application that uses table views to present three levels of hierarchy is discussed. In Section 8.9, we discuss grouped table views through an example. After that, we present the main concepts behind indexed table views in Section 8.10. Finally, we summarize the chapter in Section 8.11.

## 8.1 Overview

To use a table view in your application, you need to create an instance of the class UITableView, configure it, and add it as a subview to another view. The UITableView class is a subclass of UIScrollView; which itself is a subclass of UIView. The table view allows for only one column and zero or more rows. Each row in the table is represented by a cell. A cell is an instance of the class UITableViewCell. The cell can hold an image to the left side, text in the middle, and a view instance to the right.

The UITableView class relies on two external objects: one for providing the data that will be displayed, and the other for controlling the appearance of the table. The object supplying the data model must adopt the UITableViewDataSource protocol, while the object supplying the visual aspects of the table must adopt the UITableViewDelegate protocol.

In the following sections, we will show how to create and configure a table view starting from a simple table and gradually adding more features.

## 8.2    The Simplest Table View Application

In this section, we present the simplest table view application. This application presents, in a tabular form, a list of characters from the Simpsons show. The application accepts all the default values for the table view. It does not implement any of the table's delegate methods as all of them are optional. It does, however, use the application delegate as the data source and implements the two required methods of the UITableViewDataSource protocol.

Listing 8.1 shows the declaration of the application delegate class TVAppDelegate. As you have learned before, the class adopts the protocol by listing it after its superclass as follows: NSObject <UITableViewDataSource>. In addition to the myTable UITableView instance, we keep an array of strings representing the data model in theSimpsons instance of NSArray.

**Listing 8.1**    The application delegate declaration (TVAppDelegate.h) for a simple table view application. The application delegate manages the table view and acts as the data source.

```
#import <UIKit/UIKit.h>
#import <Foundation/Foundation.h>

@interface TVAppDelegate : NSObject<UITableViewDataSource> {
    UIWindow      *window;
    UITableView *myTable;
    NSArray       *theSimpsons;
}
@end
```

Listing 8.2 shows the implementation of the TVAppDelegate class. Inside the application-DidFinishLaunching: method, we perform all the initialization needed. After creating the main window, we create the table view instance. To initialize the table view, we use the method initWithFrame:style:. The frame used in the initialization is the area of the application frame as we want the table to occupy the whole area available to the application. The style used is UITableViewStylePlain. The style of the table must be specified during the initialization phase and cannot be changed later. If you bypass this initialization method and use the UIView's initWithFrame: initializer, the style UITableViewStylePlain will be used by default. We will look into other styles later in the chapter. After that, we populate the array theSimpsons with the names that will be displayed inside the table. Next, the data source of the table view is set to the application delegate instance. The UITableView's property for the data source is dataSource and is declared as:

```
@property(nonatomic, assign)
         id <UITableViewDataSource> dataSource;
```

Notice that this property uses `assign` rather than `retain`. Finally, the table view is added to the main window and the main window is made key and visible.

**Listing 8.2** The application delegate definition (`TVAppDelegate.m`) for a simple table view application. The application delegate manages the table view and acts as the data source.

```
#import <Foundation/Foundation.h>
#import <UIKit/UIKit.h>
#import "TVAppDelegate.h"

@implementation TVAppDelegate

- (void) applicationDidFinishLaunching:
                    (UIApplication *) application {
    window = [[UIWindow alloc] initWithFrame:
                        [[UIScreen mainScreen] bounds]] ;
    myTable = [[UITableView alloc] initWithFrame:
                    [UIScreen mainScreen].applicationFrame
                    style:UITableViewStylePlain];
    theSimpsons = [[NSArray arrayWithObjects:
            @"Homer Jay Simpson",
            @"Marjorie \"Marge\" Simpson",
            @"Bartholomew \"Bart\" J. Simpson",
            @"Lisa Marie Simpson",
            @"Margaret \"Maggie\" Simpson",
            @"Abraham J. Simpson",
            @"Santa's Little Helper",
            @"Ned Flanders",
            @"Apu Nahasapeemapetilon",
            @"Clancy Wiggum",
            @"Charles Montgomery Burns",
            nil] retain];
    myTable.dataSource = self;
    [window addSubview:myTable];
    [window makeKeyAndVisible];
}
// Data source required methods
- (NSInteger)tableView:(UITableView *)tableView
        numberOfRowsInSection:(NSInteger)section{
    return [theSimpsons count];
}
- (UITableViewCell *)tableView:(UITableView *)tableView
        cellForRowAtIndexPath:(NSIndexPath *)indexPath
{
    UITableViewCell *cell =
```

```
   [tableView
      dequeueReusableCellWithIdentifier:@"simpsons"];
 if (cell == nil) {
   cell = [[[UITableViewCell alloc]
           initWithFrame:CGRectZero
           reuseIdentifier:@"simpsons"] autorelease];
 }
 // Set up the cell
 cell.text = [theSimpsons objectAtIndex:indexPath.row];
 return cell;
}
— (void)dealloc {
 [window release];
 [myTable release];
 [theSimpsons release];
 [super dealloc];
}
@end
```

The two required methods of the `UITableViewDataSource` protocol are:

1. `tableView:numberOfRowsInSection:`. By default, the table view will have one section. You still need to specify the number of rows in that section. This method of the data source is invoked asking for that number. The method is declared as:

```
— (NSInteger)tableView:(UITableView *)table
   numberOfRowsInSection:(NSInteger)section;
```

You are given two values: the table view instance, which allows you to have the same data source method for multiple table view instances, and the section number, which in this example is always 0 (and is ignored) as we choose to take the default.

2. `tableView:cellForRowAtIndexPath:`. The table view invokes this method asking the data source for a table cell representing a specific row. The method is declared as:

```
— (UITableViewCell *)tableView:(UITableView *)tableView
   cellForRowAtIndexPath:(NSIndexPath *)indexPath;
```

In addition to the table view instance, you are given an instance of `NSIndexPath`. `NSIndexPath` is used in Cocoa as a class representing a series of indices. For example: `1.5.8.33` represents an index path. This class is extended by `UITableView` by declaring a category on it as shown in Listing 8.3.

**Listing 8.3** Extending the `NSIndexPath` for use in `UITableView`.

```
@interface NSIndexPath (UITableView)
+ (NSIndexPath *)indexPathForRow:(NSUInteger)row
        inSection:(NSUInteger)section;
```

```
@property(nonatomic,readonly) NSUInteger section;
@property(nonatomic,readonly) NSUInteger row;
@end
```

The category adds two properties: `section` and `row`.

Given the `NSIndexPath` instance, you can determine the cell configuration you want to return. In returning a cell, you can either create one from scratch, and return it autoreleased, or return a cached cell that is already created. You are encouraged to reuse cells. After creating a cell, you should use the initializer `initWithFrame:reuseIdentifier:` which is declared as:

```
- (id)initWithFrame:(CGRect)frame
        reuseIdentifier:(NSString *)reuseIdentifier;
```

The value for `frame` can be `CGRectZero` because the table will itself optimally place and size the cell. The `reuseIdentifier` is a string used to tag the cell so that it can be easily identified for reuse in the future. Our method creates a new cell in the following statement:

```
cell = [[[UITableViewCell alloc]
        initWithFrame:CGRectZero
        reuseIdentifier:@"simpsons"]
        autorelease];
```

We mentioned above that you should always reuse a cached cell as much as possible. To obtain a reused cell, use the `UITableView` instance method `dequeueReusableCell-WithIdentifier:` which is declared as:

```
- (UITableViewCell *)
dequeueReusableCellWithIdentifier:(NSString *)identifier
```

The value for `identifier` is the same tag used in creating the cell, which in our case is `@"simpsons"`. If there is an available cell, a pointer to it is returned. If, on the other hand, there are no available cells, a `nil` value is returned.

After having a `UITableViewCell` instance, we need to configure it with values appropriate to the section and row numbers. Since we are implementing a simple table view, we only set the text property of the cell by the corresponding value from the `theSimpsons` array (which represents the data model) as shown in the following statement:

```
cell.text = [theSimpsons objectAtIndex:indexPath.row];
```

Figure 8.1 shows a snapshot of the application.

## 8.3   A Table View with both Images and Text

In the previous section, we showed how to create a table view displaying text items. As we have mentioned before, each cell can have an image displayed to the left. In Listing 8.4, we show the

**Figure 8.1**   A snapshot of a simple text-only table view application.

updated `tableView:cellForRowAtIndexPath:` method that configures the cells to have images.

**Listing 8.4**   The updated method `tableView:cellForRowAtIndexPath:` for adding an image to the left side of each cell.

```
- (UITableViewCell *)tableView:(UITableView *)tableView
      cellForRowAtIndexPath:(NSIndexPath *)indexPath
{
  UITableViewCell *cell =
        [tableView dequeueReusableCellWithIdentifier:
            @"simpsons"];
  if (cell == nil) {
    cell = [[[UITableViewCell alloc]
          initWithFrame:CGRectZero
          reuseIdentifier:@"simpsons"]
          autorelease];
  }
  // Set up the cell
```

```
cell.text  = [theSimpsons objectAtIndex:indexPath.row];
NSString *imageName =
    [NSString stringWithFormat:
        @"%d.png", indexPath.row];
cell.image = [UIImage imageNamed:imageName];
return cell;
}
```

To set up an image for the cell, set the property image for the UITableViewCell instance. The property image is declared as:

```
@property(nonatomic, retain) UIImage   *image;
```

The default value is nil, indicating no image.

The image for each row is loaded from the application's bundle (see Chapter 9) using the imageNamed: class method of UIImage. The image files stored are named according to the row index. For example, the image for the first row is 0.png. The NSString class method stringWithFormat: is used to obtain the name of the image to be used in the invocation of the imageNamed: method. Figure 8.2 shows a snapshot of the application.

## 8.4   A Table View with Sections Headers and Footers

In the previous sections, we showed table views that had only one section. You can have a table with more than one section and have these sections presented with header and/or footer titles.

Let's modify our example so that it has a table with two sections. We need to have two arrays: one array, theSimpsonsFamily, holding names of the Simpsons' family, and theSimpsonsOthers, an array holding names of the others. We need to do the following modifications in order to have two sections.

First, modify the numberOfSectionsInTableView: method to return 2 for the number of sections. Second, modify tableView:numberOfRowsInSection: as follows:

```
- (NSInteger)tableView:(UITableView *)tableView
          numberOfRowsInSection:(NSInteger)section{
  if(section == 0){
    return [theSimpsonsFamily count];
  }
  else{
    return [theSimpsonsOthers count];
  }
}
```

Third, if you would like a section header, add the following Data Source method:

```
- (NSString *)tableView:(UITableView *)tableView
      titleForHeaderInSection:(NSInteger)section{
  if(section == 0){
    return @"The Simpsons Family";
```

**Figure 8.2**   A table view with both images and text. For copyright reasons, the actual images of the characters are replaced by images consisting of initial letters.

```
  }
  else{
    return @"The Others";
  }
}
```

Fourth, if you would like a section footer, add the following Data Source method:

```
- (NSString *)tableView:(UITableView *)tableView
      titleForFooterInSection:(NSInteger)section{
  if(section == 0){
    return @" End of Simpsons Family";
  }
  else{
    return @"End of The Others";
  }
}
```

Finally, modify the `tableView:cellForRowAtIndexPath:` to return the appropriate cell as follows:

```
- (UITableViewCell *)tableView:(UITableView *)tableView
        cellForRowAtIndexPath:(NSIndexPath *)indexPath
{
  UITableViewCell *cell =
      [tableView dequeueReusableCellWithIdentifier:@"simpsons"];
  if (cell == nil) {
    cell = [[[UITableViewCell alloc]
        initWithFrame:CGRectZero
        reuseIdentifier:@"simpsons"] autorelease];
  }
  // Set up the cell
  if(indexPath.section == 0){
    cell.text  = [theSimpsonsFamily objectAtIndex:indexPath.row];
  }
  else{
    cell.text  = [theSimpsonsOthers objectAtIndex:indexPath.row];
  }
  NSString *imageName =
        [NSString stringWithFormat:@"%d-%d.png",
                  indexPath.row, indexPath.section];
  cell.image = [UIImage imageNamed:imageName];
  return cell;
}
```

Figure 8.3 shows the table view with sections and section headers and footers. Notice how the headers and footers are always visible as you scroll through the table.

## 8.5  A Table View with the Ability to Delete Rows

The table view can be manipulated at runtime to enter an editing mode. In editing mode, you can delete/insert and reorder rows. In this section, we will look at a table view application that allows the user to delete rows. The application uses a button that, when tapped, will make the table view instance enter the editing mode. The user will then tap on the delete button and confirm deletion. The data source of the table view will receive a message asking for confirmation of the deletion. If the data source approves such deletion, the data model, represented by a mutable array, will be updated by the removal of the corresponding element, and the table view instance is instructed to delete the row, optionally animating the deletion. These are the basic steps taken. In the following, we elaborate more on how we can achieve that.

Listing 8.5 shows the declaration of the application delegate `TVAppDelegate`. The application delegate will create and configure the table view and act as its data source. Notice that we have a mutable array, `theSimpsons`, that will capture our data mode. A button, `editButton`, is used in the switching between editing and non-editing modes.

**Figure 8.3**    A table view with sections, section headers and footers.

**Listing 8.5**    The declaration (`TVAppDelegate.h`) of the application delegate for a table view application with the ability to delete rows. The application delegate manages the table view and acts as its data source.

```
#import <UIKit/UIKit.h>
#import <Foundation/Foundation.h>
@interface TVAppDelegate : NSObject <UITableViewDataSource> {
    UIWindow          *window;
    UITableView       *myTable;
    NSMutableArray    *theSimpsons;
    UIButton           *editButton;
}
@end
```

In Listing 8.6 we show the definition of the application delegate. We first create the edit button (see Section 5.5) that will trigger the switching between the two modes. The logic that will flip between editing and non-editing modes of the table view can be found in the action method `editAction:`. To make the table view enter editing mode, you invoke the method `setEditing:animated:` which is declared as:

− (**void**) setEditing:(BOOL)editing  animated:(BOOL)animate

If editing is equal to YES, then the table view enters the editing mode. Set animate to YES to animate the change in mode. Once the table view instance receives this message, it sends it to every visible row (cell).

In editing mode, each row can allow either deletion or insertion. If a row is in delete editing mode, it will be marked by a circled red minus sign ("–") icon to the left. If a row is in insert editing mode (addressed in Section 8.6), it will be marked by a circled green plus sign ("+") icon to the left. The question remains: how does the table view know which mode to enter? The answer is simple: an optional method in the delegate, tableView:editingStyleForRowAtIndexPath: is used to provide the editing style for a specific cell. This method is declared as:

```
- (UITableViewCellEditingStyle)
tableView:(UITableView *)tableView
editingStyleForRowAtIndexPath:(NSIndexPath *)indexPath
```

If the table view is in editing mode, it has a delegate, and if that delegate implements this method, then this method is called for every visible row asking it for the editing style of that row. The value returned can be either UITableViewCellEditingStyleDelete or UITableViewCell-EditingStyleInsert. If there is no delegate assigned (as is the case in our example) or the delegate does not implement this method, the UITableViewCellEditingStyleDelete style is assumed.

**Listing 8.6** The definition of the application delegate of a table view application with the ability to delete rows. The application delegate manages the table view and acts as its data source.

```
#import <Foundation/Foundation.h>
#import <UIKit/UIKit.h>
#import "TVAppDelegate.h"

@implementation TVAppDelegate

- (void)applicationDidFinishLaunching:
                (UIApplication *)application {
  window = [[UIWindow alloc]
        initWithFrame:[[UIScreen mainScreen] bounds]];

  editButton = [[UIButton
        buttonWithType:UIButtonTypeRoundedRect] retain];
  editButton.frame = CGRectMake(105.0, 25.0, 100, 40);
  [editButton setTitle:@"Edit" forState:UIControlStateNormal];
  [editButton addTarget:self action:@selector(editAction:)
                forControlEvents:UIControlEventTouchUpInside];
  [window addSubview:editButton];

  CGRect frame = CGRectMake(0, 70, 320, 420);
  myTable = [[UITableView alloc]
                initWithFrame:frame
```

```
                    style : UITableViewStylePlain ];
   theSimpsons = [[ NSMutableArray
                    arrayWithObjects :@"Homer Jay Simpson",
                    @"Marjorie \"Marge\" Simpson",
                    @"Bartholomew \"Bart\" J. Simpson",
                    @"Lisa Marie Simpson",
                    @"Margaret \"Maggie\" Simpson",
                    @"Abraham J. Simpson",
                    @"Santa's Little Helper",
                    @"Ned Flanders",
                    @"Apu Nahasapeemapetilon",
                    @"Clancy Wiggum",
                    @"Charles Montgomery Burns",
                    nil] retain ];
   myTable . dataSource = self ;
   [window addSubview : myTable ];
   [window makeKeyAndVisible ];
}

-(void ) editAction :( id ) sender{
   if (sender == editButton ){
      if ([ editButton . currentTitle isEqual :@"Edit"] == YES){
         [ editButton setTitle :@"Done"
            forState : UIControlStateNormal ];
         [myTable setEditing :YES animated :YES ];
      }
      else {
         [ editButton setTitle :@"Edit"
            forState : UIControlStateNormal ];
         [myTable setEditing :NO animated :YES ];
      }
   }
}

- ( void ) dealloc {
   [window release ];
   [myTable release ];
   [theSimpsons release ];
   [editButton release ];
   [super dealloc ];
}

// DataSource methods
- ( NSInteger ) tableView :( UITableView *) tableView
```

```
                numberOfRowsInSection:(NSInteger)section{
   return [theSimpsons count];
}


— (void)tableView:(UITableView *)tableView
   commitEditingStyle:(UITableViewCellEditingStyle)editingStyle
   forRowAtIndexPath:(NSIndexPath *)indexPath{

   if(editingStyle == UITableViewCellEditingStyleDelete){
     [theSimpsons removeObjectAtIndex:indexPath.row];
     [myTable
          deleteRowsAtIndexPaths:
          [NSArray arrayWithObject:indexPath]
          withRowAnimation:UITableViewRowAnimationFade];
   }
}


— (UITableViewCell *)tableView:(UITableView *)tableView
        cellForRowAtIndexPath:(NSIndexPath *)indexPath
{
   UITableViewCell *cell =
     [tableView
          dequeueReusableCellWithIdentifier:@"simpsons"];
   if (cell == nil) {
     cell = [[[UITableViewCell alloc]
          initWithFrame:CGRectZero
          reuseIdentifier:@"simpsons"]
          autorelease];
   }
   // Set up the cell
   cell.text = [theSimpsons objectAtIndex:indexPath.row];
   return cell;
}
@end
```

Whenever the user taps on the button, the editAction: method is invoked. The method first checks the current mode by examining the button's title. If the title is "Edit", the button title is changed to "Done" and the table view is asked to enter editing mode with animation. Otherwise, the button title is changed to "Edit" and the table view is asked to stop editing with animation. Figure 8.4 shows the application in non-editing mode and Fig. 8.5 shows it in editing mode (deletion).

When the user taps on the "–" icon, a "Delete" confirmation button appears to the right. If the user taps on that button, the table view sends a tableView:commitEditingStyle:forRowAt-IndexPath: message to the data source. This method is declared as:

**Figure 8.4**  A table view that allows editing. Editing can be initiated using an Edit button.

— ( **void** ) tableView : ( UITableView  ∗ ) tableView  commitEditingStyle :
( UITableViewCellEditingStyle ) editingStyle
forRowAtIndexPath : ( NSIndexPath  ∗ ) indexPath

The tableView is the table view instance asking for editing confirmation. The editingStyle is the style that the row is in (either deletion or insertion) and indexPath is the object holding the section and row numbers of the affected cell.

If the row should be deleted, the above method should update its data model, by deleting the data for that row, and invoke the table view's deleteRowsAtIndexPaths : withRowAnimation : method. The method is declared as:

— ( **void** ) deleteRowsAtIndexPaths : ( NSArray  ∗ ) indexPaths
withRowAnimation : ( UITableViewRowAnimation ) animation

indexPaths is an NSArray instance holding the instances of NSIndexPath for the rows that will be deleted. The animation value can be one of the following:

- UITableViewRowAnimationFade specifies that the deleted row should fade out of the table view.

**Figure 8.5**  A table view in editing mode. The default editing mode is deletion.

- `UITableViewRowAnimationRight` specifies that the deleted row should slide out to the right.
- `UITableViewRowAnimationLeft` specifies that the deleted row should slide out to the left.
- `UITableViewRowAnimationTop` specifies that the deleted row should slide out toward the top.
- `UITableViewRowAnimationBottom` specifies that the deleted row should slide out toward the bottom.

Figures 8.6 and 8.7 show the table view with the delete confirmation button and after a row has been deleted (while still in editing mode), respectively. Figure 8.8 shows the table view after exiting the editing mode and successfully deleting the `Lisa` row.

## 8.6   A Table View with the Ability to Insert Rows

In the previous section, we saw how we can configure the table view to enter editing mode and manage deletion of rows. In this section, we will address insertion of new rows. Listing 8.7 shows

**Figure 8.6** A table view row with delete confirmation.

the declaration of the application delegate of the demonstration application. The application delegate will create a new table view, an editing button, and a data entry view. It will also act as both the data source and the delegate of the table view.

**Listing 8.7** The application delegate TVAppDelegate class declaration in file TVAppDelegate.h. The delegate allows for insertion of new table entries and acts as both the data source and the delegate of the table view.

```
#import <UIKit/UIKit.h>
#import <Foundation/Foundation.h>

@interface TVAppDelegate :
    NSObject <UITableViewDelegate, UITableViewDataSource,
    UITextFieldDelegate> {
  UIWindow          *window;
  UITableView       *myTable;
  NSMutableArray    *theSimpsons;
  UIButton          *editButton;
  UIView            *inputACharacterView;
```

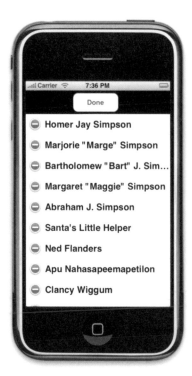

**Figure 8.7**    A table view after the deletion of a row while still in editing mode.

```
    UITextField                *characterTextField;
}
-(void)insertCharacter;
@end
```

Listing 8.8 shows the `applicationDidFinishLaunching:` method for our application delegate. First, the method creates and configures an Edit button. After that, the table view is created and configured. As we have seen in the previous section, when the user taps the edit button, the table view will enter the editing mode. The action method for the button is identical to the one you saw in the previous section. Figure 8.9 shows the starting window of the application.

**Listing 8.8**    The `applicationDidFinishLaunching:` method for the application delegate managing a table view with an insertion option.

```
- (void)
applicationDidFinishLaunching:(UIApplication *)application {
    window = [[UIWindow alloc]
            initWithFrame:[[UIScreen mainScreen] bounds]];
    editButton = [[UIButton buttonWithType:
```

**Figure 8.8**    A table view after exiting the editing mode and successfully deleting a row.

```
                        UIButtonTypeRoundedRect] retain ];
editButton.frame = CGRectMake(105.0, 25.0, 100, 40);
[editButton setTitle:@"Edit"
            forState: UIControlStateNormal ];
[editButton addTarget:self
        action: @selector(editAction :)
        forControlEvents:UIControlEventTouchUpInside ];
[window addSubview: editButton ];

CGRect frame = CGRectMake(0, 70, 320, 420);
myTable = [[UITableView alloc ]
            initWithFrame:frame
            style:UITableViewStylePlain ];
theSimpsons = [[ NSMutableArray arrayWithObjects:
                @"Homer Jay Simpson",
                @"Marjorie \"Marge\" Simpson",
                @"Bartholomew \"Bart\" J. Simpson",
```

**Figure 8.9**    A table view that allows insertion of rows.

```
                    @"Lisa Marie Simpson",
                    @"Margaret \"Maggie\" Simpson",
                    @"Abraham J. Simpson",
                    @"Santa's Little Helper",
                    @"Ned Flanders",
                    @"Apu Nahasapeemapetilon",
                    @"Clancy Wiggum",
                    @"Charles Montgomery Burns",
                     nil] retain ];
    myTable.delegate = self;
    myTable.dataSource = self;
    [window addSubview:myTable];
    inputACharacterView = nil;
    [window makeKeyAndVisible];
}
```

**Figure 8.10**    A table view after entering editing mode for insertion.

The application delegate defines the `tableView:editingStyleForRowAtIndexPath:` method needed to override the default (delete) editing style. The method simply returns `UITableViewCellEditingStyleInsert` as shown below.

```
- (UITableViewCellEditingStyle) tableView:(UITableView *)tableView
    editingStyleForRowAtIndexPath:(NSIndexPath *)indexPath{
    return UITableViewCellEditingStyleInsert;
}
```

Figure 8.10 shows the application's snapshot after entering the insert editing style.

Listing 8.9 shows the `tableView:cellForRowAtIndexPath:` method. If the image cannot be found, a generic image is used. This will allow the newly added row to have an image.

**Listing 8.9**    The data source method producing cells with text and images. It takes into account newly added entries by providing a template unknown-person image.

```
- (UITableViewCell *)tableView:(UITableView *)tableView
      cellForRowAtIndexPath:(NSIndexPath *)indexPath
{
    UITableViewCell *cell =
```

```
                [tableView dequeueReusableCellWithIdentifier:
                         @"simpsons"];
   if (cell == nil) {
     cell = [[[UITableViewCell alloc]
            initWithFrame:CGRectZero
            reuseIdentifier:@"simpsons"]
            autorelease];
   }
   // Set up the cell
   cell.text = [theSimpsons objectAtIndex:indexPath.row];
   NSString *imageName =
         [NSString stringWithFormat:@"%d.png",
             indexPath.row];
   cell.image = [UIImage imageNamed:imageName];
   if(cell.image == nil)
     cell.image =
       [UIImage imageNamed:@"unknown-person.gif"];
   return cell;
}
```

The following listing shows the `tableView:commitEditingStyle:forRowAt-IndexPath:` method. The method simply invokes the `insertCharacter` method that will actually present a data entry view to the user.

```
- (void)tableView:(UITableView *)tableView
      commitEditingStyle:(UITableViewCellEditingStyle)
      editingStyle
      forRowAtIndexPath:(NSIndexPath *)indexPath{

   if(editingStyle == UITableViewCellEditingStyleInsert){
     [self insertCharacter];
   }
}
```

Listing 8.10 shows the `insertCharacter` method. The method creates a view and adds several controls to it. A "Cancel" button is added to the view for canceling the data entry. In addition, a `UILabel` instance is added with the value "Name:" as a label to a text field. The text field is where the user enters a new name to be added to the table view. Figures 8.11 and 8.12 show the data entry view.

**Listing 8.10**    The `insertCharacter` method that will present a data entry view to the user.

```
-(void)insertCharacter{
   inputACharacterView = [[[UIView alloc]
                  initWithFrame:[[UIScreen mainScreen]
                  bounds]] autorelease];
   inputACharacterView.backgroundColor = [UIColor grayColor];
```

```
UIButton *cancelButton =
        [UIButton buttonWithType:UIButtonTypeRoundedRect];
cancelButton.frame = CGRectMake(105.0, 25.0, 100, 40);
[cancelButton setTitle:@"Cancel"
                forState:UIControlStateNormal];
[cancelButton addTarget:self
      action:@selector(cancelAction:)
      forControlEvents:UIControlEventTouchUpInside];
[inputACharacterView addSubview: cancelButton];
UILabel *label = [[[UILabel alloc]
        initWithFrame:CGRectMake(0,100, 70, 30)]
          autorelease];
label.text = @"Name:";
[inputACharacterView addSubview: label];

characterTextField = [[UITextField alloc]
          initWithFrame:CGRectMake(80,100, 250, 30)];
characterTextField.textColor = [UIColor blackColor];
characterTextField.font  = [UIFont systemFontOfSize:17.0];
characterTextField.placeholder = @"<enter a new character>";
characterTextField.backgroundColor = [UIColor whiteColor];
characterTextField.borderStyle = UITextBorderStyleBezel;
characterTextField.keyboardType = UIKeyboardTypeDefault;
characterTextField.returnKeyType = UIReturnKeyDone;
characterTextField.clearButtonMode = UITextFieldViewModeAlways;
characterTextField.enablesReturnKeyAutomatically = YES;
characterTextField.delegate = self;
[inputACharacterView addSubview: characterTextField];
[window addSubview:inputACharacterView];
}
```

The action for the cancel button is cancelAction: which is defined as follows:

```
-(void)cancelAction:(id)sender{
  [inputACharacterView removeFromSuperview];
  inputACharacterView = nil;
}
```

It simply removes the data entry view inputACharacterView from its superview, window, and sets the inputACharacterView to nil. Notice that the removeFromSuperview method does release the receiver.

The text field delegate method textFieldShouldReturn: is invoked, as you have learned in previous chapters, when the user taps the "Done" button on the keyboard. Inside this method, we add the name entered in the text field to the data model (theSimpsons mutable array) and ask the table to reload its data by sending a reloadData to the table view instance. After that, we remove the data entry view as we did above when we handled the data entry cancelation event.

**Figure 8.11**   The data entry view for adding a new entry to a table view before appearance of the keyboard.

```
− (BOOL) textFieldShouldReturn :( UITextField ∗) textField {
    [ theSimpsons addObject: textField . text ];
    [ myTable reloadData ];
    [ inputACharacterView removeFromSuperview ];
    inputACharacterView = nil ;
    return YES;
}
```

Figure 8.13 shows the application after adding a new row.

## 8.7   Reordering Table Rows

A table view can be configured to allow reordering of its rows when it enters the editing mode. By default, reordering is not enabled. To enable reordering, the data source needs to implement the method `tableView:moveRowAtIndexPath:toIndexPath:`. Once this method is defined, a reordering icon appears on the right side of each row when the table view is in editing mode. To disable reordering of specific rows, the data source needs to implement the method `tableView:canMoveRowAtIndexPath:` and exclude specific rows.

**Figure 8.12**    The data entry view for adding a new entry to a table view after appearance of the keyboard.

In the following, we give a detailed example of a table view reordering application. Listing 8.11 shows the application delegate that also acts as the data source. Notice that the data model, theSimpsons, is a mutable array because we need to change the order of the rows dynamically.

**Listing 8.11**    The file TVAppDelegate.h declaring the application delegate for the rows reordering application.

```
#import <UIKit/UIKit.h>
#import <Foundation/Foundation.h>
@interface TVAppDelegate :
        NSObject <UITableViewDataSource> {
  UIWindow          *window;
  UITableView       *myTable;
  NSMutableArray    *theSimpsons;
  UIButton           *editButton;
}
@end
```

**Figure 8.13**    A table view after the addition of a new row at the bottom.

In Listing 8.12, we show the implementation of the application delegate. The method `applicationDidFinishLaunching:` is similar to what you have seen before. It creates the table view and an edit button. In addition, the data model is populated with the values.

The `tableView:canMoveRowAtIndexPath:` method is defined to allow the reordering of all rows except two: `Bart` and `Santa's Little Helper`. To disable reordering for a given row, the method needs to return `NO`.

If the user moves a row to a new position, the method `tableView:moveRowAtIndexPath:toIndexPath:` is called. This method is declared as:

```
- (void)tableView:(UITableView *)tableView
    moveRowAtIndexPath:(NSIndexPath *)fromIndexPath
    toIndexPath:(NSIndexPath *)toIndexPath
```

The `fromIndexPath` is the current index path of the row and `toIndexPath` is the new index path. In our case, to move a name from one location in the array to a new location, we first retain the object at the current location in the statement:

```
NSString *str =
  [[theSimpsons objectAtIndex:fromIndexPath.row]
    retain];
```

This is important as we are going to remove the object from the array, and this will result in releasing it. The statement that removes the object at the current row is as follows:

```
[theSimpsons removeObjectAtIndex: fromIndexPath.row];
```

After removing the object, we need to insert it at the new location as follows:

```
[theSimpsons insertObject: str atIndex: toIndexPath.row];
```

After that, we need to release the object, `str`.

**Listing 8.12**    The file `TVAppDelegate.m` implementing the application delegate for the rows reordering application.

```
#import <Foundation/Foundation.h>
#import <UIKit/UIKit.h>
#import "TVAppDelegate.h"

@implementation TVAppDelegate

- (void)
applicationDidFinishLaunching:(UIApplication *)application {
   window = [[UIWindow alloc]
       initWithFrame:[[UIScreen mainScreen] bounds]] ;
   editButton = [[UIButton
       buttonWithType:UIButtonTypeRoundedRect] retain];
   editButton.frame = CGRectMake(105.0, 25.0, 100, 40);
   [editButton setTitle:@"Edit"
     forState:UIControlStateNormal];
   [editButton addTarget:self
       action:@selector(editAction:)
       forControlEvents:UIControlEventTouchUpInside];
   [window addSubview: editButton];

   CGRect frame = CGRectMake(0, 70, 320, 420);
   myTable = [[UITableView alloc]
       initWithFrame:frame style:UITableViewStylePlain];
   theSimpsons = [[NSMutableArray arrayWithObjects:
         @"Homer Jay Simpson",
         @"Marjorie \"Marge\" Simpson",
         @"Bartholomew \"Bart\" J. Simpson",
         @"Lisa Marie Simpson",
         @"Margaret \"Maggie\" Simpson",
         @"Abraham J. Simpson",
         @"Santa's Little Helper",
         @"Ned Flanders",
```

```objc
        @"Apu Nahasapeemapetilon",
        @"Clancy Wiggum",
        @"Charles Montgomery Burns",
         nil] retain];
  myTable.dataSource = self;
  [window addSubview:myTable];
  [window makeKeyAndVisible];
}

-(void)editAction:(id)sender{
  if(sender == editButton){
    if([editButton.currentTitle isEqual:@"Edit"] == YES){
      [editButton setTitle:@"Done"
        forState:UIControlStateNormal];
      [myTable setEditing:YES animated:YES];
    }
    else {
      [editButton setTitle:@"Edit"
        forState:UIControlStateNormal];
      [myTable setEditing:NO animated:YES];
    }

  }

}

- (void)dealloc {
  [window release];
  [myTable release];
  [theSimpsons release];
  [editButton release];
  [super dealloc];
}

// DataSource methods
- (NSInteger)tableView:(UITableView *)tableView
  numberOfRowsInSection:(NSInteger)section{
    return [theSimpsons count];
}
- (BOOL)
tableView:(UITableView *)tableView
canMoveRowAtIndexPath:(NSIndexPath *)indexPath{
  NSString *string =
    [theSimpsons objectAtIndex:indexPath.row];
```

```objc
    if ( [string  isEqual:@"Bartholomew \"Bart\" J. Simpson"]
        == YES )
            return NO;
    if ( [string  isEqual:@"Santa's Little Helper"]
        == YES )
            return NO;
    return YES;
}

- (void)
tableView:(UITableView *)tableView
    moveRowAtIndexPath:(NSIndexPath *)fromIndexPath
    toIndexPath:(NSIndexPath *)toIndexPath {
    NSString *str =
        [[theSimpsons objectAtIndex:fromIndexPath.row]
                retain];
    [theSimpsons removeObjectAtIndex:fromIndexPath.row];
    [theSimpsons insertObject:str atIndex:toIndexPath.row];
    [str release];

}

- (UITableViewCell *)
    tableView:(UITableView *)tableView
    cellForRowAtIndexPath:(NSIndexPath *)indexPath
{
    UITableViewCell *cell =
        [tableView dequeueReusableCellWithIdentifier:@"simpsons"];
    if (cell == nil) {
        cell = [[[UITableViewCell alloc]
                initWithFrame:CGRectZero
                reuseIdentifier:@"simpsons"] autorelease];
    }
    // Set up the cell
    cell.text = [theSimpsons objectAtIndex:indexPath.row];
    return cell;
}
@end
```

The method `tableView:canMoveRowAtIndexPath:` returns NO for the rows of Bart and Santa's Little Helper. It returns YES for all other rows. Figure 8.14 shows the table view while a row is being moved to a new location. Figure 8.15 shows the table view after a row has been moved to a new location.

**Figure 8.14**   A table view with reordering controls shown while a row is being moved to a new location.

## 8.8   Presenting Hierarchical Information

Table views are ideal for presenting hierarchical information. In interacting with hierarchical information, the user starts at the top level and drills down to the next level of hierarchy. The user repeats this process until he/she reaches the desired level. For example, consider a user looking at a list of names of TV shows (see Fig. 8.16). Tapping on a show name, the user will be presented with another table view holding the names of the show characters (see Fig. 8.17). Tapping on a show character, the user will be presented with a simple view with information about that character (see Fig. 8.18). The user can use the navigational buttons to go back to the previous levels of hierarchy or even edit the data of the current level. Figures 8.16, 8.17, and 8.18 show snapshots of the user drilling down to information about a specific character for a specific TV show.

There are two main classes that help you present hierarchical information to the user: (1) table view controller, and (2) navigational controller. In previous chapters, we saw how to configure and use a navigational controller. A table view controller, `UITableViewController` is a subclass of `UIViewController` that creates and manages a `UITableView` instance. You allocate a table view controller and initialize it using the `initWithStyle:` method. The table view instance created by the controller can be accessed using its property `tableView`. In addition to creating the table view and initializing it, the controller acts as both the data source and the delegate of that table

**Figure 8.15**   The table view after a row has been moved to a new location.

view. Therefore, you need to implement the table view's delegate and data source method in your subclass of that table view controller.

There are four major steps that you need to perform in order to create a working application that will present hierarchical information in the form of hierarchical table views. In the following, we present these major steps. After presenting these steps, we provide a detailed example.

Step 1.   Create a subclass of `UITableViewController` for every level of the hierarchy. Each subclass of these controllers should override the `initWithStyle:` method to configure its title and the back button title displayed in the navigation bar.

Step 2.   Choose an object that will create the navigation controller. Allocate and initialize the `UITableViewController` subclass that is the top of the hierarchy and push it onto the navigation controller as the root view controller. The object that will create these UI objects is usually the application delegate, and the work is done in its `applicationDidFinishLaunching:` method.

Step 3.   Choose a global object that is accessible from each of the table view controllers. Inside this object, provide methods to retrieve/set the data model. The application delegate is usually preferred to be such an object.

**Figure 8.16**  A table view application for displaying information about TV shows. The figure shows the top level.

Step 4.  Inside each table view controller, override the `tableView:didSelectRowAtIndex-Path:` method. Inside this method, you should: (1) store the selected row information with a global object (usually the application delegate), and (2) create an instance of the controller for the next level and push it onto the navigation controller (obtained from the global object such as the application delegate). The object that will keep track of the selected row at each level should have a separate variable for each level, for example, `level1IndexPath`, `level2IndexPath`, etc. Required and optional methods for the table view data source and delegate should be implemented in each table view controller subclass.

## 8.8.1  Detailed example

Let's illustrate the creation of a hierarchical table view application using the TV Shows example shown in Figs 8.16, 8.17, and 8.18. The TV Shows application has three levels of hierarchy. The first level presents the user with a table containing names of TV shows. The second level presents the user with a list of names of major characters for a given TV show. The third, and final, level of the hierarchy presents the user with a view showing the name and a picture of a given character.

**Figure 8.17**   The second level of the table view hierarchy. The level shows the names of major characters of a specific TV show (Lost). Notice that the back button takes the user to the previous level of hierarchy.

Clearly, we need two `UITableViewController` subclasses for the first two levels, and one `UIViewController` for the third and last level. The first table view controller subclass is called `ShowTableViewController` and it manages the table view that lists the TV shows (i.e., the first level). The declaration of the controller is shown in Listing 8.13.

**Listing 8.13**   The `ShowTableViewController` declared in `ShowTableViewController.h`. The controller represents the first level of hierarchy showing the list of TV shows.

```
#import <UIKit/UIKit.h>
@interface ShowTableViewController : UITableViewController {
}
@end
```

The implementation of the `ShowTableViewController` class is shown in Listing 8.14. The `initWithStyle:` method sets the title of the controller to `"TV Shows"`. This title will be used by the navigation controller to display in the middle of the navigation bar when the first level of hierarchy is presented to the user. The back button title is also set in this method. The value used is `"Shows"`. When the user taps on a specific show, the next level of hierarchy, showing the list of characters of that show, will be presented, and the back button title will be this value (i.e., `"Shows"`).

**Figure 8.18**   The last level of hierarchy in the TV shows application. The back button takes the user to the show that this character is part of.

The data source methods needed are implemented in the controller. We have the `tableView:numberOfRowsInSection:` method which obtains a reference to the application delegate and asks it to retrieve the number of shows. We will talk more about the data model shortly. The required data source method `tableView:cellForRowAtIndexPath:` is also implemented in the controller. To configure the cell, we ask the delegate for the show name using its method `showNameAtIndex:`. In addition, to indicate that the cell has children, the `accessoryType` property is set to `UITableViewCellAccessoryDisclosure-Indicator`.

**Listing 8.14**   The definition of the `ShowTableViewController` in the `ShowTableView-Controller.m` file. The controller manages the first level of hierarchy in the TV Shows application.

```
#import "ShowTableViewController.h"
#import "ShowCharactersTableViewController.h"
#import "TVAppDelegate.h"
@implementation ShowTableViewController
- (id)initWithStyle:(UITableViewStyle)style {
    if (self = [super initWithStyle:style]) {
```

```
      self.title = @"TV Shows";
      self.navigationItem.backBarButtonItem.title = @"Shows";
   }
   return self;
}
- (NSInteger)tableView:(UITableView *)tableView
           numberOfRowsInSection:(NSInteger)section{
   TVAppDelegate *delegate =
      [[UIApplication sharedApplication] delegate];
   return [delegate numberOfShows];
}
- (UITableViewCell *)tableView:(UITableView *)tableView
        cellForRowAtIndexPath:(NSIndexPath *)indexPath {
   static NSString *MyIdentifier = @"Show";
   UITableViewCell *cell =
      [tableView dequeueReusableCellWithIdentifier:MyIdentifier];
   if (cell == nil) {
      cell = [[[UITableViewCell alloc] initWithFrame:CGRectZero
               reuseIdentifier:MyIdentifier] autorelease];
   }
   // Configure the cell
   TVAppDelegate *delegate =
      [[UIApplication sharedApplication] delegate];
   cell.text = [delegate showNameAtIndex:indexPath.row];
   cell.accessoryType =
      UITableViewCellAccessoryDisclosureIndicator;
   return cell;
}
- (void)tableView:(UITableView *)tableView
        didSelectRowAtIndexPath:(NSIndexPath *)indexPath{
   TVAppDelegate *delegate =
      [[UIApplication sharedApplication] delegate];
   delegate.selectedShow = indexPath;
   ShowCharactersTableViewController
     *showCharactersController =
         [[ShowCharactersTableViewController alloc]
             initWithStyle:UITableViewStylePlain];
   [[delegate navigationController]
        pushViewController:showCharactersController
          animated:YES];
   [showCharactersController release];
}
@end
```

The `tableView:didSelectRowAtIndexPath:` method is where we move the user to the next level of hierarchy. First, we need to store the index path of the selected row in a location accessible by next level controller. We achieve this by setting the application delegate property `selectedShow` with the `indexPath` value passed to the method. Next, we create an instance of the next level controller and push it onto the stack of the navigation controller.

The second level controller is an instance of the class `ShowCharactersTableView-Controller`. Listing 8.15 shows the declaration of the controller.

**Listing 8.15**  The `ShowCharactersTableViewController` declared in the `ShowCharacters-TableViewController.h` file. The class manages the second level of hierarchy in the TV Shows application.

```
#import <UIKit/UIKit.h>
@interface ShowCharactersTableViewController :
     UITableViewController {
}
@end
```

The implementation of the controller is shown in Listing 8.16. As we did for the previous controller, we override the `initWithStyle:` method to update the controller's title and the title for the back button. The application delegate is asked for the show name using the method `showNameAtIndex:`. The index used in this method is the global value `selectedShow.row` managed by the application delegate which was stored in the `tableView:didSelectRowAtIndexPath:` method of the root table view controller.

**Listing 8.16**  The definition of the `ShowCharactersTableViewController` in the file `Show-CharactersTableViewController.m`.

```
#import "ShowCharactersTableViewController.h"
#import "TVAppDelegate.h"
#import "CharacterViewController.h"
@implementation ShowCharactersTableViewController −
(id)initWithStyle:(UITableViewStyle)style {
  if (self = [super initWithStyle:style]) {
    TVAppDelegate *delegate =
            [[UIApplication sharedApplication] delegate];
    self.title = [delegate
        showNameAtIndex:delegate.selectedShow.row];
    self.navigationItem.backBarButtonItem.title =
     [delegate
      showNameAtIndex:delegate.selectedShow.row];
  }
  return self;
}
− (NSInteger)tableView:(UITableView *)tableView
     numberOfRowsInSection:(NSInteger)section{
```

```
      TVAppDelegate *delegate =
            [[UIApplication sharedApplication] delegate];
      return [delegate
         numberOfCharactersForShowAtIndex:delegate.selectedShow.row];
}
- (void)tableView:(UITableView *)tableView
       didSelectRowAtIndexPath:(NSIndexPath *)indexPath{
      TVAppDelegate *delegate =
            [[UIApplication sharedApplication] delegate];
      delegate.selectedCharacter = indexPath;
      CharacterViewController *characterController =
            [[CharacterViewController alloc] init];
      [[delegate navigationController]
            pushViewController:characterController animated:YES];
      [characterController release];
}
- (UITableViewCell *)tableView:(UITableView *)tableView
       cellForRowAtIndexPath:(NSIndexPath *)indexPath {
      static NSString *MyIdentifier = @"Character";
      UITableViewCell *cell =
            [tableView dequeueReusableCellWithIdentifier:MyIdentifier];
      if (cell == nil) {
        cell = [[[UITableViewCell alloc] initWithFrame:CGRectZero
                 reuseIdentifier:MyIdentifier] autorelease];
      }
      // Configure the cell
      TVAppDelegate *delegate =
            [[UIApplication sharedApplication] delegate];
      cell.text =
       [delegate characterNameForShowIndex:delegate.selectedShow.row
            AtIndex:indexPath.row];
      cell.accessoryType =
         UITableViewCellAccessoryDisclosureIndicator;
      return cell;
}
@end
```

The method `tableView:didSelectRowAtIndexPath:` is used to push a third controller onto the navigation controller. This view controller is the leaf controller `CharacterView-Controller`. Before pushing it onto the stack, we store the index path of the selected row in the delegate `selectedCharacter` property.

The `CharacterViewController` is declared in Listing 8.17 and is implemented in Listing 8.18.

**Listing 8.17** The declaration of the `CharacterViewController` in file `CharacterView-Controller.h`. This controller manages the leaf view in the TV Shows application.

```
#import <UIKit/UIKit.h>
@interface CharacterViewController : UIViewController {
  UILabel      *nameLabel;
  UIView       *theView;
}
@end
```

The `init` method is overridden and the title is set to the character name. The character name is retrieved from the application delegate using the method `characterNameForShow-Index:AtIndex:`. The index of the show is `selectedShow.row` and the index of the character is `selectedCharacter.row`.

The `loadView` method is where we present more information about the character. To simplify things, we only use a `UILabel` instance for the name and a `UIImageView` for the picture of the character. You should be familiar with these UI objects from previous chapters by now.

**Listing 8.18** The implementation of the `CharacterViewController` in file `CharacterView-Controller.m`.

```
#import "CharacterViewController.h"
#import "TVAppDelegate.h"
@implementation CharacterViewController
- (id)init
{
  if (self = [super init]) {
    TVAppDelegate *delegate =
        [[UIApplication sharedApplication] delegate];
    self.title =
      [delegate characterNameForShowIndex:
          delegate.selectedShow.row
          AtIndex:delegate.selectedCharacter.row];
  }
  return self;
}
- (void)loadView {
  TVAppDelegate *delegate =
      [[UIApplication sharedApplication] delegate];
  theView   = [[UIView alloc]
        initWithFrame:[UIScreen mainScreen].applicationFrame];
  theView.autoresizingMask =
      UIViewAutoresizingFlexibleHeight |
      UIViewAutoresizingFlexibleWidth;
  theView.backgroundColor = [UIColor whiteColor];

  CGRect labelFrame = CGRectMake(80, 10, 190, 50);
```

```
nameLabel = [[ UILabel alloc ] initWithFrame : labelFrame ];
   nameLabel.font = [ UIFont systemFontOfSize : 25.0 ];
nameLabel.textColor = [ UIColor    blackColor ];
nameLabel.backgroundColor = [ UIColor clearColor ];
nameLabel.textAlignment = UITextAlignmentLeft;
nameLabel.lineBreakMode = UILineBreakModeWordWrap;
NSString   *theName =
      [ delegate
          characterNameForShowIndex : delegate.selectedShow.row
           AtIndex : delegate.selectedCharacter.row ];
nameLabel.text =
          [ NSString stringWithFormat : @"%@:    %@",
             @"Name", theName ];
[ theView addSubview: nameLabel ];
UIImageView    *imgView = [[ UIImageView alloc ]
                initWithImage : [ UIImage
                    imageNamed : [ NSString
                         stringWithFormat : @"%@.png",
                         theName ]]];
imgView.frame = CGRectMake(30, 70, 250, 300);
[ theView addSubview : imgView ];
[ imgView release ];
self.view = theView;
}
- (void) dealloc {
[ nameLabel release ];
[ theView  release ];
[ super dealloc ];
}
@end
```

Listing 8.19 shows the declaration of the application delegate. The delegate maintains the two properties for storing the indices of the first and second levels in selectedShow and selectedCharacter, respectively. The three view controllers access the data model for the hierarchical information through the following four application delegate methods:

```
-(NSInteger) numberOfShows ;
-(NSString *) showNameAtIndex : ( NSInteger ) index ;
-(NSInteger) numberOfCharactersForShowAtIndex : ( NSInteger ) index ;
-(NSString *) characterNameForShowIndex : ( NSInteger ) showIndex
            AtIndex : ( NSInteger ) index ;
```

We have seen how these methods are used in the presentation.

**Listing 8.19**  The declaration of the application delegate for the TV Shows application.

```objc
#import <UIKit/UIKit.h>
#import <Foundation/Foundation.h>

@interface TVAppDelegate : NSObject {
  UIWindow                  *window;
  UINavigationController     *navigationController;
  NSIndexPath               *selectedShow;
  NSIndexPath               *selectedCharacter;
  NSArray                   *theShows;
}
@property(nonatomic, retain) NSIndexPath *selectedShow;
@property(nonatomic, retain) NSIndexPath *selectedCharacter;
@property(nonatomic, retain)
        UINavigationController *navigationController;


-(NSInteger)numberOfShows;
-(NSString*)showNameAtIndex:(NSInteger) index;
-(NSInteger)numberOfCharactersForShowAtIndex:
             (NSInteger) index;
-(NSString*)characterNameForShowIndex:(NSInteger)
         showIndex AtIndex:(NSInteger) index;
@end
```

The implementation of the application delegate is shown in Listing 8.20. The first thing we do in the `applicationDidFinishLaunching:` method is prepare the data mode. The data model is represented by an array of dictionaries. Each dictionary represents a TV show and has two entries. The first entry is name of that show and the second is an array of characters for that show. After initializing the data model, we create the navigation controller and push the first level table view controller onto it. The methods called by the controllers to retrieve specific information about our data model are straightforward.

**Listing 8.20**  The implementation of the application delegate for the TV Shows application.

```objc
#import <Foundation/Foundation.h>
#import <UIKit/UIKit.h>
#import "TVAppDelegate.h"
#import "ShowTableViewController.h"
@implementation TVAppDelegate
@synthesize selectedShow;
@synthesize selectedCharacter;
@synthesize navigationController;
- (void)
  applicationDidFinishLaunching:(UIApplication *)application {
  [self prepareDataModel];
```

```objc
    window = [[UIWindow alloc]
            initWithFrame:[[UIScreen   mainScreen] bounds]];
    ShowTableViewController *showViewController =
                [[ShowTableViewController alloc]
                    initWithStyle:UITableViewStylePlain];
    navigationController = [[UINavigationController alloc]
            initWithRootViewController:showViewController];
    [showViewController release];
    [window addSubview:[navigationController view]];
    [window makeKeyAndVisible];
}
-(void) prepareDataModel{
    NSDictionary    *dic1 =
        [NSDictionary dictionaryWithObjectsAndKeys:
                @"Seinfeld",
                @"Name",
                [NSArray arrayWithObjects:
                 @"Jerry", @"George", @"Elaine", @"Kramer",
                 @"Newman", @"Frank",  @"Susan",
                 @"Peterman",  @"Bania", nil],
                @"Characters",
                  nil
                ];
    NSDictionary    *dic2 =
        [NSDictionary dictionaryWithObjectsAndKeys:
                @"Lost",
                @"Name",
                [NSArray arrayWithObjects:
                 @"Kate", @"Sayid", @"Sun", @"Hurley",
                 @"Boone", @"Claire", @"Jin",  @"Locke",
                 @"Charlie", @"Eko", @"Ben", nil],
                @"Characters",
                  nil
                ];
    theShows = [[NSArray arrayWithObjects:dic1, dic2, nil] retain];
}
-(NSInteger) numberOfShows{
    return [theShows count];
}
-(NSString *) showNameAtIndex:(NSInteger) index{
    return [[theShows objectAtIndex:index] valueForKey:@"Name"] ;
}
-(NSInteger) numberOfCharactersForShowAtIndex:
        (NSInteger) index{
```

```
    return [[[theShows objectAtIndex:index]
           valueForKey:@"Characters"] count];
}
-(NSString*)characterNameForShowIndex:(NSInteger)
        showIndex AtIndex:(NSInteger) index{
    return [[[theShows objectAtIndex:showIndex]
           valueForKey:@"Characters"] objectAtIndex:index];
}
-  (void)dealloc {
    [window release];
    [navigationController release];
    [theShows release];
    [super dealloc];
}
@end
```

## 8.9   Grouped Table Views

Until now, we have been dealing with the plain table view style. There is another style referred to as the *grouped* style that one can use to configure the table view. A grouped table view is generally used as the final level of hierarchy for presenting information about a specific item selected in the penultimate level.

The configuration of a grouped table view follows a similar approach to what we have seen so far. What you need to know is that the rows of each section are grouped together. An optional header title is used to name that group. Other than that, everything is pretty much the same.

Let's illustrate that through an example. Consider an application that presents to the user a list of favorite TV shows sorted according to their classification: comedy, political, and drama. Listing 8.21 shows the declaration of the application delegate of the demonstration application. The data model is represented in the three NSArray instances: comedyShows, politicalShows, and dramaShows. Each array will hold the shows for the corresponding section.

**Listing 8.21**   The declaration of the application delegate demonstrating the use of grouped table views.

```
#import <UIKit/UIKit.h>
#import <Foundation/Foundation.h>

@interface TVAppDelegate : NSObject <UITableViewDataSource> {
    UIWindow           *window;
    UITableView        *myTable;
    NSArray            *comedyShows, *politicalShows, *dramaShows;
}
@end
```

The implementation of the application delegate is shown in Listing 8.22. In the application-DidFinishLaunching: method, we create the table view instance as we saw before. Instead of using the plain style, we use the UITableViewStyleGrouped style. The three arrays are then populated with the data.

We saw in Section 8.4 how to configure sections and headers. There are no differences between plain and grouped styles with respect to the implementation of the configuration methods.

**Listing 8.22**  The implementation of the application delegate for the grouped table view application.

```
#import <Foundation/Foundation.h>
#import <UIKit/UIKit.h>
#import "TVAppDelegate.h"

@implementation TVAppDelegate
- (void)
applicationDidFinishLaunching:(UIApplication *)application {
  window = [[UIWindow alloc]
              initWithFrame:[[UIScreen mainScreen]
                bounds]];
  CGRect frame = CGRectMake(0, 70, 320, 420);
  myTable = [[UITableView alloc]
              initWithFrame:frame
              style:UITableViewStyleGrouped];
  comedyShows = [[NSArray arrayWithObjects:
          @"Seinfeld", @"Everybody Loves Raymond",
          nil] retain];
  politicalShows = [[NSArray arrayWithObjects:
           @"60 Minutes", @"Meet The Press",
           nil] retain];
  dramaShows = [[NSArray arrayWithObjects:
          @"Lost",
          nil] retain];

  myTable.dataSource = self;
  [window addSubview:myTable];
  [window makeKeyAndVisible];
}

- (void)dealloc {
  [window release];
  [myTable release];
  [comedyShows release];
  [politicalShows release];
  [dramaShows release];
  [super dealloc];
}
```

```
// DataSource methods

- (NSInteger)
numberOfSectionsInTableView:(UITableView *)tableView {
  return 3;
}

- (NSInteger)tableView:(UITableView *)tableView
    numberOfRowsInSection:(NSInteger)section{
  switch (section) {
    case 0:
      return [comedyShows count];
      break;
    case 1:
      return [politicalShows count];
      break;
    case 2:
      return [dramaShows count];
      break;
  }
}

- (UITableViewCell *)tableView:(UITableView *)tableView
    cellForRowAtIndexPath:(NSIndexPath *)indexPath
{
  UITableViewCell *cell =
      [tableView dequeueReusableCellWithIdentifier:@"shows"];
  if (cell == nil) {
    cell = [[[UITableViewCell alloc]
        initWithFrame:CGRectZero
        reuseIdentifier:@"shows"] autorelease];
  }
  // Set up the cell
  switch (indexPath.section) {
    case 0:
      cell.text = [comedyShows objectAtIndex:indexPath.row];
      break;
    case 1:
      cell.text = [politicalShows objectAtIndex:indexPath.row];
      break;
    case 2:
      cell.text = [dramaShows objectAtIndex:indexPath.row];
      break;
  }
```

```
    return cell;
}
- (NSString *)tableView:(UITableView *)tableView
    titleForHeaderInSection:(NSInteger)section {
    NSString *title = nil;
    switch (section) {
      case 0:
        title = @"Comedy Shows";
        break;
      case 1:
        title = @"Political Shows";
        break;
      case 2:
        title = @"Drama Shows";
        break;
      default:
        break;
    }
    return title;
}
@end
```

Figure 8.19 shows the grouped table view application.

## 8.10   Indexed Table Views

Sometimes you present a large amount of data to the user. To save the user's time when he/she is looking for a specific row, you can add an index to the table view. This index is displayed on the right-hand side of the table. When the user taps on a specific index value, the table view will scroll to the corresponding section.

In this section, we provide a demonstration application for indexed views. The application presents fives sections where each section corresponds to a US political party. Inside each section, we list some of the candidates for the office of president. Each section has an index represented by the first letter of its name. Tapping on the letter, makes the table view scroll (if necessary) to the corresponding party.

Listing 8.23 shows the declaration of the application delegate demonstrating indexed table views. Five NSArray instances are used to represent the data model.

**Listing 8.23**   The declaration of the application delegate demonstrating the indexed table view.

```
#import <UIKit/UIKit.h>
#import <Foundation/Foundation.h>
@interface TVAppDelegate:NSObject<UITableViewDataSource> {
    UIWindow            *window;
    UITableView         *myTable;
```

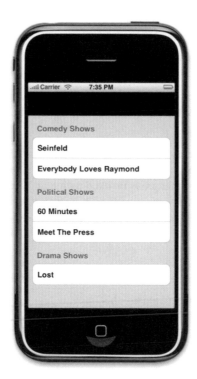

**Figure 8.19**    A grouped table view application.

NSArray                  *democratic,  *republican,  *independent,
                     *libertarian,  *socialist;
}
**@end**

Listing 8.24 shows the implementation of the application delegate for the indexed table view application. As we did before in the previous examples, the table view is created and configured, and the data model is populated with the candidates' names.

The method `tableView:titleForHeaderInSection:` was encountered in previous sections. It returns the headers for the table view's sections.

The method `sectionIndexTitlesForTableView:` is invoked by the table view asking the data source for an array of `NSString` instances. This array of strings will form the index list on the right side of the table view. The method is declared as follows:

```
- (NSArray *)
sectionIndexTitlesForTableView:(UITableView *)tableView
```

Note that the number of elements in this array does not necessarily have to be equal to the number of sections in the table view. In our example, the index list is: D, I, L, R, S. Each letter represents one political party. Note, again, that we did not have to have an index letter for every section.

The method `tableView:sectionForSectionIndexTitle:atIndex:` is invoked asking the data source for the section index corresponding to the section index title and section title index. The declaration of the method is given by:

```
— (NSInteger)
tableView:(UITableView *)tableView
sectionForSectionIndexTitle:(NSString *)title
atIndex:(NSInteger)index
```

This method is invoked when the user taps on a given index letter. Since the index of the index letter and the section index are the same, we simply return the index value passed to us. For example, if the user taps on the S index letter, the method is invoked with `title` equal to S and `index` equal to 4. Since S corresponds to the `Socialist Party USA` section which has index 4, we simply return the `index` value passed to us. If you choose not to have a one-to-one correspondence between the index letters and the sections, you will have to do some extra work in order to return the section index.

**Listing 8.24**    The implementation of the application delegate demonstrating the indexed table view.

```objc
#import <Foundation/Foundation.h>
#import <UIKit/UIKit.h>
#import "TVAppDelegate.h"
@implementation TVAppDelegate
— (void)
applicationDidFinishLaunching:(UIApplication *)application {
  window = [[UIWindow alloc]
              initWithFrame:[[UIScreen mainScreen] bounds]];
  CGRect frame = CGRectMake(0, 20, 320, 420);
  myTable = [[UITableView alloc]
              initWithFrame:frame
              style:UITableViewStylePlain];
  democratic = [[NSArray arrayWithObjects:
          @"Barack Obama", @"Joe Biden",
          @"Hillary Clinton",
          @"Christopher Dodd", @"John Edwards",
          @"Maurice Robert \"Mike\" Gravel",
          @"Dennis Kucinich",
          nil] retain];
  republican = [[NSArray arrayWithObjects:
          @"Ron Paul", @"John McCain",
          @"Mike Huckabee", @"Mitt Romney",
          nil] retain];
  independent = [[NSArray arrayWithObjects:
          @"Ralph Nader",
          nil] retain];
  libertarian = [[NSArray arrayWithObjects:
```

```
            @"Bob Barr",
            nil] retain];
  socialist   = [[NSArray arrayWithObjects:
            @"Brian Moore",
            nil] retain];
  myTable.dataSource = self;
  [window addSubview:myTable];
  [window makeKeyAndVisible];
}
- (void)dealloc {
  [window release];
  [myTable release];
  [democratic release];
  [republican release];
  [independent release];
  [libertarian release];
  [socialist release];
  [super dealloc];
}
// DataSource methods
- (NSInteger)
numberOfSectionsInTableView:(UITableView *)tableView {
  return 5;
}
- (NSInteger)tableView:(UITableView *)tableView
numberOfRowsInSection:(NSInteger)section{
  switch (section) {
    case 0:
      return [democratic count];
    case 1:
      return [independent count];
    case 2:
      return [libertarian count];
    case 3:
      return [republican count];
    case 4:
      return [socialist count];
  }
}
- (UITableViewCell *)
tableView:(UITableView *)tableView
cellForRowAtIndexPath:(NSIndexPath *)indexPath
{
  UITableViewCell *cell =
```

```objc
        [tableView dequeueReusableCellWithIdentifier:@"shows"];
    if (cell == nil) {
        cell = [[[UITableViewCell alloc]
            initWithFrame:CGRectZero
            reuseIdentifier:@"shows"] autorelease];
    }
    // Set up the cell
    switch (indexPath.section) {
        case 0:
            cell.text = [democratic objectAtIndex:indexPath.row];
            break;
        case 1:
            cell.text = [independent objectAtIndex:indexPath.row];
            break;
        case 2:
            cell.text = [libertarian objectAtIndex:indexPath.row];
            break;
        case 3:
            cell.text = [republican objectAtIndex:indexPath.row];
            break;
        case 4:
            cell.text = [socialist objectAtIndex:indexPath.row];
            break;
    }
    return cell;
}
- (NSString *)
tableView:(UITableView *)tableView
titleForHeaderInSection:(NSInteger)section {
    NSString *title = nil;
    switch (section) {
        case 0:
            title = @"Democratic";
            break;
        case 1:
            title = @"Independent";
            break;
        case 2:
            title = @"Libertarian";
            break;
        case 3:
            title = @"Republican";
            break;
        case 4:
```

**Figure 8.20**    A indexed table view application.

```
        title = @"Socialist Party USA";
        break;
    }
    return title;
}
- (NSArray *)
sectionIndexTitlesForTableView:(UITableView *)tableView {
    return[NSArray
      arrayWithObjects:@"D", @"I",
            @"L", @"R", @"S", nil];
}
- (NSInteger)
tableView:(UITableView *)tableView
sectionForSectionIndexTitle:(NSString *)title
 atIndex:(NSInteger)index {
    return index;
}
```

**Figure 8.21**    A indexed table view application after tapping on an index.

Figure 8.20 shows the indexed table view application. Figure 8.21 shows the table view after the user taps on the S index letter. The table view scrolls down, making the corresponding section visible.

## 8.11    Summary

This chapter took you through a step-by-step journey to the world of table views. We started by presenting an overview of the main concepts behind table views in Section 8.1. After that, we presented, in Section 8.2, a simple table view application and discussed the mandatory methods you need to implement in order to populate and respond to users' interactions with the table view.

In Section 8.3, we showed how easy it is to add images to table rows. Section 8.4 introduced the concept of sections and provided a table view application that has sections with section headers and footers.

In Section 8.5, we introduced the concept of editing a table view. An application that allows the user to delete rows was presented, and the main ideas were clarified. In Section 8.6, we addressed the insertion of new rows in a table view. An application was discussed that presents a data entry view to the user and adds that new data to the table's rows. In Section 8.7, we continued our discussions of the editing mode and presented an application for reordering table entries. The main concepts of reordering rows were presented.

In Section 8.8, we discussed the mechanism for presenting hierarchical information to the user. An application that uses table views to present three levels of hierarchy was discussed. In Section 8.9, we discussed grouped table views through an example. After that, we presented the main concepts behind indexed table views in Section 8.10.

# 9

# File Management

This chapter covers the topic of file management. Here, you will learn how to use both high- and low-level techniques for storing/retrieving data to/from files. To perform high-level operations on files/directories you use instances of the NSFileManager class. NSFileHandle class is used in this chapter to demonstrate low-level file access.

In Section 9.1 we talk about the Home directory of the application. Next, Section 9.2 shows how to enumerate the contents of a given directory using the high-level methods of NSFileManager. In that section, you will learn more about the structure of the Home directory and where you can store files. After that, we learn in Section 9.3 how to create and delete directories. Next, Section 9.4 covers the creation of files. Section 9.5 deals with the topic of file and directory attributes, and you will learn how to retrieve and set specific file/directory attributes. In Section 9.6 we demonstrate the use of application bundles and low-level file access. Finally, we summarize the chapter in Section 9.7.

## 9.1  The Home Directory

The application and its data are contained within a single directory called the Home directory. Your application can only access this directory and its contents. The absolute path of the home directory on the simulator is different from that on the actual device. However, the organization and content are identical.

To access the absolute path of the Home directory, you can use the function call NSHomeDirectory() which is declared as follows:

NSString ∗ NSHomeDirectory ( **void** );

It returns an NSString object holding the absolute path. As an example, the following is a home directory on the simulator:

```
/Users/ali/Library/
Application Support/iPhone Simulator/User/Applications/
F9CC3A49-997D-4523-9AFA-B553B5AE41EA
```

On the device, it is:

```
/var/mobile/Applications/F1C43BD0-1AB4-494B-B462-5A7315813D1A
```

In the next section, we will see the structure of the Home directory and where you can store files.

## 9.2   Enumerating a Directory

In this section, we will show how to enumerate (recursively) the contents of a given directory. Listing 9.1 shows the main() function for enumerating the contents of the Home directory.

The function starts by logging the absolute path of the Home directory. The log output on the simulator is:

```
Absolute path for Home Directory: /Users/ali/Library/
Application Support/iPhone Simulator/User/Applications/
F9CC3A49-997D-4523-9AFA-B553B5AE41EA
```

On the device, it is:

```
Absolute path for Home Directory: /var/mobile/Applications/
F1C43BD0-1AB4-494B-B462-5A7315813D1A
```

After that, it obtains a default NSFileManager instance for the file system using the class method defaultManager. Using this instance, we can make our high-level calls manipulating files and directories inside the Home directory.

Finding all the files and directories inside a given directory is very simple. You use the enumeratorAtPath: method declared as follows:

```
- (NSDirectoryEnumerator *)
    enumeratorAtPath:(NSString *)path;
```

You pass the path of the directory that you would like to enumerate the contents of, and receive an instance of the NSDirectoryEnumerator class. Each object in the directory enumerator is the full path of an item inside the directory used in obtaining the enumerator. The paths are all relative to this directory. You can iterate over this instance, skip subdirectories, and even access file and directory attributes.

As a subclass of NSEnumerator, you use nextObject to retrieve objects. The main() function simply retrieves all objects and logs them. The log generated on the simulator is shown below. Note that the logging timestamps are removed to save space.

```
Found Documents
Found FileMgmt5.app
Found FileMgmt5.app/FileMgmt5
Found FileMgmt5.app/Info.plist
Found FileMgmt5.app/PkgInfo
Found Library
Found Library/Preferences
Found Library/Preferences/.GlobalPreferences.plist
Found Library/Preferences/com.apple.PeoplePicker.plist
Found tmp
```

The Documents directory is available to you for storing application data. The tmp directory is used for temporary files. The other two directories AppName.app (e.g., FileMgmt5.app) and Library should not be manipulated by file system calls. You can create directories inside the

Home, tmp, and Documents. You can assume that all the contents of the Home directory will be backed up by iTunes except for the tmp directory.

**Listing 9.1**    A main() function listing the contents of the Home directory.

```
#import <Foundation/Foundation.h>

int main(int argc, char *argv[]) {
  NSAutoreleasePool * pool =
         [[NSAutoreleasePool alloc] init];
  NSLog(@"Absolute path for Home Directory: %@",
             NSHomeDirectory());
  NSFileManager *fileManager = [NSFileManager defaultManager];
  NSDirectoryEnumerator *dirEnumerator =
     [fileManager  enumeratorAtPath:NSHomeDirectory()];
  NSString *currPath;
  while (currPath = [dirEnumerator nextObject])
  {
    NSLog(@"Found %@", currPath);
  }
  [pool release];
  return 0;
}
```

The NSDirectoryEnumerator does have several convenience methods that you can use:

- directoryAttributes. You use this method to return a dictionary of the attributes of the directory you are enumerating. We will talk about file and directory attributes later in this chapter.

- fileAttributes. This method provides a dictionary of attributes for the current object of enumeration. This method works for both files and subdirectories. We will talk about file and directory attributes later in this chapter.

- skipDescendents. During enumeration, if you are not interested in the contents of a given subdirectory, you can skip it altogether by calling this method.

## 9.3    Creating and Deleting a Directory

In this section, we demonstrate the creation and deletion of subdirectories in the Home directory. Listing 9.2 shows the main() function. To create a directory, you use the createDirectoryAtPath:attributes: instance method of the NSFileManager. This method is declared as follows:

```
- (BOOL)
createDirectoryAtPath:(NSString *)path
attributes:(NSDictionary *)attributes
```

The method takes as input parameters the path of the directory to be created and the attributes of that directory. We will tackle attributes in a later section. To create a directory with default attributes, you need to pass a `nil` value for the second parameter. If the directory was created successfully, the method returns a `YES`; otherwise, it returns a `NO`.

Once the directory is successfully created, we remove it. The method for removing a file or a directory is `removeItemAtPath:error:` which is declared as follows:

```
- (BOOL)
removeItemAtPath:(NSString *)path
error:(NSError **)error
```

It takes the path for the item (a directory, file, link) to be removed, and a reference to an `NSError` object. You can pass `NULL` in the second parameter if you are not interested in knowing what may have caused the failure (return of `NO`).

---

**Listing 9.2**    A `main()` function demonstrating creation and deletion of directories.

---

```
#import <Foundation/Foundation.h>

int main(int argc, char *argv[]) {
  NSAutoreleasePool * pool = [[NSAutoreleasePool alloc] init];
  NSError *error;
  NSFileManager *fileManager = [NSFileManager defaultManager];
  NSString *newDirPath = [NSHomeDirectory()
             stringByAppendingPathComponent:@"tmp/directory"];
  BOOL success =
     [fileManager createDirectoryAtPath:newDirPath
                    attributes:nil];
  if(success == YES){
    NSLog(@"Directory %@ created successfully!", newDirPath);
    success = [fileManager removeItemAtPath:newDirPath
                            error:&error];
    if(success == YES){
      NSLog(@"Directory %@ deleted successfully!",
            newDirPath);
    }
    else{
      NSLog(@"Error deleting directory %@. %@",
            newDirPath, [error localizedDescription]);
      return -1;
    }
  }
  else{
    NSLog(@"Error creating directory %@.", newDirPath);
    return -1;
  }
}
```

```
[pool release];
return 0;
}
```

The logging output generated on the simulator is:

```
Directory /Users/ali/Library/Application Support/
iPhone Simulator/User/Applications/
BCE1C2BE-FAF0-47C2-A689-C20F630604E2/
tmp/directory created successfully!
Directory /Users/ali/Library/Application Support/
iPhone Simulator/User/Applications/
BCE1C2BE-FAF0-47C2-A689-C20F630604E2/
tmp/directory deleted successfully!
```

The logging output generated on the device is:

```
Directory /var/mobile/Applications/
2E723F14-B89B-450B-81BF-6385EFF76D05/
tmp/directory created successfully!
Directory /var/mobile/Applications/
2E723F14-B89B-450B-81BF-6385EFF76D05/
tmp/directory deleted successfully!
```

## 9.4   Creating Files

In this section, we demonstrate the creation of files in the application's Home directory. To make things interesting, we load a web page from the internet using the http protocol and store that html file in tmp. After that, we use a web view to load the html from the tmp directory and present it to the user. As you will see, these tasks can be easily achieved using the rich APIs available.

Listing 9.3 shows the declaration of the application delegate class used in our example. The class is similar to what you have seen previously in the view controllers chapter.

**Listing 9.3**   The declaration of the application delegate class used in the file creation and local file viewing example.

```
#import <UIKit/UIKit.h>

@class MainViewController;
@interface FileAppDelegate :
          NSObject <UIApplicationDelegate> {
  UIWindow *window;
  MainViewController *mainCtrl;
}
@property (nonatomic, retain) UIWindow *window;
@end
```

The implementation of the application delegate is shown in Listing 9.4. The delegate simply uses the `MainViewController` as a subview of the main window.

**Listing 9.4** The implementation of the application delegate class used in the file creation and local file viewing example.

```
#import "FileAppDelegate.h"
#import "MainViewController.h"

@implementation FileAppDelegate
@synthesize window;

- (void)applicationDidFinishLaunching:
        (UIApplication *)application {
  window = [[UIWindow alloc] initWithFrame:
                [[UIScreen mainScreen] bounds]];
  mainCtrl = [[MainViewController alloc]
                initWithNibName:nil bundle:nil];
  [window addSubview:mainCtrl.view];
   [window makeKeyAndVisible];
}

- (void)dealloc {
  [window release];
  [mainCtrl release];
  [super dealloc];
}
@end
```

The `MainViewController` class is declared in Listing 9.5. It has a reference to the `UIWebView` instance which will be used to visualize the contents of the local file in `tmp`. In addition, it declares two methods for the creation and visualization of the `html` file in `tmp`.

**Listing 9.5** The declaration of the `MainViewController` class used in the file creation and local file viewing example.

```
#import <UIKit/UIKit.h>

@interface MainViewController : UIViewController {
  UIWebView *webView;
}
-(void) createAFileInTMP;
-(void) loadWebViewWithFileInTMP;
@end
```

Listing 9.6 shows the implementation of the `MainViewController` class. The `loadView` method simply creates the web view object and makes it able to respond to zooming gestures.

The web view object is made as the view managed by the controller; thus it will be added as the subview to the main window.

The `viewDidLoad` method is invoked once the view has been loaded. It creates the file by invoking the `createAFileInTMP` method and after that it loads the web view with the downloaded file by invoking the `loadWebViewWithFileInTMP` method.

**Listing 9.6**   The implementation of the `MainViewController` class used in the file creation and local file viewing example.

```
#import <Foundation/Foundation.h>
#import <UIKit/UIKit.h>
#import "MainViewController.h"

@implementation MainViewController

- (void)loadView {
  CGRect   rectFrame =
        [UIScreen mainScreen].applicationFrame;
  webView = [[UIWebView alloc]
                initWithFrame:rectFrame];
  webView.scalesPageToFit = YES;
  self.view = webView;
}

- (void)viewDidLoad {
  [self createAFileInTMP];
  [self loadWebViewWithFileInTMP];
}

-(void) loadWebViewWithFileInTMP{
  NSFileManager   *fileManager =
            [NSFileManager defaultManager];
  NSData *data;
  NSString *fileName =
      [NSHomeDirectory() stringByAppendingPathComponent:
                    @"tmp/file.html"];
  data = [fileManager contentsAtPath:fileName];
  [webView loadData:data
            MIMEType:@"text/html"
            textEncodingName:@"UTF-8"
            baseURL:[NSURL
                URLWithString:@"http://csmonitor.com"]];
}
```

```
-(void) createAFileInTMP{
  // creating a file in tmp
  // http://www.csmonitor.com/textedition/index.html
  NSFileManager *fileManager =
        [NSFileManager defaultManager];
  NSString *fileName = [NSHomeDirectory()
            stringByAppendingPathComponent:@"tmp/file.html"];
  NSURL *theURL =
          [[NSURL alloc] initWithScheme:@"http"
              host:@"www.csmonitor.com"
              path:@"/textedition/index.html"];
  NSData *data =
          [[NSData alloc] initWithContentsOfURL:theURL];
  BOOL fileCreationSuccess =
          [fileManager createFileAtPath:fileName
              contents:data attributes:nil];
  if(fileCreationSuccess == NO){
    NSLog(@"Failed to create the html file");
  }
  [theURL release];
  [data release];
}

- (void)dealloc {
  [webView release];
  [super dealloc];
}
@end
```

The `createAFileInTMP` method first builds an NSURL object pointing to the URL `http://www.csmonitor.com/textedition/index.html` It then creates an NSData object having the contents of the `index.html` file downloaded from the server. To actually create the file on the local file system, we use the `createFileAtPath:contents:attributes:` method which is declared as follows:

```
- (BOOL)
createFileAtPath:(NSString *)path
contents:(NSData *)data attributes:(NSDictionary *)attr
```

It takes the path of the file as the first parameter, the data in the second, and the attributes in the third. Here, we use the default attributes and pass a `nil`. The path used is the absolute path of the Home directory with the `tmp/file.html` appended at the end. If there was a problem in creating the file, the return value is NO; otherwise, it is YES.

The `loadWebViewWithFileInTMP` method loads the local html file and presents it using the web view. It starts by creating an NSData object and loading it with the contents of the local file

**Figure 9.1**    A snapshot of the file creation and web visualization example.

using the NSFileManager's instance method contentsAtPath:. After that, we simply load the web view object with the contents of the NSData object.

Figure 9.1 shows a snapshot of the file creation and web visualization example.

## 9.5    Retrieving and Changing Attributes

Until now, we have been specifying nil for the dictionary attributes of files and directories. You can, however, provide a dictionary that provides attributes different from the default. Moreover, you can alter the attributes of a file system object after it has been created.

In the following, we give an example showing how you can retrieve/set the attributes of a file. Listing 9.7 shows the main() function of the program. It starts by creating file.txt file in tmp with a one-line text stored in it. We first obtain an NSData object from a string by using the NSString's instance method dataUsingEncoding: with utf-8 encoding. After that, we

create the file on the file system using the `createFileAtPath:contents:attributes:`
method which we have seen before. We use the default attributes in creating the file.

After creating the file using the default attributes, we would like to retrieve the file's
attributes to see what are the keys available and what are the values for these keys.
To retrieve the attributes of a file, we use the `NSFileManager`'s instance method
`fileAttributesAtPath:traverseLink:` which is declared as follows:

```
- (NSDictionary *)
fileAttributesAtPath:(NSString *)path
traverseLink:(BOOL)flag
```

You pass the path of the file in the first parameter. If the path points to a symbolic link, then you can
specify YES to traverse the link or NO to return the attributes of the link itself. The method returns
an NSDictionary instance if successful, or nil if not. The `attributes` variable is used to
hold on to the returned value. If `attributes` is not nil, we log the value of one attribute: the
file's size in bytes. The key in obtaining this value is `NSFileSize`. The logging output and the
(dumped) contents of the `attributes` object on the simulator just after retrieving the attributes of
the file are shown in the following log.

```
2008-08-01 08:12:06.996 FileMgmt4[394:20b] File size is 22
(gdb) po attributes
{
    NSFileCreationDate = 2008-08-01 08:11:49 -0500;
    NSFileExtensionHidden = 0;
    NSFileGroupOwnerAccountID = 20;
    NSFileGroupOwnerAccountName = staff;
    NSFileHFSCreatorCode = 0;
    NSFileHFSTypeCode = 0;
    NSFileModificationDate = 2008-08-01 08:11:49 -0500;
    NSFileOwnerAccountID = 501;
    NSFileOwnerAccountName = ali;
    NSFilePosixPermissions = 420;
    NSFileReferenceCount = 1;
    NSFileSize = 22;
    NSFileSystemFileNumber = 2436813;
    NSFileSystemNumber = 234881026;
    NSFileType = NSFileTypeRegular;
}
```

To change one or more attributes of a file or a directory, you can use the
`setAttributes:ofItemAtPath:error:` NSFileManager's method which is declared as
follows:

```
- (BOOL)
setAttributes:(NSDictionary *)attributes
ofItemAtPath:(NSString *)path
error:(NSError **)error;
```

In the first parameter, you pass a dictionary with one or more of the item's attributes that you wish to set. You pass the path of the item in the second parameter and a reference to an NSError object in the third.

The following are the attribute keys related to files and directories that are available to you:

- NSFileBusy. Use this key to specify whether the file is busy or not. The value is NSNumber with a Boolean value.

- NSFileCreationDate. Use this key to set the creation date of the file/directory. The value for this key is an NSDate object.

- NSFileExtensionHidden. Use this key to specify whether the file extension is hidden or not. The value is NSNumber with a Boolean value. The example below shows how to set this attribute.

- NSFileGroupOwnerAccountID. Use this key to specify the file's group ID. The value is specified in an NSNumber object containing an unsigned long value.

- NSFileGroupOwnerAccountName. Use this key to specify the name of the group the file owner belongs to. The value of this key is an NSString object.

- NSFileHFSCreatorCode. Use this key to specify the file's HFS creator code. The value is specified in an NSNumber object containing an unsigned long value.

- NSFileHFSTypeCode. Use this key to specify the file's HFS type code. The value is specified in an NSNumber object containing an unsigned long value.

- NSFileImmutable. Use this key to specify whether the file is mutable or not. The value is NSNumber with a Boolean value.

- NSFileModificationDate. Use this key to specify the date of the last modification of the file. The value for this key is an NSDate object.

- NSFileOwnerAccountID. Use this key to specify the account ID of the file's owner. The value is specified in an NSNumber object containing an unsigned long value.

- NSFileOwnerAccountName. Use this key to specify the name of the file's owner. The value of this key is an NSString object.

- NSFilePosixPermissions. Use this key to specify the POSIX permissions of the file. The value is specified in an NSNumber object containing an unsigned long value.

**Listing 9.7**    An example showing how to retrieve/set the attributes of a file.

```
#import <Foundation/Foundation.h>

int main(int argc, char *argv[]) {
  NSAutoreleasePool *pool = [[NSAutoreleasePool alloc] init];
  BOOL success;
  NSFileManager *fileManager = [NSFileManager defaultManager];
  NSString *filePath = [NSHomeDirectory()
            stringByAppendingPathComponent:@"tmp/file.txt"];
```

```objc
NSData *data = [@"Hello! This is a line."
                      dataUsingEncoding:NSUTF8StringEncoding];
success = [fileManager createFileAtPath:filePath
              contents:data attributes:nil];
if(success == NO){
  NSLog(@"Error creating file");
  return -1;
}
NSDictionary *attributes =
    [fileManager fileAttributesAtPath:filePath
              traverseLink:NO];
if(attributes){
  NSNumber *fSize = [attributes objectForKey:NSFileSize];
  NSLog(@"File size is %qi", [fSize longLongValue]);
}
NSDictionary *newAttributes;
NSError *error;
newAttributes =
    [NSDictionary dictionaryWithObject:
                  [NSNumber numberWithBool:YES]
                      forKey:NSFileExtensionHidden];
success = [fileManager setAttributes:newAttributes
                  ofItemAtPath:filePath
                  error:&error];
if(success == NO){
  NSLog(@"Error setting attributes of file. Error: %@",
          [error localizedDescription]);
  return -1;
}
attributes = [fileManager fileAttributesAtPath:filePath
                      traverseLink:NO];
[pool release];
return 0;
}
```

After changing the NSFileExtensionHidden to YES, the attributes object on the simulator is as follows:

```
(gdb) po attributes
{
    NSFileCreationDate = 2008-08-01 08:11:49 -0500;
    NSFileExtensionHidden = 1;
    NSFileGroupOwnerAccountID = 20;
    NSFileGroupOwnerAccountName = staff;
    NSFileHFSCreatorCode = 0;
```

```
    NSFileHFSTypeCode = 0;
    NSFileModificationDate = 2008-08-01 08:11:49 -0500;
    NSFileOwnerAccountID = 501;
    NSFileOwnerAccountName = ali;
    NSFilePosixPermissions = 420;
    NSFileReferenceCount = 1;
    NSFileSize = 22;
    NSFileSystemFileNumber = 2436813;
    NSFileSystemNumber = 234881026;
    NSFileType = NSFileTypeRegular;
}
```

The `attributes` object on the device is a little bit different. We notice several changes such as the `NSFileGroupOwnerAccountName` and `NSFileOwnerAccountID`. Although the `NSFileExtensionHidden` was successfully changed by the API call, the `NSFileExtensionHidden` key does not appear at all in the `attributes` object. It's unclear why this is the case. This serves as a reminder to always test your code on the actual device. The following are all the attributes of the file available to you on the device:

```
2008-08-01 08:17:39.982 FileMgmt4[164:20b] File size is 22
(gdb) po attributes
{
    NSFileGroupOwnerAccountID = 501;
    NSFileGroupOwnerAccountName = mobile;
    NSFileModificationDate = 2008-08-01 08:17:35 -0500;
    NSFileOwnerAccountID = 501;
    NSFileOwnerAccountName = mobile;
    NSFilePosixPermissions = 420;
    NSFileReferenceCount = 1;
    NSFileSize = 22;
    NSFileSystemFileNumber = 87161;
    NSFileSystemNumber = 234881026;
    NSFileType = NSFileTypeRegular;
}
```

## 9.6    Working with Resources and Low-Level File Access

In this section, we demonstrate the following:

1. Use of bundles. How to access files stored at the time that the application was packaged.

2. Low-level file access. How to seek and update a file.

Our application stores a text file in the application bundle as shown in the XCode's Groups and File's snapshot in Fig. 9.2. You can store data files anywhere you want, but usually you store them in the `Resources` directory as shown in Fig. 9.2.

Listing 9.8 shows the `main()` function demonstrating loading a file from a bundle and modifying it by inserting text. We have previously seen that, inside the `Home` directory of every application, there is an `XXX.app` directory (where `XXX` stands for the name of the application). Inside this directory go the data files.

To help in locating the data files inside the bundle, an instance method of the class `NSBundle` can be used to search for a specific file with a specific extension, and return the absolute path of that resource. This method is declared as follows:

```
- ( NSString *)
pathForResource :( NSString *)name ofType :( NSString *)ext ;
```

In the first parameter, you pass in the path of the resource file that you want to locate, and in the second its extension. You can pass an empty string or even `nil` for the extension if your file's name is unique in the bundle. The reason this will work is because the search algorithm returns the first occurrence of a file with the exact name, if the `ext` parameter is `nil` or empty. The location of the `file.txt` in the bundle (value of `filePath` in main() function) is:

```
/var/mobile/Applications/
5ABEB448-7634-4AE8-9833-FC846A81B418/
FileMgmt6.app/file.txt
```

Remember what we have mentioned before, that you should not change items in the `.app` directory as it will affect code signing. Therefore, to modify a file in the bundle, you need to copy it to a different directory and change it there.

After locating the file in the bundle and storing its absolute path in `filePath`, we load its contents into an NSData object using the `dataWithContentsOfFile:` method. Next, the file `Documents/fileNew.txt` is created containing the contents of the bundled file.

The original file contains a single line: `This is the contents of a file.` We would like to modify the copied file by replacing the text `"contents"` with the text `"modified"`. We would like to perform this task by using low-level file operations involving seeking, rather than loading the whole file into memory, changing it, and storing it back to disk.

To perform low-level file operations, you need to obtain an `NSFileHandle` instance. This class encapsulates the low-level mechanism for accessing files. The nature of operations that you would like to perform on the file determines the method you use to obtain the `NSFileHandle` instance. The following are the three `NSFileHandle`'s class methods available to you:

- Reading. To obtain the instance for read-only access, use the class method `fileHandle-ForReadingAtPath:` which is declared as follows:

  ```
  + ( id )
  fileHandleForReadingAtPath :( NSString *)path
  ```

- Writing. To obtain the instance for writing-only access, use the class method `fileHandleForWritingAtPath:` which is declared as follows:

  ```
  + ( id )
  fileHandleForWritingAtPath :( NSString *)path
  ```

- Reading/writing. To obtain the instance for update access, use the class method fileHandleForUpdatingAtPath: which is declared as:

+ (**id**)
fileHandleForUpdatingAtPath:(NSString *)path

When you obtain the instance using one of the three methods above, the file's pointer is set to the beginning of the file.

In our example, we open the file for updating. Since we know the location of the text that needs to be inserted, we use the seek operation on the NSFileHandle instance. To seek a file, use the seekToFileOffset: method which is declared as follows:

− (**void**)
seekToFileOffset:(**unsigned long long**)offset

The location to seek to in our example is 11. After seeking to that location, we write the "modified" text in the file by using the writeData: method. This method is declared as follows:

− (**void**)
writeData:(NSData *)data

After finishing the update on the file, we close the NSFileHandle object by using the method closeFile.

**Listing 9.8**    The main() function demonstrating loading a file from a bundle and modifying it by writing text.

```
#import <Foundation/Foundation.h>

int main(int argc, char *argv[]) {
    NSAutoreleasePool * pool =
            [[NSAutoreleasePool alloc] init];
    BOOL success;
    NSFileManager *fileManager =
        [NSFileManager defaultManager];
    NSString *filePath =
        [[NSBundle mainBundle]
            pathForResource:@"file"
            ofType:@"txt"];
    NSData *fileData =
        [NSData dataWithContentsOfFile:filePath];
    if (fileData) {
        NSString *newFilePath =
            [NSHomeDirectory()
                    stringByAppendingPathComponent:
                        @"Documents/fileNew.txt"];
        success =
            [fileManager createFileAtPath:newFilePath
```

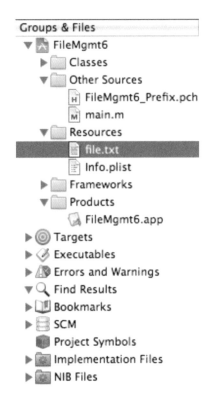

**Figure 9.2**   XCode's Groups and File's snapshot.

```
                        contents:fileData  attributes:nil];
if(success == NO){
  NSLog(@"Error creating file");
  return -1;
}
NSFileHandle   *fileHandle =
    [NSFileHandle fileHandleForUpdatingAtPath:newFilePath];
if(fileHandle){
  [fileHandle seekToFileOffset:11];
  NSData *appendedData =
    [@" modified "
        dataUsingEncoding:NSUTF8StringEncoding];
  [fileHandle writeData:appendedData];
  [fileHandle closeFile];
}
else{
```

```
      NSLog(@"Error modifying the file");
      return −1;
    }

  }
  else{
    NSLog(@"Could not load file from the app bundle");
    return −1;
  }
  [pool release];
  return 0;
}
```

## 9.7  Summary

This chapter covered the topic of file management. You have learned how to use both high- and low-level techniques for storing/retrieving data to/from files. To perform high-level operations on files/directories you used instances of the NSFileManager class. The NSFileHandle class was used in this chapter to demonstrate low-level file access.

In Section 9.1, we talked about the Home directory of the application. Next, Section 9.2 showed how to enumerate the contents of a given directory using the high-level methods of NSFileManager. In that section, you learned more about the structure of the Home directory and where you can store files. After that, you learned in Section 9.3 how to create and delete directories. Next, Section 9.4 covered the creation of files. Section 9.5 covered the topic of file and directory attributes. You also learned how to retrieve and set specific file/directory attributes in that section. In Section 9.6 we demonstrated the use of application bundles and low-level file access.

# 10

# Working with Databases

In this chapter, we will cover the basics of the SQLite database engine that is available to you using the iPhone SDK. SQLite is different from the other databases that you are familiar with. Databases, such as Oracle and Sybase, are server-based databases. In server-based databases, a server runs the database engine and serves the queries of clients running on other machines. SQLite is an embedded database in the sense that there is no server running, and the database engine is linked to your application. SQLite is 100% free to use.

This chapter is not an introduction to databases and it assumes that you know the basics of the Structured Query Language (SQL). You should know that a database is composed of a set of tables and each table has a name that uniquely identifies that table in the database. Each table consists of one or more columns and each column has a name that uniquely identifies it within that table. A row is a vector of values for each column in a given table. A row is often referred to as a record.

This chapter is organized as follows. In Section 10.1, we will describe basic SQL statements and their implementation using SQLite function calls. In Section 10.2, we discuss the handling of result sets generated by SQL statements. In Section 10.3, we address the topic of prepared statements. In Section 10.4, we talk about extensions to the SQLite API through the use of user-defined functions. In Sections 10.6 and 10.5 we present, respectively, a detailed example for storing and retrieving BLOBs to/from the database. Finally, we summarize the chapter in Section 10.7.

## 10.1 Basic Database Operations

In this section, we will talk about some of the basic SQL statements and how we can realize them in SQLite. We will present a simple program that creates a database with one table. This table will store records of stock purchases. Each record will store the stock identifier (represented by the stock symbol), the purchase price, the number of shares bought and the date of purchase. Listing 10.1 shows the `main()` function.

**Listing 10.1** The `main()` function demonstrating basic SQL statements using SQLite library function calls. The function creates a database (if one does not exist), adds a new table, and populates the table with some records.

```
#import "/usr/include/sqlite3.h"
int main(int argc, char *argv[]) {
  char    *sqlStatement;
```

```
sqlite3  *pDb;
char     *errorMsg;
int      returnCode;
char     *databaseName;

databaseName = "financial.db";
returnCode = sqlite3_open(databaseName, &pDb);
if(returnCode!=SQLITE_OK) {
  fprintf(stderr,
          "Error in opening the database. Error: %s",
          sqlite3_errmsg(pDb)
        );
  sqlite3_close(pDb);
  return -1;
}
sqlStatement =  "DROP TABLE IF EXISTS  stocks";
returnCode =
  sqlite3_exec(pDb, sqlStatement, NULL, NULL, &errorMsg);
if(returnCode!=SQLITE_OK) {
  fprintf(stderr,
    "Error in dropping table stocks. Error: %s", errorMsg);
  sqlite3_free(errorMsg);
}

sqlStatement =  "CREATE TABLE stocks (symbol VARCHAR(5), "
                  "purchasePrice FLOAT(10,4), "
                  "unitsPurchased INTEGER, "
                  "purchase_date VARCHAR(10))";
returnCode = sqlite3_exec(pDb,
    sqlStatement, NULL, NULL, &errorMsg);
if(returnCode!=SQLITE_OK) {
  fprintf(stderr,
    "Error in creating the stocks table. Error: %s",
    errorMsg);
  sqlite3_free(errorMsg);
}

insertStockPurchase(pDb, "ALU",14.23, 100, "03-17-2007");
insertStockPurchase(pDb, "GOOG",600.77, 20, "01-09-2007");
insertStockPurchase(pDb, "NT",  20.23,140, "02-05-2007");
insertStockPurchase(pDb, "MSFT", 30.23, 5, "01-03-2007");
sqlite3_close(pDb);
return 0;
}
```

The first thing that you do before working with a database is open it. The SQLite function for opening a database is `sqlite3_open()`. The function is declared as:

```
int sqlite3_open(
    const char *filename,    /* Database filename (UTF-8) */
    sqlite3 **ppDb           /* OUT: SQLite db handle */
);
```

Databases in SQLite are stored in a file. To open a database, you need to specify the filename of that database in the first parameter `filename`. Upon successful opening of the database, the function will return a value of `SQLITE_OK`. For other SQLite functions to work with this database, a handle is needed. You specify a reference to a handle pointer in the second parameter. If the database was successfully opened, a handle is written in that address. The database connection handle is of type `sqlite3`. You pass the address of a variable of type `sqlite3*` in the second parameter. It is worth noting that if the database does not exist, it is created; thus this function is used for both opening an existing database and creating a new one.

If the database was not opened successfully, you need to display an error message and close the database. The SQLite function `sqlite3_errmsg()` takes a pointer to a database handle and returns a meaningful string describing the error. Our program above uses this function in displaying the error message for failed database opening. Once you are finished with a database, you should close it. The SQLite function `sqlite3_close()` is used for that purpose. It takes, as the sole parameter, a pointer to the opened database handle (`sqlite3*`) received when you opened the database.

Once we have successfully opened a database, we would like to perform some table operations. SQLite provides a helper function that does a one-time evaluation of SQL statements. This function `sqlite3_exec()` is easy to use and works very well with many SQL statements. Later, we will talk about how this function is implemented using other SQLite functions. The `sqlite3_exec()` is declared as:

```
int sqlite3_exec(
    sqlite3 *,                                    /* An open database */
    const char *sql,            /* SQL to be evaluated */
    int (*callback)(void *,int,char **,char **),/* Callbk func */
    void *,                              /* 1st argument to callback */
    char **errmsg        /* Error msg written here */
);
```

The first parameter is the pointer to the database handle we received from the *sqlite3_open()* function. The second parameter is the C string SQL statement. If an error occurs, an error message is written into memory obtained from *sqlite3_malloc()* and *errmsg* is made to point to that message. You are responsible for freeing that space using the SQLite function `sqlite3_free()`. The third and fourth parameters are used for callback functions operating on the result of the SQL statement. The callback function, if specified, will be called for every row in the result. We will cover callback functions later, but know that the first parameter passed to this callback function can be specified in the fourth parameter of the `sqlite3_exec()` function. A return value of `SQLITE_OK` indicates successful execution of the SQL statement.

The first thing that we do in the `main()` function is to delete the table `stocks` if it exists. The SQL statement for that is:

**DROP TABLE IF EXISTS**    stocks

This SQL statement does not return records. Therefore, in the invocation of the `sqlite3_exec()` function, we pass NULL for both the callback function and its first argument. The execution of this SQL statement is achieved by the following:

```
returnCode =
    sqlite3_exec(pDb, sqlStatement, NULL, NULL, &errorMsg);
```

Once we have deleted the `stocks` table, we can go ahead and create a new one. The SQL statement for creating the `stocks` table is as follows:

**CREATE TABLE** stocks (
                        symbol **VARCHAR**(5),
                        purchasePrice **FLOAT**(10,4),
                        unitsPurchased **INTEGER**,
                        purchase_date **VARCHAR**(10)
                    )

This SQL statement should be familiar to you. It states that the `stocks` table should have four columns. The first column is of variable (maximum 5) character. The second is of type float with 10 digits in total and 4 of these digits are used after the decimal point. The third column is of type integer, and the fourth and final column is of variable character with maximum size of 10 characters.

Internally, SQLite has the following five classes for data storage:

1. INTEGER. Used to store a signed integer value. The number of bytes actually used for storage depends on the magnitude of the value and range from one to eight bytes.

2. REAL. An 8-byte IEEE floating-point storage representing a floating point number.

3. TEXT. A storage area for text. The text can be in any of the following encodings: UTF-8, UTF-16BE or UTF-16-LE.

4. BLOB. Used to store data exactly as entered, for example, an image.

5. NULL. Used to store the value NULL.

After creating the table `stocks`, we insert several records into it. The function `insertStockPurchase()` shown in Listing 10.2 is used for that purpose. As an example, the following SQL statement adds a record for purchasing 100 shares of Alcatel-Lucent's stock at $14.23 on 03-17-2007.

**INSERT INTO** stocks **VALUES** ('ALU', 14.23, 100, '03-17-2007')

We use the SQlite function `sqlite3_mprintf()` for formatted string printing. This function is similar to the standard C library function `printf()` except that it writes the result into memory obtained from the `sqlite3_malloc()` function, so you should release the string when you are finished with it using the `sqlite3_free()` function. In addition to the well-known formatting options, you have access to the options %q and %Q. You should use these options instead of the

%s options when dealing with text. The option %q works like %s except that it doubles every '
character. For example, the string "She said: 'Hey Ya'all whats up?'" will be printed
to the string as "She said: "Hey Ya"all whats up?"". The %Q option works like the
%q option except that it produces the string NULL when the value of the pointer being printed is
equal to NULL. It also surrounds the whole string with a pair of '. The previous string will be printed
as "'She said: "Hey Ya"all whats up?"'" when %Q is used.

**Listing 10.2**   The function insertStockPurchase() for adding records into the stocks table.

```
#import "/usr/include/sqlite3.h"
void insertStockPurchase(sqlite3 *pDb, const char*symbol,
            float price, int units, const char* theDate){
  char    *errorMsg;
  int     returnCode;
  char    *st;
  st  = sqlite3_mprintf("INSERT INTO stocks VALUES"
                " ('%q', %f, %d, '%q')",
                  symbol, price, units, theDate);
  returnCode =
    sqlite3_exec(pDb, st, NULL, NULL, &errorMsg);
  if(returnCode!=SQLITE_OK) {
    fprintf(stderr,
      "Error in inserting into the stocks table. Error: %s",
        errorMsg);
    sqlite3_free(errorMsg);
  }
  sqlite3_free(st);
}
```

## 10.2   Processing Row Results

In the previous section, we saw how the function sqlite3_exec() can be used in executing SQL
statements that either do not produce results, or the caller is not interested in processing the results.

If you are interested in the result set, however, you can pass a callback function pointer as the
fourth parameter to the sqlite3_exec() function. This callback function will be invoked for
every row in the result set.

The callback function should follow the following signature:

**int** (*callback)(**void** *,**int**,**char**\*\*,**char**\*\*)

The first parameter of this function is the same as the fourth parameter when the
sqlite3_exec() function is invoked. The second parameter is the number of columns in the
current row result. The third parameter is an array of pointers to strings holding the values for
each column in the current result set row. The fourth parameter is an array of pointers to strings
holding the names of result columns. If the callback function returns a value other than zero, the
sqlite3_exec() function will stop executing and will return SQLITE_ABORT.

In the function `main()` shown in Listing 10.3, we demonstrate how a callback function can be used to process the result set. The database `financial.db` is opened as we have seen before and a `SELECT` query is executed. The Query:

**SELECT** * **from** stocks

retrieves all the records in the table `stocks`. The SQLite function call for executing the statement is as follows.

```
returnCode = sqlite3_exec (pDb, sqlStatement ,
        processRow , NULL, &errorMsg );
```

The third parameter is not NULL as we saw in the previous section. Instead, we pass in the function pointer `processRow`. The function `processRow()` is shown in Listing 10.4.

Listing 10.3    The function main() for retrieving records using `sqlite3_exec()` function.

```
#import "/usr/include/sqlite3.h"
int main(int argc , char *argv[]) {
  char     *sqlStatement;
  sqlite3 *pDb;
  char     *errorMsg;
  int       returnCode;
  char     *databaseName;

  databaseName = "financial.db";
  returnCode = sqlite3_open (databaseName , &pDb);
  if (returnCode !=SQLITE_OK) {
    fprintf (stderr ,
          "Error in opening the database. Error: %s",
            sqlite3_errmsg (pDb ));
    sqlite3_close (pDb );
    return −1;
  }
  sqlStatement =  "SELECT * from stocks";
  returnCode = sqlite3_exec (pDb, sqlStatement ,
        processRow , NULL, &errorMsg );
  if (returnCode !=SQLITE_OK) {
    fprintf (stderr ,
      "Error in selecting from stocks table. Error: %s",
          errorMsg );
    sqlite3_free (errorMsg );
  }
  sqlite3_close (pDb );
  return 0;
}
```

This function follows the callback function signature. Inside the function, we have a for-loop where we display the column name, and the row value for that column.

The result of executing the program is:

```
Record Data:
The value for Column Name symbol is equal to ALU
The value for Column Name purchasePrice is equal to 14.23
The value for Column Name unitsPurchased is equal to 100
The value for Column Name purchase_date is equal to 03-17-2007

Record Data:
The value for Column Name symbol is equal to GOOG
The value for Column Name purchasePrice is equal to 600.77002
The value for Column Name unitsPurchased is equal to 20
The value for Column Name purchase_date is equal to 01-09-2007

Record Data:
The value for Column Name symbol is equal to NT
The value for Column Name purchasePrice is equal to 20.23
The value for Column Name unitsPurchased is equal to 140
The value for Column Name purchase_date is equal to 02-05-2007

Record Data:
The value for Column Name symbol is equal to MSFT
The value for Column Name purchasePrice is equal to 30.23
The value for Column Name unitsPurchased is equal to 5
The value for Column Name purchase_date is equal to 01-03-2007
```

**Listing 10.4**    The function processRow() for processing row results.

```
#import "/usr/include/sqlite3.h"

static int processRow(void *argument,
        int argc, char **argv, char **colName){
  printf("Record Data:\n");
  for(int i=0; i<argc; i++){
    printf("The value for Column Name %s is equal to %s\n",
        colName[i], argv[i] ? argv[i] : "NULL");
  }
  printf("\n");
  return 0;
}
```

## 10.3   Prepared Statements

In the previous two sections, we have used the `sqlite3_exec()` function to execute SQL statements. This function is more appropriate for SQL statements that do not return data (such as `INSERT`, `DROP`, and `CREATE`). For SQL statements that return data, such as `SELECT`, *prepared statements* are usually used.

The use of prepared statements involves three phases:

1. Preparation. In the preparation phase, you present a statement for the SQLite engine for compilation. The engine compiles this statement into byte code and reserves the resources needed for its actual execution.

2. Execution. This phase is used to actually execute the byte code and obtain rows from the result of the statement. You repeat this phase for every row in the result set.

3. Finalization. After obtaining all rows in the result set, you finalize the prepared statement so that resources reserved for it can be freed.

In the following, we discuss these three phases in detail.

### 10.3.1   Preparation

You prepare an SQL statement using `sqlite3_prepare_v2()` function. The function is declared as follows:

```
int sqlite3_prepare_v2(
    sqlite3 *db,            /* Database handle */
    const char *zSql,    /* SQL statement, UTF-8 encoded */
    int nBytes,            /* Length of zSql in bytes. */
    sqlite3_stmt **ppStmt,    /* OUT: Statement handle */
    const char **pzTail    /*OUT: Ptr to unused portion of zSql */
)
```

The first parameter, db, is the pointer to the database handle obtained from a prior *sqlite3_open()* call. The SQL statement (e.g., `SELECT` statement) is passed in the zSql parameter. You pass the length (in bytes) of that statement in the third parameter. The fourth parameter is used to obtain a statement handle. You pass a reference to a variable of type `sqlite3_stmt*`, and on successful preparation of the SQL statement, that variable will hold the statement handle. In the case that *zSql points to multiple SQL statements, the function will make *pzTail point to the first byte past the first SQL statement in zSql. If *zSql points to a single SQL statement, passing a NULL for the fifth parameter is appropriate.

### 10.3.2   Execution

Once you have compiled the SQL statement, you need to execute it and retrieve the first row result. The SQL statement is executed using the function `sqlite3_step()`. The declaration of the function is as follows:

```
int sqlite3_step(sqlite3_stmt *);
```

The function takes a pointer to the statement handle as its sole parameter. As long as there is a new row in the result set, the function returns SQLITE_ROW. When all rows have been exhausted, the function returns SQLITE_DONE.

### 10.3.3  Finalization

After retrieving the last row, the statement is finalized by calling sqlite3_finalize(). The function's declaration is as follows:

```
int sqlite3_finalize(sqlite3_stmt *pStmt);
```

It takes as the sole parameter a pointer to the statement handle. Finalization closes the statement and frees resources.

Let's demonstrate these concepts by showing a small working example. The function main() in Listing 10.5 is where we open a database, select some records from a table, and print them one by one.

**Listing 10.5**   The function main() demonstrating prepared statements.

```
#import "/usr/include/sqlite3.h"
int main(int argc, char *argv[]) {
  char      *sqlStatement;
  sqlite3 *database;
  int        returnCode;
  char      *databaseName;
  sqlite3_stmt *statement;

  databaseName = "financial.db";
  returnCode = sqlite3_open(databaseName, &database);
  if(returnCode!=SQLITE_OK) {
    fprintf(stderr,
            "Error in opening the database. Error: %s",
            sqlite3_errmsg(database));
    sqlite3_close(database);
    return -1;
  }
  sqlStatement = sqlite3_mprintf(
            "SELECT S.symbol, S.unitsPurchased, "
            "S.purchasePrice FROM stocks AS S WHERE "
            "S.purchasePrice  >= %f", 30.0);
  returnCode =
          sqlite3_prepare_v2(database,
          sqlStatement, strlen(sqlStatement),
          &statement, NULL);
```

```
if (returnCode != SQLITE_OK) {
  fprintf(stderr,
      "Error in preparation of query. Error: %s",
      sqlite3_errmsg(database));
  sqlite3_close(database);
  return -1;
}
returnCode = sqlite3_step(statement);
while (returnCode == SQLITE_ROW){
  char *symbol;
  int   units;
  double price;
  symbol = sqlite3_column_text(statement, 0);
  units  = sqlite3_column_int(statement, 1);
  price  = sqlite3_column_double(statement, 2);
  printf("We bought %d from %s at a price "
    "equal to %.4f\n",
    units, symbol, price);
  returnCode = sqlite3_step(statement);
}
sqlite3_finalize(statement);
sqlite3_free(sqlStatement);
return 0;
}
```

After opening the database, we invoke the `sqlite3_prepare_v2()` function on the following SQL statement:

```
SELECT
        S.symbol, S.unitsPurchased, S.purchasePrice
        FROM stocks AS S
        WHERE S.purchasePrice  >=  30.0
```

The SQL statement will result in a set of records from the table `stocks` whose `purchasePrice` is greater than or equal to $30. The statement is compiled as follows:

```
returnCode = sqlite3_prepare_v2(database,
        sqlStatement, strlen(sqlStatement),
        &statement, NULL);
```

Notice that we pass NULL for the last parameter as we only have one SQL statement to compile. If the statement compilation is successful, the return code will be equal to SQLITE_OK. If there is an error, we display the error message and exit the `main()` function.

After compiling the statement, we execute the statement to retrieve the first result record. The function used in the execution of the statement is `sqlite3_step()`. If there is a successful retrieval of a row, the return code will be SQLITE_ROW. If we receive an SQLITE_ROW return code, we retrieve the values for the columns in that row. To retrieve a column value, you use an SQLite function of the form `sqlite3_column_XXX()`. The first parameter to this function is a pointer to the SQL statement (type `sqlite3_stmt`) that was returned by the `sqlite3_prepare_v2()` function. The second parameter is the column index, where the left most column has an index of 0. The return value depends on the version of the function.

We have the following three statements corresponding to the three columns.

```
symbol = sqlite3_column_text(statement, 0);
units  = sqlite3_column_int(statement, 1);
price  = sqlite3_column_double(statement, 2);
```

The first statement corresponds to the `S.symbol` column. The column belongs to the `TEXT` storage class. The function `sqlite3_column_text()` will return a C-string of the `symbol` column that is stored in that row. The other functions, `sqlite3_column_int()` and `sqlite3_column_double()`, work in the same way except that they return an integer and a double value, respectively.

After printing the values for the columns constituting the row, we move to the next row in the result by again invoking the `sqlite3_step()` function. When we are finished with the result, we exit the while-loop and finalize the statement by invoking the `sqlite3_finalize()` function. The result of running this query, provided that the `stocks` table was populated as in the previous sections, is as follows:

```
We bought 20 from GOOG at a price equal to 600.7700
We bought 5 from MSFT at a price equal to 30.2300
```

## 10.4   User-defined Functions

Often, you are faced with a situation requiring you to use a function that the SQL engine does not implement. SQLite provides a mechanism for extending the C API and allows for user-defined functions. The user can define new custom functions for use in SQL statements for a specific database connection. Such functions are transient in that they are only available during the life of a database connection. They are not stored in the database.

In this section, we demonstrate the use of user-defined functions by adding the function `Palindrome()` to a database connection. The function `Palindrome(t)` takes a text-based parameter, `t`, and checks to see if `t` is the same whether it is read from the right or from the left. Listing 10.6 shows the `main()` function demonstrating the installation of a user-defined function for an opened database connection.

**Listing 10.6**   The `main()` function demonstrating the installation of a user-defined function for an opened database connection.

```
int main(int argc, char *argv[]) {
  char      *sqlStatement;
  sqlite3   *database;
  int       returnCode;
  char      *databaseName;
  sqlite3_stmt *statement;
```

```
databaseName = "financial.db";
returnCode = sqlite3_open(databaseName, &database);
if(returnCode!=SQLITE_OK) {
  fprintf(stderr,
      "Error in opening the database. Error: %s",
      sqlite3_errmsg(database));
  sqlite3_close(database);
  return -1;
}
sqlite3_create_function(database, "Palindrome", 1,
    SQLITE_UTF8, NULL, palindrome, NULL, NULL);
sqlStatement = sqlite3_mprintf(
    "SELECT S.symbol, S.unitsPurchased, S.purchasePrice "
    "FROM stocks AS S WHERE "
    "Palindrome(S.symbol) = 1 AND S.purchasePrice  >= %f",
    30.0);

returnCode = sqlite3_prepare_v2(
        database, sqlStatement, strlen(sqlStatement),
        &statement, NULL);
if(returnCode!=SQLITE_OK) {
  fprintf(stderr,
      "Error in preparation of query. Error: %s",
      sqlite3_errmsg(database));
  sqlite3_close(database);
  return -1;
}
returnCode = sqlite3_step(statement);
while(returnCode == SQLITE_ROW){
  char *symbol;
  int   units;
  double price;
  symbol = sqlite3_column_text(statement, 0);
  units  = sqlite3_column_int(statement, 1);
  price  = sqlite3_column_double(statement, 2);
  printf("We bought %d from %s at a price equal to %.4f\n",
        units, symbol, price);
  returnCode = sqlite3_step(statement);
}
sqlite3_finalize(statement);
sqlite3_free(sqlStatement);
return 0;
}
```

The user-defined function is installed for a given connection by calling `sqlite3_create_function()`. The function is declared as:

```
int sqlite3_create_function(
  sqlite3 *connectionHandle,
  const char *zFunctionName,
  int nArg,
  int eTextRep,
  void *,
  void (*xFunc)(sqlite3_context *,int,sqlite3_value **),
  void (*xStep)(sqlite3_context *,int,sqlite3_value **),
  void (*xFinal)(sqlite3_context *)
)
```

The first parameter of this function is the connection (database) handle. The second parameter is the function name as it is used in SQL statements. This name can be different from the C function name that actually implements the function. The third parameter is used to specify the number of parameters for the custom function being created. The fourth parameter is used to specify the encoding of the parameters. You can install different versions of the same function that use different encodings. The SQLite engine will be able to route the calls to the appropriate function. The fifth parameter is an arbitrary pointer. Inside your user-defined function, you can access this pointer using `sqlite3_user_data()`. The seventh parameter is a pointer to the C function implementing the behaviour whose logical name is the second parameter, `zFunctionName`. More on this in a moment. The eighth and ninth parameters are aggregate step and finalize functions, respectively. These two functions are used in executing aggregate SQL statements.

All user-defined functions have the same signature:

```
void (sqlite3_context *context, int nargs,
  sqlite3_value **values)
```

The function returns `void` and all its three parameters are input parameters. The first parameter is the SQL function context. Think of it as a channel ID for the function and the SQL engine to communicate on. The second parameter is the number of arguments used when the logical function was called from within the SQL statement. The third parameter is the array of parameter values passed to the function.

Since all user-defined functions are `void`, the results/errors are signaled back using SQLite3 routines. To signal back an error message to the caller, you use the function `sqlite3_result_error()`. The first parameter in this function is the context (so that the engine knows which SQL statement this error is related to). The second parameter is a C-string providing the error message in text. Finally, the last parameter is the length of the error message.

The SELECT statement we use here is similar to the one in the previous section, except that we require that the stock transaction to have a palindrome symbol. The SELECT statement is as follows:

```
SELECT
    S.symbol, S.unitsPurchased, S.purchasePrice
    FROM stocks AS S
```

```
WHERE  Palindrome(S.symbol) = 1 AND
       S.purchasePrice  >=  30.0
```

For the SQLite engine to execute this query, the Palindrome() needs to be defined for this connection. We define the function by the following statement:

```
sqlite3_create_function(database, "Palindrome", 1,
    SQLITE_UTF8, NULL, palindrome, NULL, NULL);
```

Listing 10.7 shows the implementation of the palindrome() function.

**Listing 10.7**   The user-defined function palindrome() and its implementation.

```
#import "/usr/include/sqlite3.h"
int isPalindrome(char *text){
  unsigned char *p1, *p2;
  p1 = text;
  p2 = p1+strlen(text)-1;
  while (*p1==*p2 && (p1<=p2)){
    p1++;p2--;
  }
  if(p1>= p2)
    return 1;
  return 0;
}


void palindrome(sqlite3_context *context,
        int nargs, sqlite3_value **values){
  char *errorMessage;
  if(nargs != 1){
    errorMessage =
     "Incorrect no of arguments. palindrome(string)";
    sqlite3_result_error(context, errorMessage,
                      strlen(errorMessage));
    return;
  }
  if (
    (sqlite3_value_type(values[0]) != SQLITE_TEXT)){
    errorMessage = "Argument must be of type text.";
    sqlite3_result_error(context, errorMessage,
                      strlen(errorMessage));
    return;
  }
  unsigned char *text;
  text = sqlite3_value_text(values[0]);
  sqlite3_result_int(context, isPalindrome(text));
}
```

The palindrome() function first checks to see that the number of parameters is equal to 1. If not, an error message is signaled back and the function returns. The function also checks the type of the parameter passed as we are expecting a TEXT value. The function sqlite3_value_type() returns the type of the parameter. The function is declared as:

```
int sqlite3_value_type(sqlite3_value *)
```

It takes a pointer to a value of type sqlite3_value and returns one of the following types: SQLITE_INTEGER, SQLITE_FLOAT, SQLITE_BLOB, SQLITE_NULL, or SQLITE3_TEXT.

After making sure that the type of the parameter is TEXT, we need to obtain the actual text value. The SQLite function sqlite3_value_text() is used for that purpose. There are other similar functions (e.g., sqlite3_value_int()) for the other types. Once we have the string passed to us, we check if it is a palindrome using the function isPalindrome(). You should be familiar with this function from introductory computer science classes.

To send the result back to the SQLite engine, you use a function of the form sqlite3_result_XXX(), which takes the context as the first parameter and the result value as the second parameter. For example, we use the function sqlite3_result_int() to return an integer as follows:

```
sqlite3_result_int(context, isPalindrome(text))
```

## 10.5  Storing BLOBs

In the previous sections, we have dealt primarily with simple data types (strings, integers, and floating points). In addition to scalar and text data types, the SQLite database engine also supports the BLOB data type. A BLOB storage class allows you to store binary data (e.g., image files) as-is. We will demonstrate the mechanism for storing BLOBs in this section, and retrieving them in the next section.

To explain the main concepts behind inserting BLOB values in a database, we consider a new table in the database that stores information about the companies we are investing in. In addition to the company's symbol and name, we add an image column of type BLOB that stores the logo of the company in PNG format.

Listing 10.8 shows the main() function. It creates a new companies table using the following SQL statement:

```
CREATE TABLE  companies
      (symbol VARCHAR(5)  PRIMARY KEY,
       name VARCHAR(128), image BLOB)
```

**Listing 10.8**    The main() function demonstrating storing BLOBs into a table.

```
#import "/usr/include/sqlite3.h"
int main(int argc, char *argv[]) {

  char     *sqlStatement;
```

```
sqlite3    *pDb;
char      *errorMsg;
int       returnCode;
char      *databaseName;

NSAutoreleasePool * pool =
      [[NSAutoreleasePool alloc] init];
databaseName = "financial.db";
returnCode = sqlite3_open(databaseName, &pDb);
if(returnCode!=SQLITE_OK) {
  fprintf(stderr,
    "Error in opening the database. Error: %s",
    sqlite3_errmsg(pDb));
  sqlite3_close(pDb);
  return -1;
}
sqlStatement = "DROP TABLE IF EXISTS  companies";
returnCode = sqlite3_exec(pDb, sqlStatement,
      NULL, NULL, &errorMsg);
if(returnCode!=SQLITE_OK) {
  fprintf(stderr,
    "Error in dropping table companies. Error: %s",
    errorMsg);
  sqlite3_free(errorMsg);
}

sqlStatement =
      "CREATE TABLE companies "
      "(symbol VARCHAR(5)  PRIMARY KEY, "
      " name VARCHAR(128), image BLOB)";
returnCode = sqlite3_exec(pDb,
    sqlStatement, NULL, NULL, &errorMsg);
if(returnCode!=SQLITE_OK) {
  fprintf(stderr,
    "Error in creating the companies table. Error: %s",
    errorMsg);
  sqlite3_free(errorMsg);
  return -1;
}
insertCompany(pDb, "ALU", "Alcatel-Lucent");
insertCompany(pDb, "GOOG", "Google");
insertCompany(pDb, "MSFT", "Microsoft");
insertCompany(pDb, "NT", "Nortel");
sqlite3_close(pDb);
```

```
[pool release];

return 0;
}
```

After creating the `companies` table, we add four records by invoking the `insertCompany()` function shown in Listing 10.9. The `insertCompany()` function starts by compiling the following `INSERT` statement:

INSERT INTO companies VALUES (?, ?, ?)

This statement is a little bit different from what we have used before. This type of statement is called a parametrized statement. It uses "?" indicating that a value that will be bound later. To actually bind a parameter to a specific value, you use one of several functions that have the form `sqlite3_bind_xxxx()`. For example, to bind an integer, you use `sqlite3_bind_int()`. The following are the important bind functions:

1. Binding BLOBs. The bind function for BLOBs is declared as:

   ```
   int sqlite3_bind_blob(sqlite3_stmt*, int,
        const void*, int n, void(*)(void*))
   ```

   The first parameter of this, and all bind functions, is a pointer to a statement handle received from the statement preparation function `sqlite3_prepare_v2()`. The second parameter is the index of the SQL statement's parameter that you want to bind. Note that the index starts at 1. The third parameter is the number of bytes in the BLOB. The fourth parameter is a pointer to a function that will be invoked when the SQLite engine finishes with the execution of the statement to release the BLOB's memory. There are two special values for this parameter:

   (a) `SQLITE_STATIC`. This special value informs the SQLite engine that the BLOB is static and does not need to be freed.
   (b) `SQLITE_TRANSIENT`. This special value informs the SQLite engine that the BLOB is transient and needs to be copied. SQLite engine makes a copy of the BLOB before the bind function returns.

2. Binding Text. The bind function for text is very similar to the one for BLOBs.

   ```
   int sqlite3_bind_text(sqlite3_stmt*, int, const char*,
                         int n, void(*)(void*))
   ```

   The first two parameters, as well as the last one, are the same as the BLOB's bind function. The third parameter is the zero-terminated text that you would like to bind. The fourth parameter is the length (in bytes) of the text, excluding the zero-terminator. If the value is negative, then the number of bytes up to the first zero terminator is used.

3. Binding Integers. The bind function for integers is very simple:

   ```
   int sqlite3_bind_int(sqlite3_stmt*, int, int)
   ```

   The first two parameters are the same as above. The last parameter is the integer value.

4. Binding Reals. The bind function for real numbers is also very simple, and is similar to binding integers:

```
int sqlite3_bind_double(sqlite3_stmt*, int, double)
```

The first two parameters are the same as above. The last parameter is the real number value.

5. Binding a NULL. This is the simplest of them all:

```
int sqlite3_bind_null(sqlite3_stmt*, int)
```

The first two parameters are the same as above and the value is, of course, implicit.

The insertCompany() (see Listing 10.9) function assumes that a PNG file for each company is available. The files names are assumed to have the same name as the symbol. For example, for Alcatel-Lucent, the logo is stored in the ALU.png file. To retrieve the bytes of an image file, we create an NSData object using NSData's class method dataWithContentsOfFile:. This method retrieves the contents of a file and builds an NSData around it. Once we have the bytes in the Objective-C object, we retrieve them into a C-string using the following two statements:

```
buffer = malloc([pData length]);
[pData getBytes:buffer];
```

The first statement allocates a buffer of length equal to the NSData object length. To retrieve the bytes, we use the instance method getBytes: in the second statement.

Now that we have the three values for the three SQL parameters, we use the appropriate bind function in order to complete the SQL statement. Executing the INSERT statement is the same as any prepared statement: just use sqlite3_step(). Lastly, we finalize the statement and free the allocated buffer since we have specified SQLITE_STATIC in the BLOB bind function.

**Listing 10.9**   The insertCompany() function for inserting a company record that includes a BLOB image.

```
#import "/usr/include/sqlite3.h"

void insertCompany(sqlite3 *pDb, const char* symbol,
                   const char* name){
  int        returnCode;
  sqlite3_stmt *pStmt;
  unsigned char *buffer;

  char    *st = "INSERT INTO companies VALUES (?, ?, ?)";
  returnCode = sqlite3_prepare_v2(pDb, st, -1, &pStmt, 0);
  if(returnCode != SQLITE_OK) {
    fprintf(stderr, "Error in inserting into companies table.");
    return;
  }

  NSMutableString *imageFileName =
      [NSMutableString stringWithCString:symbol];
```

```
[imageFileName appendString:@".png"];
NSData * pData =
    [NSData dataWithContentsOfFile:imageFileName];
buffer = malloc([pData length]);
[pData getBytes:buffer];

sqlite3_bind_text(pStmt, 1, symbol, -1, SQLITE_STATIC);
sqlite3_bind_text(pStmt, 2, name, -1, SQLITE_STATIC);
  sqlite3_bind_blob(pStmt, 3, buffer,
        [pData length], SQLITE_STATIC);
returnCode = sqlite3_step(pStmt);
if(returnCode != SQLITE_DONE) {
  fprintf(stderr,
        "Error in inserting into companies table.");
}
returnCode = sqlite3_finalize(pStmt);
if(returnCode != SQLITE_OK) {
  fprintf(stderr,
        "Error in inserting into companies table. ");
}
free(buffer);
}
```

## 10.6   Retrieving BLOBs

In the previous section, we saw how we can populate a table with records containing BLOB columns. In this section, we will learn how we can retrieve these BLOB columns. The presentation will use the same `companies` table populated before.

Listing 10.10 shows the `main()` function used to demonstrate the retrieval of BLOBs. What we would like to do is to retrieve these images and write them to the file system with a different name. The `main()` function opens the database and retrieves the images by invoking the `retrieveCompany()` function shown in Listing 10.11.

**Listing 10.10**   The `main()` function demonstrating the retrieval of BLOB columns from a database.

```
int main(int argc, char *argv[]) {
  sqlite3    *pDb;
  int        returnCode;
  char       *databaseName;
  NSAutoreleasePool * pool =
      [[NSAutoreleasePool alloc] init];
  databaseName = "financial.db";
  returnCode = sqlite3_open(databaseName, &pDb);
  if(returnCode!=SQLITE_OK) {
```

```
    fprintf(stderr,
      "Error in opening the database. Error: %s",
      sqlite3_errmsg(pDb));
    sqlite3_close(pDb);
    return -1;
  }
  retrieveCompany(pDb, "ALU");
  retrieveCompany(pDb, "GOOG");
  retrieveCompany(pDb, "MSFT");
  retrieveCompany(pDb, "NT");
  sqlite3_close(pDb);
  [pool release];

  return 0;
}
```

We start by preparing the following parametrized SQL statement:

```
SELECT image FROM companies WHERE symbol = ?
```

After that, we bind the sole parameter with the `symbol` parameter of the function. Note that we could have just used `sqlite3_mprintf()` to do that job without using parametrized queries. We then execute the query and check for a row result. Since there should be at most one record (the symbol is a primary key), we retrieve the BLOB column value at most once. We use `NSData` as a wrapper of the image bytes as in the following statement:

```
NSData * pData =
         [NSData dataWithBytes:
                 sqlite3_column_blob(pStmt, 0)
                 length:sqlite3_column_bytes(pStmt, 0)];
```

The class method `dataWithBytes:length:` is declared as follows:

```
+ (id)dataWithBytes:(const void *)bytes
       length:(NSUInteger)length
```

It takes the bytes and length as two parameters. To retrieve the BLOB bytes from the column result, we use the function `sqlite3_column_blob()`. This function takes a pointer to the statement handle we received when we invoked the `sqlite3_prepare_v2()` function and the column index (starting from 0). The length of the BLOB bytes can be retrieved by the function `sqlite3_column_bytes()`.

Once we have retrieved the image from the database and have used an `NSData` instance as a wrapper around it, we can use the `NSData`'s instance method `writeToFile:atomically:` to write the contents of this data to a file. The method is declared as:

```
- (BOOL)writeToFile:(NSString *)path
         atomically:(BOOL)useAuxiliaryFile
```

In addition to the file path, the useAuxiliaryFile is used to specify whether a temporary file should be used. If the value is YES, the data will be written first to a temporary file and then that temporary file will be renamed to the new name. Once we have written the file, we finalize the statement and return from the function.

**Listing 10.11**  The retrieveCompany() function used to retrieve BLOB images from the database and write them back to the file system.

```
#import "/usr/include/sqlite3.h"
void retrieveCompany(sqlite3 *pDb, const char* symbol){
  int      returnCode;
  sqlite3_stmt *pStmt;
  char     *st =
      "SELECT image FROM companies WHERE symbol = ?";
  returnCode = sqlite3_prepare_v2(pDb, st, -1, &pStmt, 0);
  if(returnCode!=SQLITE_OK) {
    fprintf(stderr, "Error retrieving image from companies.");
    return;
  }
  sqlite3_bind_text(pStmt, 1, symbol, -1, SQLITE_STATIC);
  returnCode = sqlite3_step(pStmt);
  if(returnCode == SQLITE_ROW){
    NSData * pData =
          [NSData dataWithBytes:
                  sqlite3_column_blob(pStmt, 0)
                  length:sqlite3_column_bytes(pStmt, 0)];
    NSMutableString *imageFileName  =
        [NSMutableString stringWithCString:symbol];
    [imageFileName appendString:@"-2.png"];
    [pData writeToFile:imageFileName  atomically:YES];
  }
  returnCode = sqlite3_finalize(pStmt);
  if(returnCode != SQLITE_OK) {
    fprintf(stderr, "Error inserting into companies.");
  }
}
```

## 10.7  Summary

This chapter covered the main aspects of using the SQLite database engine from within an iPhone application.

We presented the main concepts through concrete examples. We started by talking about the basic SQL statements and their implementation using SQLite function calls. Then, we discussed the handling of result sets generated by SQL statements. After that, we addressed the topic of prepared statements. Next, we talked about extensions to the SQLite C API and demonstrated that through the use of a simple user-defined function. Finally, we presented detailed treatment of BLOB handling through the storage and retrieval of image files.

# 11

# XML Processing

In this chapter, you will learn how to effectively use XML in your iPhone application. The chapter follows the same theme used in others chapters and exposes the main concepts through a working iPhone application: an RSS feed reader.

The chapter is organized as follows. Section 11.1 explains the main concepts behind XML and RSS. Section 11.2 presents a detailed discussion of DOM parsing. Section 11.3 offers another, different XML parsing technique, SAX, and shows how you can write a SAX iPhone client. In Section 11.4 we look at a table-based RSS reader application. Finally, Section 11.5 provides a summary of the main steps you need to take in order to effectively harness the power of XML from within your native iPhone application.

## 11.1   XML and RSS

### *11.1.1   XML*

Extensible Markup Language (XML) is a meta-language specification for exchanging information over the internet. As a meta-language, it can be used to define application-specific languages which are then used to instantiate XML documents that adhere to the semantics of these languages.

The power behind XML is due to: (1) its extensibility, which allows anyone to define new XML elements, and (2) it being based on text, thus opening your application data to being used on any computing system.

To create/use an XML language, you need to identify the elements used in that language. An XML element uses: (1) a begin-tag, (2) text content, and (3) an end-tag. For example, the element `person` can appear in an XML document as:

```
<person>
content  ...
</person>
```

Where `<person>` is the begin-tag and `</person>` is the end-tag. The content can itself be composed of text and other elements. For example:

```
<person>
  <name>content of name...</name>
  <address>content of address...</address>
</person>
```

If the text content of a given element contains characters that are difficult to include (e.g., "<", ">", "&", etc.), entities can be used for their representation. For example, "<" can be represented by the entity reference &lt;.

The fact that an XML document must have exactly one root element, and that any given element may contain other elements, allows us to naturally represent the XML document as a tree. For example, the following XML document can be represented as a tree (see Fig 11.1).

```
<?xml version="1.0"?>
<person>
   <name>
         <first>Homer</first>
         <last>Simpson</last>
   </name>
   <address>
         <street>1094 Evergreen Terrace</street>
         <city>Springfield</city>
         <state>TA</state>
   </address>
</person>
```

To work with an XML document, you need to be able to parse it (e.g., construct a tree representation of the document in memory as shown in Fig. 11.1). There are several techniques for parsing and we will cover those shortly. libxml2 is an XML parser written in C that is available on, and recommended for use with, the iPhone OS. As we will see shortly, working with this library is very easy. You will be able to use a few function calls to the library in order to construct a tree similar to the one shown in Fig. 11.1.

We need to remember that white spaces are not ignored in XML. In Fig. 11.1, we show the white spaces as TEXT nodes. In libxml2, text nodes are of type XML_TEXT_NODE, while element nodes are of type XML_ELEMENT_NODE.

Now that we have an understanding of what XML is, let's look at one of its applications: RSS.

## 11.1.2   RSS

Really Simple Syndication (RSS) is an XML language used for sharing web content. As a content publisher, RSS gives you the power to inform your readers about new content on your information channel. As a content consumer, RSS allows you to target your web activities towards information that you are actually interested in. For example, if you are mainly interested in health news, you do not want to spend a lot of time on cnn.com or msnbc.com looking for health articles. What you want is a way for cnn.com or msnbc.com to tell you when new health articles on their websites become available. The news channel can set up an XML instance file based on the RSS language advertising the newest health articles on its website. You use RSS reader software to subscribe to

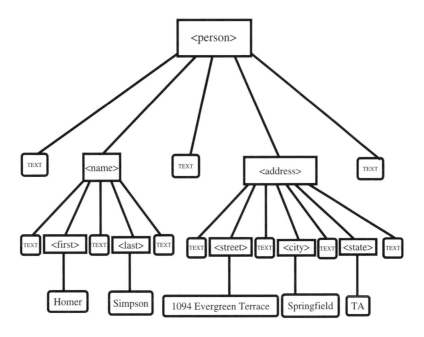

**Figure 11.1**    A tree representation of an XML document.

**Figure 11.2**    Several RSS icons. The *universal feed icon* (bottom icon) is gaining wide acceptance.

this XML file. The reader can refresh the copy of this XML file and present it to you. This scheme provides you with efficiency and also privacy as the website does not have to know your email address in order to inform you of new content. RSS can be thought of as both a push and a pull technology. The producer pushes filtered content that the consumer pulls.

Websites advertise the existence of specific channels using several icons. Figure 11.2 shows some of these icons. The *universal feed icon* (bottom icon) is gaining wide acceptance.

Let's illustrate the basics of an RSS feed through an example. The Nebraska State Patrol provides an RSS feed for absconded offenders. Individuals can subscribe to this channel to stay informed. Like everything else on the internet, an RSS feed has a URL. For example, the URL for absconded offenders in the state of Nebraska is: http://www.nsp.state.ne.us/SOR/Abscondedrss.xml. Listing 11.1 shows a sample XML document of this feed.

**Listing 11.1**    An example of an RSS document.

```xml
<?xml version="1.0" encoding="UTF-8"?>
<rss version="2.0">
   <channel>
    <title>
        Nebraska State Patrol | Absconded Offenders
    </title>
    <link>
        http://www.nsp.state.ne.us/sor/
    </link>
    <description>
        The Nebraska State Patrol is currently
        seeking information on the location of the
      following individuals to determine if they are in
      compliance with the Nebraska Sex Offender
      Registration Act. This site is intended to
      generate information on these individuals
      and should not be used solely for the purpose
      of arrest. Anyone with information
      please call 402-471-8647.
    </description>
    <image>
        <title>Nebraska State Patrol | SOR</title>
        <url>http://www.nsp.state.ne.us/sor/rsslogo.jpg
        </url>
        <link>http://www.nsp.state.ne.us/sor/</link>
    </image>

        <item>
         <title>Austen, Kate</title>
         <link>
         http://www.nsp.state.ne.us/sor/200403KA2
         </link>
         <description>
         Absconded - Jefe de una loca mujer
         </description>
        </item>

   </channel>
   </rss>
```

Every RSS feed document starts with the following :

```
<?xml version="1.0" encoding="UTF-8"?>
```

This line indicates that this is an XML document. The `version` attribute is mandatory while the encoding is not.

The root of the RSS feed is the `rss` element. This root element has only one child: the `channel` element. The `channel` element has three mandatory child elements: `title`, `link`, and `description`. In addition, it can hold several optional child elements such as: `webMaster`, `image`, `copyright`.

The mandatory elements are required for an RSS feed to be valid. However, valid does not necessarily mean useful. To be useful, the channel element should have one or more `item` child elements. Each story in an RSS feed file is represented by an `item` element. An `item` element contains three child elements: (1) a `title` element, (2) a `link` element, and (3) an optional `description` element. The reader presents to you the title of the story, its link, and, optionally, its description. If you are interested in the story, you click the link (a URL) to visit the web page of that story.

Now that we know the structure of an RSS feed document, let's use the `libxml2` library to extract information from an RSS feed. First, we present a reader using DOM, then one using SAX.

## 11.2    Document Object Model (DOM)

Using this model, the parser will load the whole XML document to memory and present it to the client as a tree. You can navigate the nodes of this tree and extract relevant information.

Listing 11.2 shows Objective-C code that first fetches the RSS XML document from a URL, puts it into a string that the `libxml2` library can work with, and uses `libxml2`'s functions to navigate the parsed tree and extract the relevant information.

**Listing 11.2**    DOM XML Parsing.

```
1  #include <libxml/xmlmemory.h>
2  #include <libxml/parser.h>
3
4  -(void)fetchAbsconders{
5    NSAutoreleasePool * pool =
6              [[NSAutoreleasePool alloc] init];
7    NSError *err = nil;
8    NSURL * url = [NSURL URLWithString:feedURL];
9    NSString *URLContents =
10       [NSString stringWithContentsOfURL:url
11        encoding:NSUTF8StringEncoding error:&err];
12   if (!URLContents)
13     return;
14   const char *XMLChars =
15   [URLContents cStringUsingEncoding:NSUTF8StringEncoding];
16
```

```
17    if ( parser == XML_PARSER_DOM) {
18      xmlDocPtr doc =
19          xmlParseMemory(XMLChars, strlen(XMLChars));
20      xmlNodePtr cur;
21      if (doc == NULL ) {
22        return;
23      }
24      cur = xmlDocGetRootElement(doc);
25      cur = findNextItem(cur);
26      while (cur) {
27        XOAbsconder *absconder = getitem(doc, cur);
28        if (absconder) {
29          [absconders addObject:absconder];
30        }
31        cur = findNextItem(cur->next);
32      }
33      xmlFreeDoc(doc);
34    }
```

On line 8, we create an NSURL object from the URL address string representation, feedURL, of the RSS feed address. The statement on lines 9, 10, and 11 uses the NSString's class method stringWithContentsOfURL:encoding:error: to create a string containing the contents of the URL. The method fetches the RSS feed file from the server and puts it in the NSString instance, URLContents.

On line 12, we check to see if the string was successfully created. If it was not, the fetchAbsconders method returns without changing the absconders array. Of course, in a production code, you will use the error object to propagate the error to the client.

Once we have an NSString object with the contents of the RSS feed file, we need to convert it to a C-string (char*), the format that libxml2 works with. The statement on lines 14 and 15 does just that. We use the NSString instance method cStringUsingEncoding: with the encoding NSUTF8StringEncoding.

The fetchAbsconders method demonstrates the use of two XML parsing schemes. Listing 11.2 shows the first half of this method and it covers the DOM parsing.

To work with any XML document using DOM, you first need to load it into memory in the form of a tree. The function to achieve that is xmlParseMemory(). The function is declared in parser.h as:

```
xmlDocPtr
xmlParseMemory (const char * buffer, int size)
```

It takes the XML document, represented by a C-string, and the size of this string as input. It returns a pointer to the tree representation of the parsed document in the form of xmlDocPtr (a pointer to xmlDoc).

The xmlDoc is a structure defined in tree.h. The following shows the first few lines of this structure.

```
struct _xmlDoc {
    void           *_private; /* application data */
    xmlElementType   type;         /* XML_DOCUMENT_NODE */
    char    *name;  /* name/filename/URI of the document */
    struct _xmlNode *children;  /* the document tree */
    struct _xmlNode *last;  /* last child link */
    struct _xmlNode *parent;  /* child->parent link */
...
};
```

Now that we have a tree representation of the XML document, we can start traversing it. To begin traversing, line 24 obtains the root node using the function `xmlDocGetRootElement()`. The function returns `xmlNodePtr`, which is a pointer to the root node, `xmlNode`.

Every node is represented by the `xmlNode` structure defined in `tree.h` as follows:

```
typedef struct _xmlNode xmlNode;
typedef xmlNode *xmlNodePtr;

struct _xmlNode {
    void           *_private; /* application data */
    xmlElementType   type;/* type number */
    const xmlChar   *name; /* name of the node, or entity */
    struct _xmlNode *children;/* parent->children link */
    struct _xmlNode *last;  /* last child link */
    struct _xmlNode *parent;/* child->parent link */
    struct _xmlNode *next;/* next sibling link */
    struct _xmlNode *prev;  /* previous sibling link */
    struct _xmlDoc  *doc;  /* the containing document */

    /* End of common part */
    xmlNs    *ns; /* pointer to the associated namespace */
    xmlChar  *content;    /* the content */
    struct _xmlAttr *properties;/* properties list */
    xmlNs    *nsDef; /* namespace definitions on this node */
    void    *psvi; /* for type/PSVI informations */
    unsigned short   line;  /* line number */
    unsigned short   extra; /* extra data for XPath/XSLT */
};
```

Most of these fields are self-explanatory. You will be dealing mostly with the fields which link to other nodes. If you are at a given node, you can go to its parent using the `parent` field. If you want its children, use `children`. If you want the siblings (i.e., those nodes with same parent as your parent), use the `next` field.

Figure 11.3 shows a graphical representation of the navigational links available for various nodes in the document tree.

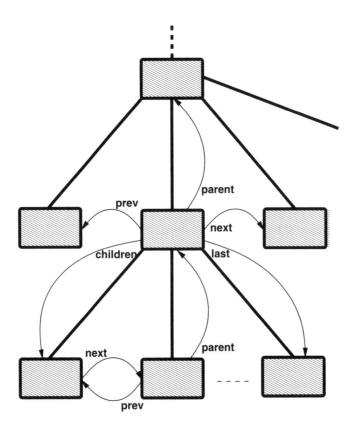

**Figure 11.3**    Representation of the navigational links available for various nodes in the document tree.

Now that we have a pointer to the root of the document, we search for the first item in the RSS feed. This is shown in the statement on line 25: cur = findNextItem(cur). The function findNextItem() is defined in Listing 11.3.

**Listing 11.3**    Searching for an item element in the RSS feed.

```
xmlNodePtr findNextItem(xmlNodePtr curr){
  if(!curr)
    return curr;
  if ((!xmlStrcmp(curr->name, (const xmlChar *)"item")) &&
  (curr->type == XML_ELEMENT_NODE)) {
    return curr;
  }
  if(curr->type == XML_TEXT_NODE){
    return findNextItem(curr->next);
  }
```

```
if ( curr –>type  ==  XML_ELEMENT_NODE ){
    if  ((! xmlStrcmp( curr –>name,  ( const  xmlChar  *)"channel"))
        || (! xmlStrcmp( curr –>name,  ( const  xmlChar  *)"rss" ))){
            return   findNextItem( curr –>xmlChildrenNode );
    }
}
if ( curr –>type  ==  XML_ELEMENT_NODE ){
    if ((! xmlStrcmp( curr –>name,  ( const  xmlChar  *)"title"))
        || (! xmlStrcmp( curr –>name,  ( const  xmlChar  *)"link"))
        || (! xmlStrcmp( curr –>name,
            ( const  xmlChar  *)"description"))
        || (! xmlStrcmp( curr –>name,  ( const  xmlChar  *)"image"))
        ){
        return   findNextItem( curr –>next );
    }
}
return  NULL;
}
```

The function makes recursive calls to itself as long as the item tag has not been found. At the beginning, we check for the termination condition. We use the xmlStrcmp() function to see if the node's name is "item". If yes, we return the pointer to that node. The rest of the code has similar logic. The only difference is that, when we are interested in a given subtree, we use the xmlChildrenNode link to traverse that subtree. If we are not interested in the node, we skip the subtree altogether and go to the next sibling using the next link.

Now that we have a pointer to an item element node, we retrieve the three element children and build an Objective-C object from the data. The function getitem() is where such logic is found. The function is called as follows:

```
XOAbsconder *absconder =  getitem(doc, cur);
```

getitem() takes the document and node pointers and returns either the XOAbsconder object or nil. Listing 11.4 presents the implementation of the getitem() function.

**Listing 11.4**    Building an XOAbsconder object from an item element.

```
XOAbsconder*
getitem (xmlDocPtr doc,  xmlNodePtr  curr ){

    xmlChar *name,  *link,  *description;
    curr = curr –>xmlChildrenNode;
    if (! curr )
        return  nil;
    while  (curr && (curr –>type  ==  XML_TEXT_NODE))
        curr = curr –>next;
    if (! curr )
```

```
      return nil;
  if ((!xmlStrcmp(curr->name,
  (const xmlChar *)"title")) &&
  (curr->type == XML_ELEMENT_NODE)) {
    name =
      xmlNodeListGetString(doc, curr->xmlChildrenNode, 1);
    curr = curr->next;
    while (curr && (curr->type == XML_TEXT_NODE))
      curr = curr->next;
    if(!curr){
      xmlFree(name);
      return nil;
    }
  }
  else
    return nil;
  if ((!xmlStrcmp(curr->name,
  (const xmlChar *)"link")) &&
  (curr->type == XML_ELEMENT_NODE)) {
    link =
      xmlNodeListGetString(doc, curr->xmlChildrenNode, 1);
    curr = curr->next;
    while (curr && (curr->type == XML_TEXT_NODE))
      curr = curr->next;
    if(!curr){
      xmlFree(name);
      xmlFree(link);
      return nil;
    }
  }
  else
    return nil;
  if ((!xmlStrcmp(curr->name,
  (const xmlChar *)"description")) &&
  (curr->type == XML_ELEMENT_NODE)) {
    description =
      xmlNodeListGetString(doc, curr->xmlChildrenNode, 1);
  }
  else{
    xmlFree(name);
    xmlFree(link);
    xmlFree(description);
    return nil;
  }
```

```
XOAbsconder *abscender = [[XOAbsconder alloc]
  initWithName:[NSString stringWithCString:name]
  andURL:[NSString stringWithCString:link]
  andDescription:[NSString stringWithCString:description]];
[abscender autorelease];
xmlFree(name);
xmlFree(link);
xmlFree(description);
return abscender;
}
```

We traverse all the children of the node. Since in XML a whitespace is recognized as a valid child node, we skip those at the beginning:

```
while (curr && (curr->type == XML_TEXT_NODE))
  curr = curr->next;
```

Once we have skipped the text nodes, we check for the three elements: title, link, and description. The function requires that they appear in that order.

To retrieve the text value for each of these three elements, we can use xmlNodeListGet-String function. The function is declared in tree.h as:

```
xmlChar *
xmlNodeListGetString  (xmlDocPtr doc,
                       xmlNodePtr list,
                       int inLine)
```

The function constructs a string from the node list. If inLine is 1, the entity contents are replaced. The function returns the string and the caller is responsible for freeing the memory of the string using the xmlFree() function.

After retrieving the text of the three elements, we create the XOAbsconder, autorelease it, free the memory of the three strings and return the XOAbsconder object.

Back to Listing 11.2, the fetchAbsconders method keeps calling the getitem() function and adding the objects to the absconders array in the statement:

```
[absconders addObject:absconder];
```

When the fetchAbsconders method is finished, the absconders array contains the absconder objects created and populated from the RSS feed document.


## 11.3    Simple API for XML (SAX)

We have seen in Section 11.2 how DOM loads the entire XML document to memory and allows you to navigate the nodes. In some applications, the size of the XML document may prevent loading the whole document due to limited device memory. The Simple API for XML (SAX) is another XML parsing model that is different from DOM. In SAX, you configure the parser with call-back functions. The SAX parser will use these function pointers to call your functions, informing you of important events. For example, if you are interested in the event Start of Document, you set up a function for this event and give the parser a pointer to it.

Listing 11.5 shows the remainder of the fetchAbsconders method pertaining to SAX parsing.

**Listing 11.5**    SAX XML Parsing. Remainder of fetchAbsconders method.

```
else if(parser == XML_PARSER_SAX){
    xmlParserCtxtPtr ctxt = xmlCreateDocParserCtxt(XMLChars);
    int parseResult =
        xmlSAXUserParseMemory(&rssSAXHandler,
                              self, XMLChars,
                              strlen(XMLChars));
    xmlFreeParserCtxt(ctxt);
    xmlCleanupParser();
}
[pool release];
}
```

To use SAX in libxml2, you first set up a parser context using the function xmlCreateDocParserCtxt(), which takes a single parameter: the XML document represented as a C-string. After that, you start the SAX parser by calling the xmlSAXUserParseMemory() function. The function is declared in parser.h as:

```
int xmlSAXUserParseMemory          (xmlSAXHandlerPtr sax,
            void * user_data,
            const char * buffer,
            int size)
```

This function parses an in-memory buffer and calls your registered functions as necessary. The first parameter to this function is a pointer to the SAX handler. The SAX handler is a structure holding the pointers to your call-back functions. The second parameter is an optional pointer that is application specific. The value specified will be used as the context when the SAX parser calls your call-back functions. The third and fourth parameters are used for the C-string XML document in memory and its length, respectively.

The SAX handler is where you store the pointers to your call-back functions. If you are not interested in an event type, just store a NULL value in its field. The following is the definition of the structure in tree.h:

```
struct _xmlSAXHandler {
    internalSubsetSAXFunc internalSubset
    isStandaloneSAXFunc isStandalone
    hasInternalSubsetSAXFunc   hasInternalSubset
    hasExternalSubsetSAXFunc   hasExternalSubset
    resolveEntitySAXFunc   resolveEntity
    getEntitySAXFunc   getEntity
    entityDeclSAXFunc entityDecl
```

notationDeclSAXFunc  notationDecl
attributeDeclSAXFunc   attributeDecl
elementDeclSAXFunc  elementDecl
unparsedEntityDeclSAXFunc unparsedEntityDecl
setDocumentLocatorSAXFunc setDocumentLocator
startDocumentSAXFunc  startDocument
endDocumentSAXFunc  endDocument
startElementSAXFunc startElement
endElementSAXFunc endElement
referenceSAXFunc  reference
charactersSAXFunc  characters
ignorableWhitespaceSAXFunc  ignorableWhitespace
processingInstructionSAXFunc  processingInstruction
commentSAXFunc  comment
warningSAXFunc  warning
errorSAXFunc  error
fatalErrorSAXFunc fatalError  :get all the errors
getParameterEntitySAXFunc getParameterEntity
cdataBlockSAXFunc  cdataBlock
externalSubsetSAXFunc  externalSubset
**unsigned int**  initialized
*// The following fields are extensions*
**void** ∗  _private
startElementNsSAX2Func  startElementNs
endElementNsSAX2Func  endElementNs
xmlStructuredErrorFunc  serror
}

Listing 11.6 shows our SAX handler.

---

**Listing 11.6**  Our SAX handler.

---

```
static  xmlSAXHandler rssSAXHandler ={
NULL,                           /* internalSubset */
NULL,                           /* isStandalone    */
NULL,                           /* hasInternalSubset */
NULL,                           /* hasExternalSubset */
NULL,                           /* resolveEntity */
NULL,                           /* getEntity */
NULL,                           /* entityDecl */
NULL,                           /* notationDecl */
NULL,                           /* attributeDecl */
NULL,                           /* elementDecl */
NULL,                           /* unparsedEntityDecl */
NULL,                           /* setDocumentLocator */
NULL,                           /* startDocument */
```

```
NULL,                              /* endDocument */
NULL,                              /* startElement */
NULL,                              /* endElement */
NULL,                              /* reference */
charactersFoundSAX ,               /* characters */
NULL,                              /* ignorableWhitespace */
NULL,                              /* processingInstruction */
NULL,                              /* comment */
NULL,                              /* warning */
errorEncounteredSAX ,              /* error */
fatalErrorEncounteredSAX ,         /* fatalError */
NULL,                              /* getParameterEntity */
NULL,                              /* cdataBlock */
NULL,                              /* externalSubset */
XML_SAX2_MAGIC,                    //
NULL,
startElementSAX ,                  /* startElementNs */
endElementSAX ,                    /* endElementNs */
NULL,                              /* serror */
};
```

Aside from the function pointers, the `initialized` field should be set to the value `XML_SAX2_MAGIC` in order to indicate that the handler is used for a SAX2 parser. Once you call the `xmlSAXUserParseMemory()`, the SAX parser starts the parsing of the document and calling your registered call-back functions.

We are mainly interested in three functions: `startElementNsSAX2Func()`, `endElement-NsSAX2Func()`, and `charactersSAXFunc()`.

`startElementNsSAX2Func()` is called when the parser encounters the start of a new element. `startElementNsSAX2Func()` is defined in `tree.h` as:

```
void    startElementNsSAX2Func    (void * ctx ,
          const xmlChar * localname ,
          const xmlChar * prefix ,
          const xmlChar * URI ,
          int nb_namespaces ,
          const xmlChar ** namespaces ,
          int nb_attributes ,
          int nb_defaulted ,
          const xmlChar ** attributes )
```

`ctx` is user data and it is the second value you used when you called the function `xmlSAXUser-ParseMemory()`. In our case, it is a pointer to the class `XORSSFeedNebraska`. `localname` is the local name of the element. `prefix` is the element namespace prefix (if available). `URI` is the element namespace name (if available). `nb_namespaces` is number of namespace definitions on that node. `namespaces` is a pointer to the array of prefix/URI pair namespace definitions. `nb_attributes` is the number of attributes on that node. `nb_defaulted` is the number of defaulted attributes. The defaulted ones are at the end of the array. `attributes` is a pointer to the array of (localname/prefix/URI/value/end) attribute values.

Listing 11.7 shows the definition of our `startElementNsSAX2Func()` function.

**Listing 11.7**   The `startElementSAX()` call-back function.

```
static void
startElementSAX(void *ctx,
                const xmlChar *localname,
                const xmlChar *prefix,
                const xmlChar *URI,
                int nb_namespaces,
                const xmlChar **namespaces,
                int nb_attributes,
                int nb_defaulted,
                const xmlChar **attributes)
{
    NSAutoreleasePool *pool = [[NSAutoreleasePool alloc] init];
    XORSSFeedNebraska *feedNebraska =
                (XORSSFeedNebraska*) ctx;
    if (feedNebraska.currentElementContent) {
        [feedNebraska.currentElementContent release];
        feedNebraska.currentElementContent = nil;
    }

    if ((!xmlStrcmp(localname, (const xmlChar *)"item"))) {
        feedNebraska.currAbsconder =
                [[XOAbsconder alloc] init];
    }
    [pool release];
}
```

It's a good practice to have an autorelease pool per function. We first start by casting the `ctx` to a pointer to our class `XORSSFeedNebraska`. The class and its parent are declared in Listings 11.8 and 11.9.

**Listing 11.8**   The `XORSSFeedNebraska` class declaration.

```
#import "XORSSFeed.h"
@interface XORSSFeedNebraska : XORSSFeed {
}
@end
```

**Listing 11.9**   The `XORSSFeed` class declaration.

```
@class XOAbsconder;
typedef enum {
```

```
  XML_PARSER_DOM,
  XML_PARSER_SAX
} XMLParser;
@interface XORSSFeed : NSObject {
  NSString *feedURL;
  NSMutableArray *absconders;
  XMLParser   parser;
  NSMutableString *currentElementContent;
   XOAbsconder *currAbsconder;
}
@property(nonatomic, copy) NSString *feedURL;
@property(nonatomic, assign) XMLParser parser;
@property(nonatomic, assign)
        NSMutableString *currentElementContent;
@property(nonatomic, assign) XOAbsconder *currAbsconder;
-(id)init;
-(id)initWithURL:(NSString*) feedURL;
-(void)fetchAbsconders;
-(NSUInteger)numberOfAbsconders;
-(XOAbsconder*)absconderAtIndex:(NSUInteger) index;
-(void)addAbsconder:(XOAbsconder*)absconder;
@end
```

The XORSSFeedNebraska object has an instance variable of type NSMutableString called currentElementContent. This variable holds the text value inside an element. It's constructed in our charactersFoundSAX() function and used in the endElementSAX() function. The function startElementSAX() always releases and so we set this instance variable to nil (if it is not already nil). This will ensure that we start with an empty string for holding the text. If the element name is item, we create a new object of the XOAbsconder class. This is a simple class holding the three pieces of data information about an individual absconder. Listing 11.10 shows the declaration of the XOAbsconder and Listing 11.11 shows its definition.

**Listing 11.10**   The XOAbsconder class declaration.

```
#import <UIKit/UIKit.h>
@interface XOAbsconder : NSObject {
NSString *name;
NSString *furtherInfoURL;
NSString *desc;
}

@property(copy) NSString *name;
@property(copy) NSString *furtherInfoURL;
@property(copy) NSString *desc;
-(id)init;
-(id)initWithName:(NSString *)name
```

```objc
        andURL:(NSString*)url
        andDescription:(NSString*)desc;
-(NSString*)description;
@end
```

**Listing 11.11**    The XOAbsconder class definition.

```objc
#import "XOAbsconder.h"

@implementation XOAbsconder
@synthesize name;
@synthesize furtherInfoURL;
@synthesize desc;

-(id)initWithName:(NSString*)name
        andURL:(NSString*)url
        andDescription:(NSString*)description{
  self = [super init];
  if(self){
    self.name = name;
    self.furtherInfoURL = url;
    self.desc = description;
  }
  return self;
}

-(id)init{
  return [self initWithName:@""
            andURL:@""
            andDescription:@""];
}

-(NSString*)description{
  return [NSString stringWithString:name];
}

-(void)dealloc{
  [name release];
  [furtherInfoURL release];
  [desc release];
  [super dealloc];
}
@end
```

Our endElementNsSAX2Func() function is called endElementSAX() and is shown in Listing 11.12.

**Listing 11.12**    The endElementSAX() function definition.

```
static void
endElementSAX (void *ctx,
                const xmlChar *localname,
                const xmlChar *prefix,
                const xmlChar *URI)
{
  NSAutoreleasePool *pool = [[NSAutoreleasePool alloc] init];
  XORSSFeedNebraska *feedNebraska = (XORSSFeedNebraska*) ctx;
  if ((!xmlStrcmp(localname, (const xmlChar *)"item"))) {

    if (feedNebraska.currAbsconder){
      [feedNebraska    addAbsconder:feedNebraska.currAbsconder];
    }
    [feedNebraska.currAbsconder release];
    feedNebraska.currAbsconder = nil;
  }
  else if ((!xmlStrcmp(localname,
                (const xmlChar *)"title"))) {
    if (feedNebraska.currAbsconder){
      feedNebraska.currAbsconder.name =
          feedNebraska.currentElementContent;
    }
  }
  else if ((!xmlStrcmp(localname,
          (const xmlChar *)"link"))) {
    if (feedNebraska.currAbsconder){
      feedNebraska.currAbsconder.furtherInfoURL =
          feedNebraska.currentElementContent;
    }
  }
  else if ((!xmlStrcmp(localname,
          (const xmlChar *)"description"))) {
    if (feedNebraska.currAbsconder){
      feedNebraska.currAbsconder.desc =
          feedNebraska.currentElementContent;
    }
  }

  if (feedNebraska.currentElementContent) {
      [feedNebraska.currentElementContent release];
```

```
        feedNebraska.currentElementContent = nil;
    }
  [pool release];
}
```

The function first checks to see if the element's name is `item`. If it is, then we add the `XOAbsconder` object which was constructed by the other call-back functions. Otherwise, we check for the three element names: `title`, `link`, and `description`. For each of these elements, we set its respective text value gathered by the `charactersSAXFunc()` function. For example, the following sets the `desc` instance variable with the current text value.

```
feedNebraska.currAbsconder.desc =
        feedNebraska.currentElementContent;
```

The text of the element is stored in `charactersSAXFunc()`. The function is declared in `parser.h` as:

```
void   charactersSAXFunc        (void * ctx,
            const xmlChar * ch,
            int len)
```

This function is called by the parser informing you of new found characters. In addition to the context, you receive the string of characters and its length. Between the start of an element and the end of that element, this function might be called several times. Your function should take this into account and append the new text to the current string.

Our function `charactersFoundSAX()` is shown in Listing 11.13.

**Listing 11.13**  The `charactersFoundSAX()` function definition.

```
static void
charactersFoundSAX(void * ctx, const xmlChar * ch, int len)
{
    NSAutoreleasePool *pool =
                [[NSAutoreleasePool alloc] init];
    XORSSFeedNebraska  *feedNebraska =
                (XORSSFeedNebraska*) ctx;
    CFStringRef str =
          CFStringCreateWithBytes(kCFAllocatorSystemDefault,
              ch, len, kCFStringEncodingUTF8, false)
    if (!feedNebraska.currentElementContent) {
      feedNebraska.currentElementContent =
            [[NSMutableString alloc] init];
    }
    [feedNebraska.currentElementContent
            appendString:(NSString *)str];
    CFRelease(str);
     [pool release];
}
```

The function starts by casting the `ctx` into a `XORSSFeedNebraska` instance. Using this pointer, we can call our Objective-C class. After that, we create a string from received characters by using the function `CFStringCreateWithBytes()`, which is declared as follows:

```
CFStringRef CFStringCreateWithBytes (
   CFAllocatorRef alloc,
   const UInt8 *bytes,
   CFIndex numBytes,
   CFStringEncoding encoding,
   Boolean isExternalRepresentation
);
```

The first parameter is used to specify the memory allocator. `kCFAllocatorDefault` is used for the current default allocator. The second parameter is the buffer which contains the characters. The third parameter specifies the number of bytes. The fourth parameter is the encoding. We use `kCFStringEncodingUTF8` for UTF8 encoding. The fifth parameter is used to specify if the characters in the buffer are in an external representation format. Since they are not, we use `false`.

Once we have the string representation of the characters, we check to see if this is the first time `charactersFoundSAX` has been called for the current element. Recall that the parser can call this function multiple times, supplying the content of a single element. If it is the first time, we allocate our mutable string. After that, we append the string we created from the character buffer to the mutable string. When the `endElementSAX()` function is called, we retrieve this string to build our Objective-C object, `currAbsconder`. When we are finished with the string `str`, we use the `CFRelease()` function to deallocate it.

Finally, the error handling functions are shown in Listing 11.14 and 11.15. As in all other event functions, what you do for error-handling depends on your application. In our example, we release the `currAbsconder` object that we are constructing and log the problem.

**Listing 11.14**   The `errorEncounteredSAX()` function definition.

```
static void
errorEncounteredSAX (void * ctx, const char * msg, ...)
{
XORSSFeedNebraska  *feedNebraska = (XORSSFeedNebraska*) ctx;
  if (feedNebraska.currAbsconder){
    [feedNebraska.currAbsconder release];
    feedNebraska.currAbsconder = nil;
  }
    NSLog(@"errorEncountered: %s", msg);
}
```

**Listing 11.15**   The `fatalErrorEncounteredSAX()` function definition.

```
static void
fatalErrorEncounteredSAX (void * ctx, const char * msg, ...)
{
XORSSFeedNebraska  *feedNebraska = (XORSSFeedNebraska*) ctx;
```

```
if (feedNebraska.currAbsconder){
    [feedNebraska.currAbsconder release];
    feedNebraska.currAbsconder = nil;
}
    NSLog(@"fatalErrorEncountered: %s", msg);
}
```

## 11.4   An RSS Reader Application

In this section, we present a working iPhone application based on the code developed so far. The application will present the contents of an RSS feed to the user in a scrollable table view.

Listing 11.16 shows the application delegate declaration and definition. The application delegate uses an instance of the class XORSSFeedNebraska to retrieve the XML document and parse it to generate the items.

The delegate's applicationDidFinishLaunching: method creates a window and the table view controller. It then asks the instance of XORSSFeedNebraska to fetch the XML and parse it by calling fetchAbsconders method. The table view controller's declaration and definition are shown in Listing 11.17.

**Listing 11.16**   The RSS reader application delegate declaration and definition.

```
#import <UIKit/UIKit.h>
#import "XORSSFeedNebraska.h"
@interface XORSSFeedAppDelegate : NSObject {
 UIWindow *window;
 UINavigationController *navigationController;
 XORSSFeedNebraska *rssFeed;
}
@property (nonatomic, retain)
    UINavigationController *navigationController;
@end

#import "XORSSFeedAppDelegate.h"
#import "XORSSFeedNebraska.h"
#import "RootViewController.h"

@implementation XORSSFeedAppDelegate
@synthesize navigationController;
- (void)applicationDidFinishLaunching:
    (UIApplication *)application {
        window = [[UIWindow alloc] initWithFrame:
            [[UIScreen mainScreen] bounds]] ;
    // Create the navigation and view controllers
    RootViewController *rootViewController =
```

```
      [[ RootViewController alloc ] init ];
   UINavigationController *aNavigationController =
      [[ UINavigationController alloc ]
        initWithRootViewController : rootViewController ];
   self . navigationController = aNavigationController ;
   [ aNavigationController release ];
   [ rootViewController release ];
   // Configure and show the window
   [ window addSubview : [ navigationController view ]];
   rssFeed = [[ XORSSFeedNebraska alloc ] init ];
   [ rssFeed fetchAbsconders ];
   // Make the window key and visible
   [ window makeKeyAndVisible ];
}
-(NSString *) xoTitle {
   return @"Nebraska Absconders";
}
- ( NSInteger ) countOfList {
     return [ rssFeed numberOfAbsconders ];
}
- ( id ) objectInListAtIndex : ( NSUInteger ) theIndex {
     return [ rssFeed absconderAtIndex : theIndex ];
}
- ( void ) dealloc {
   [ window release ];
   [ navigationController release ];
   [ rssFeed release ];
   [ super dealloc ];
}
@end
```

As you have learned from previous chapters, the table view controller is the data source and delegate of the table view. It uses the application delegate to respond to the queries about the table's data model (e.g., number of rows, etc).

Figure 11.4 shows the application main window.

**Listing 11.17**    *The RSS reader table controller declaration and definition.*

```
#import <UIKit/UIKit.h>
@interface RootViewController : UITableViewController {
}
@end

#import "RootViewController.h"
#import "XOAbsconder.h"
#import "XORSSFeedAppDelegate.h"
```

```
@implementation RootViewController
- init {
  if (self = [super init]) {
    XORSSFeedAppDelegate *appDelegate =
      (XORSSFeedAppDelegate *)
        [[UIApplication sharedApplication] delegate];
    self.title = [appDelegate xoTitle];
  }
  return self;
}
- (NSInteger)numberOfSectionsInTableView:
    (UITableView *)tableView {
  return 1;
}
- (NSInteger)tableView:(UITableView *)tableView
    numberOfRowsInSection:(NSInteger)section {
  XORSSFeedAppDelegate *appDelegate =
    (XORSSFeedAppDelegate *)
      [[UIApplication sharedApplication] delegate];
  return [appDelegate countOfList];
}
- (UITableViewCell *)tableView:(UITableView *)tableView
  cellForRowAtIndexPath:(NSIndexPath *)indexPath
{
  UITableViewCell *cell =
    [tableView dequeueReusableCellWithIdentifier:@"XO"];
  if (cell == nil) {
    cell = [[[UITableViewCell alloc]
      initWithFrame:CGRectZero
        reuseIdentifier:@"XO"] autorelease];
  }
  XORSSFeedAppDelegate *appDelegate =
    (XORSSFeedAppDelegate *)
      [[UIApplication sharedApplication] delegate];
  XOAbsconder *absconder =
    [appDelegate objectInListAtIndex:indexPath.row];
  cell.text = [absconder description];
  return cell;
}
@end
```

**Figure 11.4**    The Nebraska Absconders RSS reader application.

## 11.5  Summary

There are two approaches to XML parsing: DOM and SAX. DOM builds a tree representation of the XML document and allows you to navigate the nodes. SAX sequentially parses the document, calling your registered functions appropriately. If you like to write the least amount of code, use DOM. If the XML document is large, use SAX. If you are interested in a couple of nodes in the XML document, use SAX. If you will process most of the document, use DOM. If you would like to write the XML document back to a file, use DOM. If the application accesses the XML document sequentially, use SAX. If you want to make a lot of modifications to the XML document, use DOM. If the XML document is central to your application and you have many methods/objects working on it, use DOM.

To use DOM parsing in your application, follow the following steps:

1. Create an `NSURL` object from the XML document URL address.

2. Create an `NSString` instance to hold the actual XML document by calling `NSString`'s class method `stringWithContentsOfURL:encoding:error:`. This method will fetch the XML document from the internet and store it in a Cocoa string.

3. Convert the Cocoa string to a C-based string using the `NSString` instance method `cStringUsingEncoding:`, and use `NSUTF8StringEncoding`.

4. Use `libxml2` function `xmlParseMemory()` to load the C-string XML document into memory in the form of a tree.

5. Obtain a pointer to the root element and start traversing the tree according to your application's requirements.

6. To obtain the text value of an element, use the function `xmlNodeListGetString()`.

7. Any time you retrieve a string value from `libxml2`, know that it is your responsibility to deallocate it. Use `xmlFree()` function to do just that. Call `xmlFreeDoc()` when you are finished.

To use SAX parsing in your application, follow the following steps:

1. Create a structure of type `xmlSAXHandler`. Fill the entries representing the events that you are interested in receiving with pointers to your event functions. Make sure that the `initialized` entry is set to `XML_SAX2_MAGIC`.

2. Different events have different function signatures. For example, `charactersFoundSAX()` is declared as:

```
charactersFoundSAX(
        void * ctx, const xmlChar * ch, int len)
```

Locate the appropriate function signature in `libxml2`'s `tree.h` file.

3. For meaningful XML parsing, create at least three functions:

   (a) `startElementNsSAX2Func`. This function is called when the parser encounters a begin-tag.

   (b) `endElementNsSAX2Func`. This function is called when the parser encounters an end-tag.

   (c) `charactersSAXFunc`. This function is called (potentially more than once for a given element) to provide you with characters found inside the element.

4. Before you start parsing the document, create a document parser context by calling `xmlCreateDocParserCtxt()` and passing the C-string XML document as the sole argument.

5. After setting up the event functions and the SAX handler, call `libxml2`'s function `xmlSAXUserParseMemory()` passing in:

   (a) A pointer to the handler.

   (b) A pointer to a context. The context can point to any object (e.g., a Cocoa object).

   (c) The C-string representing the XML document and its length in bytes.

6. The parser will start parsing the document and firing the events. If you have registered in the handler a function for a given event, that function will be called.

7. Following the call to `xmlSAXUserParseMemory()`, free the context by calling `xmlFreeParserCtxt()`, and clear the parser by calling `xmlCleanupParser()`.

## Problems

(1) There are several web services available on http://ws.geonames.org/. The *Wikipedia Full-text Search* returns the Wikipedia entries found for a given query. The returned result of executing this web service is an XML document. There are several parameters for this web service. The parameter q is where you specify the query. maxRows is the maximum number of records that can be returned. The full description of the web service can be found at: http://www.geonames.org/export/wikipedia-webservice.html#wikipediaSearch.

As an example, the following URL request:
http://ws.geonames.org/wikipediaSearch?q=plano,texas&maxRows=10
will return an XML document with result entries. Here is a partial listing of the XML document:

**Listing 11.18**    An example of wikipediaSearch web service XML result.

```
<?xml version="1.0" encoding="UTF-8" standalone="no"?>
<geonames>
<entry>
<lang>en</lang>
<title>Plano, Texas</title>
<summary>
Plano  is  a  city  in  Collin  and  Denton  Counties  in
the  U.S.  state  of  Texas.  Located  mainly  within
Collin  County,  it  is  a  wealthy  northern  suburb
of  Dallas.  The  population  was  222,030  at  the
2000  census,  making  it  the  ninth  largest  city  in
Texas.  According  to  a  2005  census  estimate,
Plano  had  grown  to  250,096  making
Plano  the  sixty−ninth  most  populous  city  in  the
United  States  (...)
</summary>
<feature>city</feature>
<countryCode>US</countryCode>
<population>245411</population>
<elevation>0</elevation>
<lat>33.0193</lat>
<lng>−96.7008</lng>
<wikipediaUrl>
http://en.wikipedia.org/wiki/Plano%2C_Texas
</wikipediaUrl>
<thumbnailImg/>
</entry>
.
.
.
</geonames>
```

Write an iPhone application that presents this information in a tabular form.

(2) XPath (XML Path Language) is a language for selecting nodes from an XML document. Read more about it at `www.w3.org/TR/xpath` and investigate how you can use the `libxml2` library to perform XPath operations.

# 12

# Location Awareness

In this chapter, we will address the topic of Location Awareness. First, we will talk in Section 12.1 about the Core Location framework and how to use it to build location-aware applications. After that, Section 12.2 discusses a simple location-aware application. Next, Section 12.3 covers the topic of geocoding. In that section, you will learn how to translate postal addresses into geographical locations. In Section 12.4, you will learn how to sample movement of the device and display that information on maps. Finally, Section 12.5 discusses how to relate zip codes to geographical information. In that section, you will also learn the actual formula that implements the distance between two locations.

## 12.1 The Core Location Framework

The second generation of the iPhone (iPhone 3G) is equipped with a Global Positioning System (GPS) chip. GPS utilizes three or four satellites to triangulate the position of a point on earth. The accuracy of the point's position using this technique ranges from 5 to 40 meters.

The first generation of the iPhone uses non-GPS techniques for identifying the location of the device. Non-GPS techniques such as Cell-Identification, Time-of-Arrival (TOA) and Enhanced Observed Time Difference (E-TOD) can be used in conjunction with Wi-Fi and Bluetooth to provide a reasonable substitute for the lack of a GPS chip [3]. Of course, the location accuracy of these methods is much lower than GPS and ranges from 100 to 500 meters.

Regardless of the technique used, the iPhone provides the Core Location framework [4] as a software interface with whatever technique(s) is/are used to find the location. The framework provides classes and protocols that you can use to get the current location within a specified accuracy as well as to schedule future updates of the current location.

The main class of the Core Location framework is `CLLocationManager`. `CLLocationManager` is the entry point that the developer uses to gain current and future location information. You use an instance of `CLLocationManager` to schedule future updates of the current location of the device.

To gain access to the current location's information, follow these steps:

1. You only need to create an instance of `CLLocationManager` if one does not exist.

2. Configure the `CLLocationManager` instance. You need to configure the instance of the manager with the following parameters:

---

- desiredAccuracy. Using this property, you tell the framework about your needs with respect to the accuracy of the location (in terms of meters). The desiredAccuracy property is declared as follows:

@property(assign , nonatomic)
    CLLocationAccuracy  desiredAccuracy

Different applications require different accuracies. The framework tries to deliver location accuracies according to the value of this property, but it cannot guarantee that. There are several values you can choose from:

- kCLLocationAccuracyBest. This specifies the best accuracy available and it is the default.
- kCLLocationAccuracyNearestTenMeters. This represents an accuracy within ten meters.
- kCLLocationAccuracyHundredMeter. This represents an accuracy within a hundred meters.
- kCLLocationAccuracyKilometer. This value represents an accuracy within 1000 meters.
- kCLLocationAccuracyThreeKilometers. This value represents an accuracy within 3000 meters.

- distanceFilter. The value of this property determines how often you will receive location updates. You will receive a new update only when the device moves a distance greater than or equal to this distance. If a more accurate reading is available, this value is ignored and you will receive a new location update. This property is declared as:

@property(assign , nonatomic)
        CLLocationDistance  distanceFilter

Where CLLocationDistance is declared as:

**typedef double** CLLocationDistance

All values are in meters. If you specify kCLDistanceFilterNone, you will get updates for all device movements.

- delegate. This property specifies the delegate object receiving the updates. The property is declared as:

@property(assign , nonatomic)
    **id**<CLLocationManagerDelegate > delegate

The delegate implements the CLLocationManagerDelegate protocol. This protocol has two optional methods:

(a) locationManager:didUpdateToLocation:fromLocation:.
    This method is invoked whenever the location manager wants to update you with a location. The method is declared as follows:

> – ( **void** ) locationManager : ( CLLocationManager ∗ ) manager
>   didUpdateToLocation : ( CLLocation ∗ ) newLocation
>   fromLocation : ( CLLocation ∗ ) oldLocation

You receive a reference to the location manager in the first parameter. The second parameter is an instance of the CLLocation class encapsulating the new location. The third parameter is another, possibly nil, CLLocation object holding the previous location.

(b) locationManager:didFailWithError:. This method of the delegate gets called whenever the manager fails to compute the current location. The method is declared as follows:

> – ( **void** ) locationManager : ( CLLocationManager ∗ ) manager
>   didFailWithError : ( NSError ∗ ) error

You should implement a class that adopts the CLLocationManagerDelegate protocol and assign the instance of this class to the delegate property of the CLLocationManager instance.

3. Invoke startUpdatingLocation. Call the startUpdatingLocation method of the CLLocationManager instance to start receiving location updates.

4. Invoke stopUpdatingLocation. You should call stopUpdatingLocation as soon as you are satisfied with the current location information.

The previous steps represent the basic usage of the location services.

## 12.1.1   The CLLocation class

Latitude and longitude define a logical grid system of the world. They are developed and implemented to locate places on earth. Latitude lines are parallel with equal distance from each other. The equator is 0 degrees, the north and south poles are 90 degrees. A degree is approximately 69 miles. Longitude lines run from north to south. The range for longitudes is 0 to 180 degrees east and 0 to 180 degrees west.

To locate a point on earth, you can describe it by a (latitude, longitude) pair. For example, $(33°1'12'', -96°44'19.67'')$. This degree-minute-second format can be converted to decimal format. The previous location can be written in decimal form as: $(33.02, -96.7388)$.

The location of the device is encapsulated by the class CLLocation, which contains the geographical position of the device represented by the latitude and longitude. In addition, it holds the altitude of the device and various values describing the location measurement. You typically receive objects of this kind from the location manager.

The following are some of the important properties of this class:

• coordinate. The latitude and longitude of the device in degrees. This property is declared as follows:

@property ( readonly , nonatomic )
  CLLocationCoordinate2D coordinate

CLLocationCoordinate2D is a structure declared as follows:

```
typedef struct {
    CLLocationDegrees latitude;
    CLLocationDegrees longitude;
} CLLocationCoordinate2D;
```

Where CLLocationDegrees is of type double.

- altitude. Returns the altitude of the device in meters. Positive values indicate above sea level while negative ones indicate below sea level. The property is declared as follows:

```
@property(readonly, nonatomic) CLLocationDistance altitude
```

- horizontalAccuracy. If you imagine that the latitude and longitude were the coordinates of the center of a circle, and the horizontalAccuracy is the radius of that circle, then the device can be within any point inside that circle. The property is declared as:

```
@property(readonly, nonatomic)
    CLLocationAccuracy horizontalAccuracy
```

The property is of type CLLocationAccuracy, which is defined as double. A negative value indicates an invalid lateral location.

- verticalAccuracy. This property provides the vertical accuracy of the location. The altitude is within $+/-$ of this value. The property is declared as follows:

```
@property(readonly, nonatomic)
    CLLocationAccuracy verticalAccuracy
```

Negative values indicate an invalid altitude reading.

- timestamp. This provides the time when the location was determined. The property is declared as follows:

```
@property(readonly, nonatomic) NSDate *timestamp
```

Most of the time, you receive CLLocation objects from the location manager. If you would like to cache objects of this type, then you need to allocate and initialize a new location object. You can use one of the following two initialization methods depending on your situation:

- initWithLatitude:longitude:. This method is declared as follows:

  - (id)initWithLatitude:(CLLocationDegrees)latitude
    longitude:(CLLocationDegrees)longitude

- initWithCoordinate:altitude:horizontalAccuracy:
  verticalAccuracy:timestamp:. This method is declared as follows:

```
- (id)initWithCoordinate:(CLLocationCoordinate2D)coordinate
  altitude:(CLLocationDistance)altitude
  horizontalAccuracy:(CLLocationAccuracy)hAccuracy
  verticalAccuracy:(CLLocationAccuracy)vAccuracy
  timestamp:(NSDate *)timestamp;
```

There is one last method that can be useful in finding the distance (in meters) from one given location to another. This method is `getDistanceFrom:` and it returns the lateral distance from the location provided in the first parameter to the location encapsulated by the receiver. The method is declared as follows:

```
- (CLLocationDistance)
getDistanceFrom:(const CLLocation *)location
```

Later in this chapter, we will show how such a method can be implemented and used within a database engine.

## 12.2   A Simple Location-aware Application

In this section, we will start by providing a simple location-aware application. The application will configure a location manager and display the updates in a text view. To keep things simple, we implement the functionality of the application in one class: the application delegate.

Listing 12.1 shows the declaration of the application delegate class. The class maintains references to the text view and the location manager. The `noUpdates` instance variable is used to count the number of location updates received by the application delegate so far. We stop the location updates when we reach ten updates. Notice that we have added a new `#import` statement for the Core Location framework.

**Listing 12.1**   The declaration of the application delegate class used in the simple location-aware example.

```
#import <UIKit/UIKit.h>
#import <CoreLocation/CoreLocation.h>

@interface Location1AppDelegate : NSObject
<UIApplicationDelegate, CLLocationManagerDelegate> {
  UIWindow            *window;
  UITextView          *textView;
  CLLocationManager   *locationMgr;
  NSUInteger          noUpdates;
}
@property (nonatomic, retain) UIWindow *window;
@end
```

Listing 12.2 shows the implementation of the application delegate class. The `application-DidFinishLaunching:` method configures a text view and adds it as a subview to the main window. An instance of the location manager is created, and its `delegate` property is set to the application delegate instance. The location manager is made to start updating and the window is made visible.

Location updates are received by the CLLocationManagerDelegate's method locationManager:didUpdateToLocation:fromLocation:. In our implementation of this method, we simply concatenate the text in the text view with the description of the new location object. The text view's text property is then set to this value. When ten updates have been received, the location manager is made to stop updating us by invoking its stopUpdatingLocation method.

**Listing 12.2**    The implementation of the application delegate class used in the simple location-aware example.

```
#import "Location1AppDelegate.h"

@implementation Location1AppDelegate
@synthesize window;

- (void)locationManager:(CLLocationManager *)manager
  didUpdateToLocation:(CLLocation *)newLocation
       fromLocation:(CLLocation *)oldLocation{
  noUpdates++;
  if(noUpdates >= 10){
    [locationMgr stopUpdatingLocation];
  }
  [self updateLocation:[newLocation description]];
}

-(void) updateLocation:(NSString *) update{
  NSMutableString *newMessage =
      [[NSMutableString alloc] initWithCapacity:100];
  [newMessage appendString:
    [NSString stringWithFormat:@"Update #:%i\n", noUpdates]];
  [newMessage appendString:update];
  [newMessage appendString:@"\n"];
  [newMessage appendString:[textView text]];
  textView.text = newMessage;
  [newMessage release];
}

- (void)
applicationDidFinishLaunching:(UIApplication *)application {
  window = [[UIWindow alloc]
    initWithFrame:[[UIScreen mainScreen] bounds]];
  CGRect rectFrame =
    [UIScreen mainScreen].applicationFrame;
  textView = [[UITextView alloc] initWithFrame:rectFrame];
```

**Figure 12.1**  `Project->Edit Active Target` menu.

```
    textView . editable  = NO;
    locationMgr = [[ CLLocationManager  alloc ]  init ];
    locationMgr . delegate  = self ;
    noUpdates  =  0;
    [ locationMgr  startUpdatingLocation ];
    [ window  addSubview : textView ];
    [ window  makeKeyAndVisible ];
}

−  ( void ) dealloc  {
    [ textView  release ];
    [ locationMgr  release ];
    [ window  release ];
    [ super  dealloc ];
}
@end
```

For this code to build successfully, you need to add a reference to the `Core Location` library. In XCode, select the `Project->Edit Active Target` menu as shown in Fig. 12.1. The `Target Info` window will appear as shown in Fig. 12.2. Click on the "+" button located at the bottom left side. A list of libraries will be shown. Scroll down and locate the `CoreLocation.framework` as shown in Fig. 12.3. Select it and click "Add". Figure 12.4 shows the added `Core Location` library in the `Linked Libraries` section.

Figure 12.5 shows a snapshot of the application after receiving ten location updates.

**Figure 12.2** `Target Info` window.

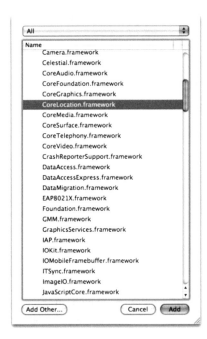

**Figure 12.3** The `CoreLocation.framework` library.

**Figure 12.4**    The added `Core Location` library in the `Linked Libraries` section.

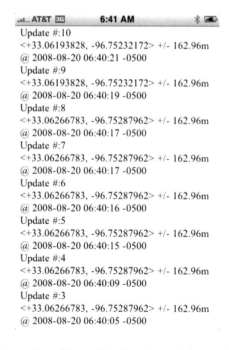

**Figure 12.5**    A snapshot of the application after receiving ten location updates.

## 12.3  Google Maps API

Google provides an HTTP interface for geocoding. Geocoding is a translation process where addresses such as: `3400 W Plano Pkwy, Plano, TX 75075` can be converted to actual geographic coordinates in latitude and longitude. To access this service, the client sends an HTTP request to `http://maps.google.com/maps/geo?` with the following parameters:

- `q`. This parameter represents the address for which you want to find its geo data.

- `output`. The format of the result to be sent back to you. Several formats exist such as `xml` and `csv`. The comma separated values (`csv`) is the easiest to deal with.

- `key`. To access the service, you need an API key from Google. At the time of writing, the usage is free for public websites. Google does, however, police the service.

For example, sending the following HTTP request:

```
http://maps.google.com/maps/geo?q=3400+W+Plano+Pkwy+Plano,
+TX+75075&output=csv&
key=ABQIAAAAERNgBiSqUogvAN307LdVDxSkQMtcTv75TNsQ97PejimT5pm-
BxST0Gma_YCBaUccn3pRis8XjkxM8w
```

will, provided you use a different key, return:

```
200,8,33.010003,-96.757923
```

There are four comma-separated values received from Google when you use `csv` format. The first value is the HTTP protocol status code. 200 is `OK` (see `RFC 2616` for more information). The second value is the `accuracy`. A value of 8 means `Address Level Accuracy`. For a complete list, see `GGeoAddressAccuracy` in the Google Maps API reference. The last two pieces of the result, which is what we are really interested in, are the `latitude` and `longitude`, respectively.

### 12.3.1  A geocoding application

In this section, we will build an application that finds the distance between two addresses. First, we build the `GoogleMapsWrapper` helper class, a class which encapsulates the geocoding service. After that, we show an application delegate that uses this helper class to display the distance between two addresses using a text view.

Listing 12.3 shows the declaration of the `GoogleMapsWrapper` class. The main method declared by this class is the `findGeoInfoForAddress:andReturnLatitude:and-Longitude:` method. This method takes the address as an input parameter and returns the latitude and longitude as output parameters. The return code for success is 0.

The `GoogleMapsWrapper` also maintains a set of Google Maps keys. These keys can be used to load-balance the HTTP requests as Google puts a limit on the number of queries used per key. The method `addKey:` is used to store a key, and the method `getKey` is used to retrieve one.

**Listing 12.3**   The declaration of the `GoogleMapsWrapper` class used in the geocoding application.

```
#import <UIKit/UIKit.h>

@interface GoogleMapsWrapper : NSObject {
    NSMutableArray *keys;
}
- (id)init;
-(void)addKey:(NSString*) key;
-(NSString*)getKey;
-(int)
findGeoInfoForAddress:(NSString*)address
andReturnLatitude:(float*) latitude
andLongitude:(float*) longitude;
@end
```

Listing 12.4 shows the implementation of the `GoogleMapsWrapper` class. The `find-GeoInfoForAddress:andReturnLatitude:andLongitude:` method first builds the query to be used in the HTTP request. After creating an `NSURL` object for the request, it contacts Google by invoking the `initWithContentsOfURL:` of `NSData`.

The response of the query is in comma-separated format (`csv`) that needs to be parsed. To retrieve the four values in the response, we utilize the Cocoa class `NSScanner`. An `NSScanner` class is used to scan an `NSString` object for strings and numbers by progressing through the string. In addition, you can use it to skip over characters in a given set. The response of the query is first converted to an `NSString` object, `contents`. After that, an `NSScanner` object is created by invoking the `scannerWithString:` class method of `NSScanner` passing in that string.

First, we need to check the status code value of the response. To retrieve the status code, we ask the scanner to extract all characters starting from the current position (beginning of string) up to the first comma. The method `scanUpToCharactersFromSet:intoString:` is used for that purpose. Once we have the status code in the string `statusCode`, we check to see if it is equal to the value 200. If it is not, we return a −1, indicating an error. If the status code is equal to 200, we retrieve the latitude and longitude values using the `scanFloat:` method.

The `GoogleMapsWrapper` class does not implement load-balancing (e.g., a simple randomization algorithm). We use only one key in our application.

**Listing 12.4**   The implementation of the `GoogleMapsWrapper` class used in the geocoding application.

```
#import "GoogleMapsWrapper.h"

#define GEO_QUERY      @"http://maps.google.com/maps/geo?q="
#define GEO_CSV_KEY    @"&output=csv&key="
@implementation GoogleMapsWrapper

-(int)findGeoInfoForAddress:(NSString*)address
andReturnLatitude:(float*) latitude
andLongitude:(float*) longitude{
```

```objc
if (! address || ! latitude || ! longitude ){
  return −1;
}
NSMutableString *query =
  [[NSMutableString  alloc] initWithString :GEO_QUERY];
[query appendString : address ];
[query appendString :GEO_CSV_KEY];
[query appendString :[ self getKey ]];
[query replaceOccurrencesOfString :@" "
       withString :@"%20" options : NSLiteralSearch
       range :NSMakeRange(0, [query length ])];
NSURL *url= [[NSURL alloc] initWithString : query ];
if (! url ){
  [query release ];
  return −1;
}
NSData *data = [[NSData alloc] initWithContentsOfURL : url ];
if (! data ){
  [query release ];
  [url release ];
  *latitude = *longitude = 404;
  return −1;
}
NSString *contents = [[NSString alloc] initWithData : data
                      encoding : NSUTF8StringEncoding ];
if (! contents ){
  [query release ];
  [url release ];
  [data release ];
  return −1;
}
/*
 A reply returned in the csv format consists of four numbers,
 separated by commas:
 HTTP status code
 accuracy (See accuracy constants )
 latitude
 longitude
 example:  200,6,42.730070, −73.690570
 */
NSScanner *theScanner ;
NSCharacterSet *comma =
    [NSCharacterSet characterSetWithCharactersInString :@"," ];
NSString *statusCode ;
```

```
theScanner = [NSScanner scannerWithString : contents ];
if ([ theScanner scanUpToCharactersFromSet : comma
      intoString :& statusCode ]){
  if ([ statusCode intValue ] != 200){
    *latitude = *longitude = 404;
    [ query release ];
    [ url release ];
    [ data release ];
    [ contents release ];
    return -1;
  }
}
if (
    [ theScanner scanCharactersFromSet : comma intoString :NULL]
    &&
    [ theScanner scanUpToCharactersFromSet : comma
        intoString :NULL] &&
    [ theScanner scanCharactersFromSet : comma intoString :NULL]
    &&
    [ theScanner scanFloat : latitude ] &&
    [ theScanner scanCharactersFromSet : comma  intoString :NULL]
    &&
    [ theScanner scanFloat : longitude ]
    ){
  [ query release ];
  [ url release ];
  [ data release ];
  [ contents release ];
  return 0;
}
[ query release ];
[ url release ];
[ data release ];
[ contents release ];
return -1;
}

-(NSString *) getKey {
  if ([ keys count ] < 1){
    return @"NULL_KEY";
  }
  return [ keys objectAtIndex :0];
}
```

```
-(void)addKey:(NSString*) key{
  [keys addObject:key];
}

- (id)init{
  self = [super init];
  keys = [[NSMutableArray arrayWithCapacity:1] retain];
  return self;
}

- (void)dealloc {
  [keys release];
  [super dealloc];
}
@end
```

Listing 12.5 shows the declaration of the application delegate class. As we have mentioned before, the application delegate will create the main window and attach a text view to it. It then will use the `GoogleMapsWrapper` class to find the distance between two addresses and display that information to the user in a text view as shown in Fig. 12.6. The class maintains references to the `UITextView` and the `GoogleMapsWrapper` classes.

**Listing 12.5**    The declaration of the application delegate class used in the geocoding example.

```
#import <UIKit/UIKit.h>
#import <CoreLocation/CoreLocation.h>
#import "GoogleMapsWrapper.h"

@interface Location2AppDelegate :
    NSObject <UIApplicationDelegate> {
  UIWindow           *window;
  UITextView            *textView ;
  GoogleMapsWrapper    *gWrapper;
}
@property (nonatomic, retain) UIWindow *window;
@end
```

Listing 12.6 shows the implementation of the application delegate class. The `application-DidFinishLaunching:` method configures the GUI and invokes the method `findDistance-FromAddress:toAddress:` to find the distance between the White House and the Pentagon. The result is then formatted and assigned to the `text` property of the text view object.

Listing 12.6   The implementation of the application delegate class used in the geocoding example.

```
#import "Location2AppDelegate.h"
#import "GoogleMapsWrapper.h"

#define FROM_ADDRESS
        @"1600 Pennsylvania Ave NW, Washington, DC 20500"
#define TO_ADDRESS @"Army Navy Dr & Fern St, Arlington, VA 22202"

@implementation Location2AppDelegate

@synthesize window;

-(double) findDistanceFromAddress:(NSString*) from
 toAddress:(NSString *) to{
  float lat, lon;
  CLLocation *fromLocation;
  CLLocation *toLocation;
  if(
     [gWrapper findGeoInfoForAddress:from
          andReturnLatitude:&lat andLongitude:&lon] == 0
     ){
     fromLocation = [[CLLocation alloc]
       initWithLatitude:lat longitude:lon];
    if([gWrapper findGeoInfoForAddress:to
            andReturnLatitude:&lat
            andLongitude:&lon] == 0){

     toLocation =[[[CLLocation alloc]
        initWithLatitude:lat longitude:lon] autorelease];
      return [toLocation getDistanceFrom:fromLocation];
    }
    return -1;
  }
  return -1;
}

- (void)
  applicationDidFinishLaunching:(UIApplication *)application {
    window = [[UIWindow alloc]
      initWithFrame:[[UIScreen mainScreen] bounds]];
  CGRect rectFrame =
    [UIScreen mainScreen].applicationFrame;
  textView = [[UITextView alloc] initWithFrame:rectFrame];
  textView.editable = NO;
```

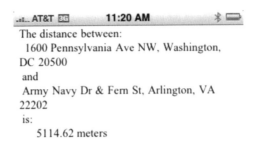

**Figure 12.6**    A snapshot of the geocoding application showing the distance between two addresses.

```
gWrapper = [[GoogleMapsWrapper alloc] init];
[gWrapper addKey:
   @"ABQIAAAAERNgBiSqUogvAN307LdVDx"
    "SkQMtcTv75TNsQ97PejimT5pm-MAxST0Gma_Y"
    "CBaUccn3pRis8XjkxM8w"];

NSMutableString *outStr =
  [[NSMutableString alloc]
    initWithFormat:@"The distance between: \n  %@ \n and"
            "\n %@ \n is:\n \t \t  %.2f meters\n",
            FROM_ADDRESS, TO_ADDRESS,
            [self findDistanceFromAddress:FROM_ADDRESS
                          toAddress:TO_ADDRESS]
            ];
textView.text = outStr;
[window addSubview:textView];
[window makeKeyAndVisible];
}

- (void)dealloc {
  [gWrapper release];
  [textView release];
  [window release];
  [super dealloc];
}
@end
```

## 12.4    A Tracking Application with Maps

Many of the iPhone applications require the display of a map. If you are faced with the task of developing one of these applications, you can use Google Maps API and the UIWebView class for that purpose.

In this section, we will develop a tracking application. The application will first track and store the movement of the device for a configurable number of movements. The user can interrupt the tracking or wait until a specified number of movements have been recorded. In either case, the user is able to go through these movements and visualize (in a map) the geographic location and the time of the recording of each movement.

Listing 12.7 shows the declaration of the application delegate class. The application delegate will have a navigation controller for the GUI; thus, it maintains references to a view and a navigation controller.

**Listing 12.7**    The declaration of the application delegate class used in the tracking application.

```
#import <UIKit/UIKit.h>
#import "LocationsViewController.h"

@interface Location3AppDelegate :
  NSObject <UIApplicationDelegate> {
  UIWindow                    *window;
  LocationsViewController *ctrl;
  UINavigationController      *navCtrl;
}
@property (nonatomic, retain) UIWindow *window;
@end
```

Listing 12.8 shows the implementation of the application delegate class. The `application-DidFinishLaunching:` method simply creates a view controller of type `LocationsView-Controller` and uses it as the root controller for a navigation controller. The view of the navigation controller is then added as a subview to the main window and the main window is made visible.

**Listing 12.8**    The implementation of the application delegate class used in the tracking application.

```
#import "Location3AppDelegate.h"
@implementation Location3AppDelegate
@synthesize window;

- (void)applicationDidFinishLaunching:
    (UIApplication *)application {  window = [[UIWindow alloc]
      initWithFrame:[[UIScreen mainScreen] bounds]];
  ctrl = [[LocationsViewController alloc]
      initWithNibName:nil bundle:nil];
  navCtrl = [[UINavigationController alloc]
      initWithRootViewController:ctrl];
  [window addSubview:navCtrl.view];
  [window makeKeyAndVisible];
}

- (void)dealloc {
```

```
[ ctrl  release ];
[ navCtrl  release ];
[ window  release ];
[ super  dealloc ];
}
@end
```

Our view controller is declared in Listing 12.9. The view controller adopts the CLLocation-ManagerDelegate as it will be the delegate of the location manager that it will create. It declares two bar buttons for stopping the sampling of movements, navigating to the next recording, and navigating to the previous recording. The right bar button will be used for both stopping the sampling of movements and as a "Next" button. In addition, the view controller maintains a reference to a web view for visualizing the locations sampled.

**Listing 12.9**   The declaration of LocationsViewController view controller class used in the tracking application.

```
#import  <UIKit/UIKit.h>
#import  <CoreLocation/CoreLocation.h>

@interface  LocationsViewController  :
     UIViewController  <CLLocationManagerDelegate >{
  CLLocationManager  *locationMgr;
  NSUInteger          noUpdates;
  NSMutableArray      *locations;
  UIWebView           *webView;
  UIBarButtonItem     *rightButton, *leftButton;
  NSUInteger          current;
}
@end
```

Listing 12.11 shows the implementation of the view controller. In the initialization method, initWithNibName:bundle:, we create two bar buttons. The right button is labelled "Stop" and the left "Previous". The left button is made disabled.

The loadView method creates and configures a location manager. The distance needed to receive an update is made to be equal to MIN_DISTANCE. In addition, a web view is created and initialized with the contents of an HTML file stored in the bundle. The file map3.html is shown in Listing 12.10. This file is one of many sample files demonstrating the use of the Google Maps API provided by Google. As you will see shortly, we will use Javascript to modify the appearance of the map dynamically.

**Listing 12.10**   The HTML page used for displaying a Google map for the geo-tracking application

```
<!DOCTYPE html PUBLIC "-//W3C//DTD XHTML 1.0 Strict//EN"
     "http://www.w3.org/TR/xhtml1/DTD/xhtml1-strict.dtd">
<html xmlns="http://www.w3.org/1999/xhtml"
     xmlns:v="urn:schemas-microsoft-com:vml">
```

```
<head>
<meta http-equiv="content-type" content="text/html;
        charset=utf-8"/>
<title>Geo-tracking Example</title>
<script
src="http://maps.google.com/maps?file=api&amp;v=2&amp;key=K"
        type="text/javascript">
</script>
<script type="text/javascript">
function initialize() {
  }
   </script>
</head>
<body onload="initialize()" onunload="GUnload()">
    <div id="map_canvas" style="width: 500px; height: 500px">
    </div>
</body>
</html>
```

On receiving location updates, we store these locations in an array. When we have sampled NO_OF_LOCATIONS locations, we enable the left bar button, change the title of the right button to "Next" and point out the first location in the map.

The method centerMap: is used to display the location in the map. The method takes as an input parameter the index of the location in the array of sampled locations. It extracts the latitude and longitude information from the location, sets the center of the map to that location, and pans to the center. In addition, it opens an information window with the time of the sampling of the location. All of this is done in Javascript such as the one shown below. Finally, we execute the Javascript code using the web view's method stringByEvaluatingJavaScriptFromString:.

```
var map = new GMap2(document.getElementById("map_canvas"));
map.setMapType(G_HYBRID_MAP);
map.setCenter(new GLatLng(37.331689, -122.030731), 18);
map.panTo(map.getCenter());
map.openInfoWindow(map.getCenter(),
      document.createTextNode("Loc: (1/1),
Time: 2008-08-06 19:51:27 -0500"));
```

Figure 12.7 shows a snapshot of the tracking application while sampling movements, and Fig. 12.8 shows a snapshot of the tracking application while viewing one of those sampled locations.

The application poses some ethical (and maybe legal) issues. If you find a need to launch this application and hide it in someone's car or bag, you should think again! Spying is not nice and it may end you in jail. Moms, of course, are an exception! One may want to modify the application and add real-time reporting of movements to interested parties. This is left to the reader as an exercise.

**Listing 12.11**  The implementation of `LocationsViewController` view controller class used in the tracking application.

```objc
#import "LocationsViewController.h"

#define NO_OF_LOCATIONS 100
#define MIN_DISTANCE    100

@implementation LocationsViewController

- (void)locationManager:(CLLocationManager *)manager
  didUpdateToLocation:(CLLocation *)newLocation
      fromLocation:(CLLocation *)oldLocation{
  noUpdates++;
  [locations addObject:newLocation];
  self.title = [NSString
      stringWithFormat:@"Locations: %i", noUpdates];
  if(noUpdates == 1){
    [self centerMap:0];
  }
  if(noUpdates >= NO_OF_LOCATIONS){
    [locationMgr stopUpdatingLocation];
    leftButton.enabled = YES;
    rightButton.title = @"Next";
    current = 0;
    [self centerMap:current];
  }

}

-(void) centerMap:(NSUInteger) index{
  CLLocation *loc = [locations objectAtIndex:index];
  NSString *js =
  [NSString stringWithFormat:
   @"var map = "
   "new GMap2(document.getElementById(\"map_canvas\"));"
   "map.setMapType(G_HYBRID_MAP);"
   "map.setCenter(new GLatLng(%lf, %lf), 18);"
   "map.panTo(map.getCenter());"
   "map.openInfoWindow(map.getCenter(),"
   "document.createTextNode(\"Loc: (%i/%i), Time: %@\"));",
   [loc coordinate].latitude, [loc coordinate].longitude,
   index+1, [locations count],
   [loc timestamp]];
  [webView stringByEvaluatingJavaScriptFromString:js];
```

```objc
}

- (id)initWithNibName:(NSString *)nibNameOrNil
        bundle:(NSBundle *)nibBundleOrNil {
  if (self = [super initWithNibName:nibNameOrNil
        bundle:nibBundleOrNil]) {
    rightButton =
    [[UIBarButtonItem alloc]
     initWithTitle:@"Stop"
     style:UIBarButtonItemStyleDone
     target:self
     action:@selector(stopOrNext)
     ];
    self.navigationItem.rightBarButtonItem = rightButton;

    leftButton =
    [[UIBarButtonItem alloc]
     initWithTitle:@"Previous"
     style:UIBarButtonItemStyleDone
     target:self
     action:@selector(prev)
     ];
    self.navigationItem.leftBarButtonItem = leftButton;
    leftButton.enabled = NO;

  }
  return self;
}

-(void)stopOrNext{
  if ([rightButton.title isEqualToString:@"Stop"] == YES){
    [locationMgr stopUpdatingLocation];
    leftButton.enabled = YES;
    rightButton.title = @"Next";
    current = 0;
    [self centerMap:current];
  }
  else
  if(current < ([locations count]-1)){
    [self centerMap:++current];
  }
}
```

```objc
-(void) prev {
  if (current > 0 && (current < [locations  count])){
    current = current -1;
    [self centerMap:current];
  }
}

- (void) loadView {
  locations = [[NSMutableArray arrayWithCapacity:10] retain];
  locationMgr = [[CLLocationManager alloc] init];
  locationMgr.distanceFilter  = MIN_DISTANCE;
  locationMgr.delegate = self;
  noUpdates = 0;

  CGRect  rectFrame = [UIScreen mainScreen].applicationFrame;
  webView = [[UIWebView alloc] initWithFrame:rectFrame];
  NSString *htmlFilePath =
    [[NSBundle mainBundle]
       pathForResource:@"map3" ofType:@"html"];
  NSData *data =
       [NSData dataWithContentsOfFile:htmlFilePath];
  [webView loadData:data
      MIMEType:@"text/html"
   textEncodingName:@"utf-8"
       baseURL:[NSURL
            URLWithString:@"http://maps.google.com/"]
   ];
  [locationMgr startUpdatingLocation];
  self.view = webView;
}

- (void) dealloc {
  [rightButton release];
  [leftButton release];
  [locationMgr release];
  [locations release];
  [super dealloc];
}
@end
```

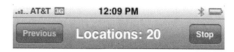

**Figure 12.7**    A snapshot of the tracking application while sampling movements.

## 12.5   Working with ZIP Codes

The United States Postal Service (USPS) uses a coding system to help in the efficient distribution of mail in the US. Each potential recipient of mail is thought to live in a specific zone represented by a Zone Improvement Plan (ZIP) code. ZIP codes are, in theory, tied to geographical locations. Figure 12.9 shows the zip code zones of the United States.

There are various databases available on ZIP codes. These databases differ in their accuracy and pricing. Databases referring to the latitude and longitude of a given ZIP code can be thought to describe the center of the ZIP code servicing area. There are several places where one can buy US ZIP code databases. You can download a recent database for free from the site in [1].

The contents of the US ZIP codes file [1] is comma-separated. For example, the last few entries in the file are as follows:

```
89508,Reno,NV,39.5296329,-119.8138027,Washoe
91008,Duarte,CA,34.1394513,-117.9772873,Los Angeles
92058,Oceanside,CA,33.1958696,-117.3794834,San Diego
94505,Discovery Bay,CA,37.9085357,-121.6002291,Contra Costa
95811,Sacramento,CA,38.5815719,-121.4943996,Sacramento
```

In the following, we present the major steps that you can take in order to answer questions like the following: give me all ZIP codes that are within 10 miles from 68508.

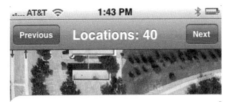

**Figure 12.8** A snapshot of the tracking application while viewing a sampled location.

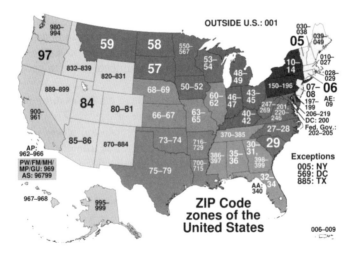

**Figure 12.9** Zip code zones of the United States [2].

1. Create an SQLite `zipcodes` table. To efficiently search, it is advisable to represent your data in a database. The following table can be used to store the ZIP code data.

```
CREATE  TABLE  zipcodes (
    zipcode int NOT NULL PRIMARY KEY,
    latitude   float(10,8),  longitude   float(10,8),
    state  varchar(2),  city  varchar(128),
    county  varchar(128)
)
```

The `zipcode` will be our primary key and for each ZIP code, we have the `latitude`, `longitude`, `state`, `city`, and `county`.

2. Populate the `zipcodes` table. Populate the table with the ZIP code geographical data obtained from the text file. The data stored in a comma-separated ASCII file. Use an `NSScanner` object for value extraction. The extracted tokens of each line are used as input to an `INSERT` SQL statement.

3. Construct an Objective-C class for answering questions. After you have produced the database for online use, you need to develop a new class that will answer geographical queries. A major query that one would like to ask is: give me all ZIP codes that are within 10 miles from 20007. This query might be implemented with a method having the following signature:

```
-(NSArray *)
zipcodesNearLatitude:(float)lat andLongitude:
    (float) lon withinDistance:(float)distance;
```

Let's take a look at a possible implementation of the above method. The method's main focus is the execution and the manipulation of results of the following SQL statement:

```
SELECT Z.zipcode FROM zipcodes AS Z WHERE
Distance(latitude1 , latitude2 , Z.latitude , Z.longitude)
    <= distance
```

This `SELECT` statement finds all ZIP codes such that the distance between a ZIP code's (latitude, longitude) and a given point (latitude1, longitude1) is within the value `distance` (in kilometers).

You have learned how to write code for these SQL statement. You have also learned how to create C-functions and use them in SQL queries. The `Distance()` function in the above SQL statement must be implemented by you. Listing 12.12 presents the C-implementation.

**Listing 12.12**    The C implementation of the `Distance` user-defined function.

```
void distance(sqlite3_context *context, int nargs,
            sqlite3_value **values){
    char *errorMessage;
    double pi = 3.14159265358979323846;
    if(nargs != 4){
```

```
        errorMessage =
          "Wrong # of args. Distance(lat1, lon1, lat2, lon2)";
        sqlite3_result_error(context, errorMessage,
               strlen(errorMessage));
        return;
    }
    if (
        (sqlite3_value_type(values[0]) != SQLITE_FLOAT)   ||
        (sqlite3_value_type(values[1]) != SQLITE_FLOAT)   ||
        (sqlite3_value_type(values[2]) != SQLITE_FLOAT)   ||
        (sqlite3_value_type(values[3]) != SQLITE_FLOAT)
        ){
        errorMessage =
          "All four arguments must be of type float.";
        sqlite3_result_error(context, errorMessage,
          strlen(errorMessage));
        return;
    }
    double latitude1, longitude1, latitude2, longitude2;
    latitude1 = sqlite3_value_double(values[0]);
    longitude1 = sqlite3_value_double(values[1]);
    latitude2 = sqlite3_value_double(values[2]);
    longitude2 = sqlite3_value_double(values[3]);

    double x = sin( latitude1 * pi/180 ) *
    sin( latitude2 * pi/180  ) + cos(latitude1 *pi/180 ) *
    cos( latitude2 * pi/180 ) *
    cos( abs( (longitude2 * pi/180) −
    (longitude1 *pi/180) ) );
    x = atan( ( sqrt( 1− pow( x, 2 ) ) ) ) / x );
    x = ( 1.852 * 60.0 * ((x/pi)*180) ) / 1.609344;

    sqlite3_result_double(context, x);
}
```

## 12.6   Summary

In this chapter, we addressed the topic of Location Awareness. First, we talked in Section 12.1 about
the Core Location framework and how to use it to build location-aware applications. After that,
Section 12.2 discussed a simple location-aware application. Next, Section 12.3 covered the topic of
geocoding. In that section, you learned how to translate postal addresses into geographical locations.
In Section 12.4, you learned how to sample movement of the device and display that information on
maps. Finally, Section 12.5 discussed how to relate ZIP codes to geographical information. In that
section, you also learned the actual formula that implements the distance between two locations.

# 13

# Working with Devices

In this chapter, we demonstrate the use of the several devices available on the iPhone. Section 13.1 discusses the usage of the accelerometer. In Section 13.2, we show how to play small sound files. Next, Section 13.3 shows how to play video files. After that, Section 13.4 shows how to obtain iPhone/iPod touch device information. Using the camera and the photo library is described in Section 13.5. Finally, we summarize the chapter in Section 13.6

## 13.1 Working with the Accelerometer

The iPhone is equipped with an easy-to-use accelerometer. The accelerometer provides you with the current orientation of the device in 3D space. You subscribe to these updates with a given frequency (10 updates/s to 100 updates/s) and you receive three floating-point values in each update. These values represent the acceleration of x, y, and z in space. The acceleration on each axis is measured in $g$s, where $g$ is the acceleration due to gravity on earth at sea-level ($1g$ is equal to $9.80$ m s$^{-2}$).

If you hold the iPhone in front of you and imagine an axis that goes through the Home button and the earpiece that is orthogonal to the floor, then that axis is the y-axis. Positive values of y indicate that the phone is accelerating up and negative values indicate that it is accelerating down towards the floor. The x-axis goes from right to left perpendicular to the y-axis. Positive values indicate that the force is towards your right side and negative values indicate that the force is towards the left. The z-axis passes through the device. Negative values indicate that the device is moving away from you and positive values indicate that the force is moving the device towards you.

Due to the force of gravity, the device will report non-zero values on some or all of the axes even if the device is stationary. For example, if you hold the device in front of you in portrait mode as shown in Fig. 13.1, the x- and z-axes will report $0g$ while the y-axis will report $-1g$. This basically says that there is no force moving the device to the right/left or forward/backward, but there is a $1g$ force on the device downwards. This force, of course, is gravity.

If you hold the device in landscape mode as shown in Fig. 13.2, the x-axis becomes the axis affected by the force of gravity. The value of the $x$ component of the vector reported by the accelerometer will be $1g$. If you hold the device as in Fig. 13.3, the value will be $-1g$. If you rest the iPhone face up on the table, the z reading will be $-1g$ and if you put it face down, it will report $1g$.

*iPhone SDK Programming*   Maher Ali
© 2009 John Wiley & Sons, Ltd

**Figure 13.1**   Stationary iPhone reporting an accelerometer vector of $(0, -1, 0)$.

If you hold the iPhone facing you as shown in Fig. 13.1 and tilt it to the right, the y value will start increasing and the x value increasing. If you tilt it to the left, the y value will start increasing and the x value decreasing.

### 13.1.1   Example

In this section, we present a simple application that demonstrates the use of the accelerometer. The example will show you how to configure the accelerometer and how to intercept a *shake*, a *hug* and a *push*. In addition, the application will report when the iPhone is in portrait mode with Home button up or down while being perpendicular to the floor.

To use the accelerometer, use the following steps:

1. Obtain the shared accelerometer object. The application has one accelerometer object. Use the sharedAccelerometer method to obtain that object. The method is declared as follows:

   + (UIAccelerometer *)      sharedAccelerometer

2. Configure the accelerometer. Configure the frequency of updates. The property specifying the frequency of updates is updateInterval, which is declared as follows:

**Figure 13.2**    Stationary iPhone reporting an accelerometer vector of (1, 0, 0).

**Figure 13.3**    Stationary iPhone reporting an accelerometer vector of (−1, 0, 0).

```
@property(nonatomic) NSTimeInterval updateInterval;
```

`NSTimeInterval` is declared as `double`. The value you specify for this property ranges from 0.1 (a frequency of 10Hz) to 0.01 (a frequency of 100Hz) seconds.

You also need to configure the delegate property `delegate` which is declared as follows:

```
@property(nonatomic, assign)
    id<UIAccelerometerDelegate> delegate
```

The protocol `UIAccelerometerDelegate` has a single optional method `accelerometer:didAccelerate:`, which is declared as follows:

```
- (void)
accelerometer:(UIAccelerometer *)accelerometer
didAccelerate:(UIAcceleration *)acceleration;
```

The method receives the accelerometer object and a `UIAcceleration` instance. The `UIAcceleration` object holds the values for the 3D vector (x, y, and z) and a timestamp (`timestamp`).

Listing 13.1 shows the application delegate class declaration for the accelerometer example. The application delegate adopts both `UIApplicationDelegate` and `UIAccelerometerDelegate` protocols. In addition, it maintains the previous accelerometer reading in the `accelerationValues` instance variable.

**Listing 13.1**    The application delegate class declaration for the accelerometer example.

```
#import <UIKit/UIKit.h>

@interface AccelAppDelegate :
  NSObject <UIApplicationDelegate, UIAccelerometerDelegate> {
  UIWindow *window;
  UIAccelerationValue accelerationValues[3];
}
@end
```

Listing 13.2 shows the implementation of the application delegate class. The `applicationDidFinishLaunching:` method starts by configuring the accelerometer to a 10Hz frequency of updates and setting the delegate to the application delegate.

The `accelerometer:didAccelerate:` method is where we have the recognition logic for the movements described above. To recognize a shake, it suffices to observe an alteration of acceleration on at least two axes. We use a $3g$ value-difference for each axis. For example, the statement:

```
BOOL x_big_difference = (fabs(x - accelerationValues[0]) >3);
```

Will result in the value `YES` (1) if the difference between the previous and the current acceleration on the x-axis is larger than $3g$.

To recognize that the iPhone is in portrait mode with the axis of the Home-earpiece orthogonal to the floor while the Home button is at the bottom, we make sure that the x and z values are 0 with some tolerance interval, and the y value is about $-1$. Similarly, to recognize that the iPhone is upside-down, the value of y must be around $1g$.

To check for an iPhone hug/punch, the method checks to see a major acceleration on the z-axis with a negligible change on the x- and y-axes. If the z value has changed towards a negative acceleration, we interpret that as a punch. If, on the other hand, the value has changed to a positive acceleration, we interpret that as a hug.

**Listing 13.2**   The implementation of the application delegate class used in the accelerometer example.

```
#import "AccelAppDelegate.h"

#define BETWEEN(arg, v1, v2) ((arg >= v1) && (arg <= v2 ))

@implementation AccelAppDelegate

- (void)accelerometer:(UIAccelerometer *)accelerometer
didAccelerate:(UIAcceleration *)acceleration{
  UIAccelerationValue x, y, z;
  x = acceleration.x;
  y = acceleration.y;
  z = acceleration.z;

  NSLog(@"X: %4.2f, Y:%4.2f, Z:%4.2f", x, y, z);

  // shake
  BOOL x_big_difference = (fabs(x - accelerationValues[0]) >3);
  BOOL y_big_difference = (fabs(y - accelerationValues[1]) >3);
  BOOL z_big_difference = (fabs(z - accelerationValues[2]) >3);
  int axes = x_big_difference + y_big_difference +
                z_big_difference;
  if(axes>= 2){
    NSLog(@"iPhone Shaken!");
  }

// orientation
  if(BETWEEN(x, -0.05, 0.05) && BETWEEN(y, -1, -0.95) &&
      BETWEEN(z, -0.05, 0.05)){
    NSLog(@"iPhone perpendicular to ground, Home button down");
  }

  if(BETWEEN(x, -0.05, 0.05) && BETWEEN(y, 0.95, 1) &&
      BETWEEN(z, -0.05, 0.05)){
    NSLog(@"iPhone perpendicular to ground, Home button up");
  }

// hug/punch
  BOOL x_change = (fabs(x - accelerationValues[0]) < 1);
  BOOL y_change = (fabs(y - accelerationValues[1]) < 1);
  BOOL z_change = (fabs(z - accelerationValues[2]) >= 3);
  if(x_change && y_change && z_change){
    if(z > accelerationValues[2])
      NSLog(@"hug");
```

```
    else
      NSLog(@"punch");
  }

  accelerationValues[0] = x;
  accelerationValues[1] = y;
  accelerationValues[2] = z;
}

- (void)
applicationDidFinishLaunching:(UIApplication *)application {
  CGRect fullScreen = [[UIScreen mainScreen] bounds];
  window = [[UIWindow alloc] initWithFrame:fullScreen];
  UIAccelerometer *accelerometer =
      [UIAccelerometer sharedAccelerometer];
  accelerometer.updateInterval = 0.1; // 10Hz
  accelerometer.delegate = self;
  [window makeKeyAndVisible];
}

- (void)dealloc {
  [window release];
  [super dealloc];
}
@end
```

## 13.2  Audio

In this section, we demonstrate the playing of small audio files ($<$ 30 seconds in length) using Cocoa
APIs. To play a short sound file, you first register the file as a system sound and obtain a handle. After
that you can play the sound using this handle. When you are finished and do not want to play this
sound again, you deallocate that system sound.

To register a sound file as a system sound, use the function AudioServicesCreateSystem-
SoundID() which is declared as follows:

```
OSStatus
AudioServicesCreateSystemSoundID (
        CFURLRef            inFileURL,
        SystemSoundID    * outSystemSoundID)
```

The first parameter is a CFURLRef (or its counterpart NSURL instance). This parameter specifies
the URL of the sound file. The second parameter is a reference to a SystemSoundID. In it, a 32-bit
unsigned integer, representing the ID of the system sound, will be stored. The return value must be
0 to indicate successful registration of the system sound.

To play the system sound, use the `AudioServicesPlaySystemSound()` function which is declared as:

**void**
AudioServicesPlaySystemSound (
  SystemSoundID inSystemSoundID
)

You pass in the system sound handle you obtained from the previous function. The predefined identifier `kSystemSoundID_Vibrate` can be used to trigger vibration.

To deallocate the system sound, use the function `AudioServicesDisposeSystem-SoundID()`, which is declared as follows:

OSStatus
AudioServicesDisposeSystemSoundID (
  SystemSoundID inSystemSoundID
)

You pass in the system sound handle which you obtained from the registration function.

### 13.2.1  Example

In this section, we build an application that plays a sound file every minute. Listing 13.3 shows the declaration of the application delegate class. Notice the include for the `<AudioToolbox/AudioToolbox.h>` header file. Also, you need to add the `Audio-Toolbox.framework` linked library to the project in XCode.

**Listing 13.3**  The declaration of the application delegate class demonstrating the playing of small audio files.

```
#import <UIKit/UIKit.h>
#include <AudioToolbox/AudioToolbox.h>


@interface AudioAppDelegate :
        NSObject <UIApplicationDelegate> {
  UIWindow      *window;
  SystemSoundID    audioSID;
}
@end
```

Listing 13.4 shows the implementation of the application delegate class. The sound file is stored in the application bundle. In the `applicationDidFinishLaunching:` method, we first obtain the absolute file path of the `sound.caf` file. Then, an `NSURL` object is created from this file path using the method `fileURLWithPath:isDirectory:`. The system sound is then registered. The types `CFURL` and `NSURL` are interchangeable or, in Cocoa's terminology, "toll-free bridged". Therefore, we pass in the `NSURL` object in place of the reference to `CFURL`, `CFURLRef`. If there is no error, the sound is played.

The `play:` method plays the sound and then schedules a timer to invoke the `play:` method in one minute.

**Listing 13.4**   The implementation of the application delegate class demonstrating the playing of small audio files.

```
#import "AudioAppDelegate.h"

@implementation AudioAppDelegate

- (void)
applicationDidFinishLaunching:(UIApplication *)application {
  CGRect screenFrame = [[UIScreen  mainScreen] bounds];
  window = [[UIWindow alloc] initWithFrame:screenFrame];

  NSString *filePath = [[NSBundle mainBundle]
                              pathForResource:@"sound"
                              ofType:@"caf"];
  NSURL *aFileURL = [NSURL fileURLWithPath:filePath
                                  isDirectory:NO];
  OSStatus error = AudioServicesCreateSystemSoundID(
                        (CFURLRef)aFileURL, &audioSID);
  if(error == 0)
    [self play:nil];
  [window makeKeyAndVisible];
}

- (void)play:(NSTimer*)theTimer {
  AudioServicesPlaySystemSound(audioSID);
  // schedule a 1 minute play
  [NSTimer scheduledTimerWithTimeInterval:60.0
             target:self selector:@selector(play:)
             userInfo:nil repeats:NO];
}

- (void)dealloc {
  AudioServicesDisposeSystemSoundID (audioSID);
  [window release];
  [super dealloc];
}
@end
```

## 13.3   Video

To play video from within your application, you can use the MPMoviePlayerController class. You create and initialize an instance of this class and ask it to play. This controller plays the video file in full-screen mode. When playback is finished, the applications screen will become visible.

The following code plays the movie `MyMovie.m4v` stored in the application's bundle:

```
NSString *filePath =
[[NSBundle mainBundle] pathForResource:@"MyMovie"
            ofType:@"m4v"];
 NSURL     *fileUrl = [NSURL fileURLWithPath:filePath];
 MPMoviePlayerController *movieController =
      [[MPMoviePlayerController alloc]
            initWithContentURL:fileUrl];
 movieController.backgroundColor = [UIColor grayColor];
 movieController.movieControlMode =
         MPMovieControlModeVolumeOnly;
[movieController play];
```

The code above first finds the full path of the movie in the bundle and uses it to create an NSURL instance. The MPMoviePlayerController is created afterwards and initialized using the initializer initWithContentURL:, passing in the NSURL instance. Optionally, you can set the background color and the control mode. For the movieControlMode property, you can specify (or accept the default of) MPMovieControlModeDefault to allow for the standard controls (e.g., play, pause, timeline, etc.) to appear. To hide all controls, use MPMovieControl-ModeHidden. The code above uses MPMovieControlModeVolumeOnly to show only the volume control. After that, the controller is asked to play the movie using the method play.

## 13.4   Device Information

The UIDevice class is used to provide information about the iPhone/iPod Touch. There is a single instance of this class that can be obtained using the class method currentDevice. The following are some of the pieces of information you can obtain using this instance:

- Unique identifier. You can obtain a string that uniquely identifies the iPhone device using the property uniqueIdentifier. This property is declared as follows:

  ```
  @property(nonatomic, readonly, retain)
      NSString     *uniqueIdentifier
  ```

- Operating system. You can obtain the name of the operating system using the systemName property. This property is declared as follows:

  ```
  @property(nonatomic, readonly, retain)
      NSString     *systemName
  ```

- Operating system version. You can obtain the OS version using the systemVersion property. This property is declared as follows:

  ```
  @property(nonatomic, readonly, retain)
      NSString     *systemVersion
  ```

- The model. You can distinguish between iPhone and iPod Touch using the `model` property. This property is declared as follows:

  `@property(nonatomic, readonly, retain) NSString *model`

- Orientation. The orientation of the device can be obtained using the `orientation` property. This property is declared as follows:

  `@property(nonatomic, readonly)`
  `    UIDeviceOrientation orientation`

  Possible values are: `UIDeviceOrientationUnknown`, `UIDeviceOrientationPortrait`, `UIDeviceOrientationPortraitUpsideDown`, `UIDeviceOrientationLandscapeLeft`, `UIDeviceOrientationLandscapeRight`, `UIDeviceOrientationFaceUp`, and `UIDeviceOrientationFaceDown`.

## 13.5   Taking and Selecting Pictures

In this section, you will learn how to use the camera for taking pictures. You will learn that you do not have direct access to the camera or the image library, but rather you use a supplied controller that handles user's interaction for taking and editing the picture. The controller will provide you with the final image when the user finishes. The same controller can be used to pick images stored in the user's library. You will master the use of this controller in this section. This section is organized as follows. In Section 13.5.1, we outline the major steps needed to access the camera and the image library. Then, in Section 13.5.2 we provide a detailed example demonstrating taking and picking pictures.

### 13.5.1   Overall approach

To access the camera or to select pictures from the user's library, you have to use a system-supplied interface that is provided to you. The main class used for either taking new pictures or selecting existing ones is `UIImagePickerController`. The major steps for taking/selecting pictures are as follows:

1. Check availability of action. Whether you would like to take a new picture or select an existing one, you need to check if this function is available to you. The `UIImagePickerController`'s class method used for this purpose is `isSourceTypeAvailable:`.

2. If the specified function is available, you need to create an instance of `UIImagePickerController`, initialize it, and configure it with the specified function.

3. Set the delegate. The `UIImagePickerController` will be responsible for the user's interaction while picking or taking a new picture. You need to set the delegate to an object and implement specific methods in order to receive the result. The delegate follows the `UIImagePickerControllerDelegate` protocol.

4. Present the controller. You modally present the controller to the user by calling `presentModalViewController:animated:` on an existing view controller, passing the `UIImagePickerController` instance as the first parameter.

5. Handle picture selection. When the user picks an image, the delegate's method `image-PickerController:didFinishPickingImage:editingInfo:` is called. You should retrieve the image and dismiss the picker controller that was modally presented.

6. Handle picture cancellation. If the user cancels the operation, the method `imagePicker-ControllerDidCancel:` of the delegate is called. You should dismiss the picker controller that was presented modally.

## 13.5.2 Detailed example

In this section, we present a detailed application demonstrating the use of the `UIImagePicker-Controller` class. The application presents the user with an action sheet with two options: taking a new picture or selecting an existing one. Depending on the user's selection, the application configures an instance of the `UIImagePickerController` class and presents it to the user. After the user finishes his/her task, the result (if any) is used as a background to the main window.

The application implements two classes: an application delegate class and a simple view controller. Listing 13.5 shows the declaration of the application delegate class `CameraAppDelegate`. The application delegate uses an instance of the `MainController` class for managing the user interface.

**Listing 13.5**   Application delegate declaration for the simple camera application.

```
#import <UIKit/UIKit.h>
#import "MainController.h"

@interface CameraAppDelegate :
    NSObject <UIApplicationDelegate> {
  UIWindow *window;
  MainController    *viewController;
}
@property (nonatomic, retain) UIWindow *window;
@end
```

Listing 13.6 shows the implementation of the application delegate. The `application-DidFinishLaunching:` method creates the main window and an instance of the `MainController` view controller. It then adds the view controller's view as a subview of the window and makes the window key and visible.

**Listing 13.6**   Application delegate implementation for the simple camera application.

```
#import "CameraAppDelegate.h"

@implementation CameraAppDelegate
@synthesize window;
```

```
— (void)applicationDidFinishLaunching:
        (UIApplication *)application {
    window = [[UIWindow alloc]
        initWithFrame:[[UIScreen mainScreen] bounds]];
    viewController = [MainController alloc];
    [window addSubview:viewController.view];
    [window makeKeyAndVisible];
}
— (void)dealloc {
    [window release];
    [super dealloc];
}
@end
```

Listing 13.7 shows the declaration of the `MainController` view controller. It adopts two protocols: (1) the `UIImagePickerControllerDelegate` for handling communications with the `UIImagePickerController` instance, and (2) `UIActionSheetDelegate` for handling communications with the action sheet.

**Listing 13.7**  Declaration of the `MainController` class for the simple camera application.

```
#import <UIKit/UIKit.h>

@interface MainController :
    UIViewController<UIImagePickerControllerDelegate,
                        UIActionSheetDelegate> {
}
@end
```

Listing 13.8 shows the `loadView` method of the `MainController` class. This method simply creates a full-size view, configures it, and assigns it to the `view` property of the view controller.

**Listing 13.8**  The `loadView` method of the `MainController` class for the simple camera application.

```
— (void)loadView {
    CGRect rectFrame =
        [UIScreen mainScreen].applicationFrame;
    UIView *theView =
        [[UIView alloc] initWithFrame:rectFrame];
    theView.backgroundColor = [UIColor darkGrayColor];
    theView.autoresizingMask = UIViewAutoresizingFlexibleHeight |
                        UIViewAutoresizingFlexibleWidth;
    self.view = theView;
    [theView release];
}
```

When the view has finished loading, the method `viewDidLoad` is invoked automatically. Inside this method, we create an action sheet that asks the user to choose whether to take a new picture or select an existing one. The method sets the view controller as the delegate and shows the action sheet in the controller's view.

**Listing 13.9**   The `viewDidLoad` method for the view controller.

```
- (void) viewDidLoad {
  UIActionSheet *
  actionSheet = [[UIActionSheet alloc]
          initWithTitle :@"Choose an option:"
          delegate: self cancelButtonTitle: nil
          destructiveButtonTitle: nil
          otherButtonTitles :@"New Picture",
              @"Select a Picture", nil];
  [actionSheet showInView: self.view];
}
```

Listing 13.10 shows the `actionSheet:clickedButtonAtIndex:` that handles button clicks for the action sheet. If the first button is tapped, we check to make sure that the camera is available. The class method `isSourceTypeAvailable:` of the `UIImagePicker-Controller` class is used. The method is declared as:

```
+ (BOOL) isSourceTypeAvailable:
  (UIImagePickerControllerSourceType) sourceType
```

The only parameter is of type `UIImagePickerControllerSourceType` and can have the following values:

- `UIImagePickerControllerSourceTypePhotoLibrary` specifies the source as the photo library.

- `UIImagePickerControllerSourceTypeSavedPhotosAlbum` specifies the source as the camera's roll.

- `UIImagePickerControllerSourceTypeCamera` specifies the source as the built-in camera.

The method returns YES if the specified source is available, and NO, otherwise. If the camera is available, the method creates a new instance of the `UIImagePickerController` class and sets its source type property (`sourceType`) to the value `UIImagePickerControllerSource-TypeCamera`. The `sourceType` property is declared as:

```
@property (nonatomic)
  UIImagePickerControllerSourceType sourceType
```

If, on the other hand, the second button is tapped, we repeat the previous steps except that we use the source `UIImagePickerControllerSourceTypePhotoLibrary` instead. After that, we set the delegate of the image picker controller to the view controller instance, set the `allowsImageEditing` property to YES, and present the image picker controller by invoking the view controller's `presentModalViewController:animated:` method. The `allowsImageEditing` property is used to determine whether the user is allowed to edit the image before returning it to our code.

**Listing 13.10**  The `actionSheet:clickedButtonAtIndex:` method handling button clicks for the action sheet of the simple camera application.

```objc
- (void) actionSheet :( UIActionSheet *) actionSheet
    clickedButtonAtIndex :( NSInteger) buttonIndex
{
  [ actionSheet release ];
  UIImagePickerController *picker ;
  if ( buttonIndex == 0){
    if ( (![ UIImagePickerController
        isSourceTypeAvailable :
          UIImagePickerControllerSourceTypeCamera ])
    ){
      return ;
    }
    picker = [[ UIImagePickerController alloc ] init ];
    picker . sourceType =
      UIImagePickerControllerSourceTypeCamera ;
  }
  else {
    if ( (![ UIImagePickerController
        isSourceTypeAvailable :
          UIImagePickerControllerSourceTypePhotoLibrary ])
    ){
      return ;
    }
    picker = [[ UIImagePickerController alloc ] init ];
    picker . sourceType =
      UIImagePickerControllerSourceTypePhotoLibrary ;
  }
  picker . delegate = self ;
  picker . allowsImageEditing = YES ;
  [ self presentModalViewController : picker animated : YES ];
}
```

As we have mentioned before, the image picker controller informs us when the user has picked an image by invoking the method `imagePickerController:didFinishPicking-Image:editingInfo:` of its delegate. The method is declared as follows:

```objc
- (void )
imagePickerController :( UIImagePickerController *) picker
didFinishPickingImage :( UIImage *) image
editingInfo :( NSDictionary *) editingInfo
```

The first parameter, `picker`, is the picker object controlling the image picker interface. The second parameter is the image picked by the user (possibly after editing). The third parameter is a dictionary used to hold editing information (if editing is enabled). Two keys are used to obtain relevant values in the dictionary:

- `UIImagePickerControllerOriginalImage`. Use this key to obtain the original image (instance of `UIImage`) before the user's edit.

- `UIImagePickerControllerCropRect`. Use this key to obtain an `NSValue` object containing a value of type `CGRect` holding the cropping rectangle applied to the original image.

Listing 13.11 shows the implementation of the `imagePickerController:didFinish-PickingImage:editingInfo:` method. The method simply creates an image view using the passed image and adds that view as a subview to the main controller's view. It also dismisses the image picker view controller by calling the `dismissModalViewControllerAnimated:` method.

**Listing 13.11**    Handling successful image picking for the simple camera application.

```
- (void)
imagePickerController:(UIImagePickerController *)picker
    didFinishPickingImage:(UIImage *)image
          editingInfo:(NSDictionary *)editingInfo
{
  UIImageView *imgView =
      [[UIImageView alloc] initWithImage:image];
  [self.view addSubview:imgView];
  [self dismissModalViewControllerAnimated:YES];
  [picker release];
  [imgView release];
}
```

Listing 13.12 shows handling the event that the user cancels the image picking. We simply dismiss the image picker and release it.

**Listing 13.12**    Handling user's cancellation of image picking for the simple camera application.

```
- (void)imagePickerControllerDidCancel:
      (UIImagePickerController *)picker
{
  [self dismissModalViewControllerAnimated:YES];
  [picker release];
}
@end
```

Figure 13.4 shows the main screen that the user sees when the application is launched. Figure 13.5 shows the view when the user is in the process of taking a picture. Figure 13.6 shows the view just after the user has taken a picture and the image picker is still in control. The user can confirm that he/she wants this picture (and it will be saved and returned to our application as seen in Fig. 13.7) or tap on "Retake" to take another one. Figure 13.8 shows the view when the image picker exited and

**Figure 13.4**   The main screen that the user sees when the simple camera application is launched.

**Figure 13.5**   The view when the user is in the process of taking a picture.

**Figure 13.6**   The view just after the user has taken a picture. The image picker is still in control. The user can confirm that he/she wants this picture or tap on "Retake" to take another one.

**Figure 13.7**   The view image picker saving the picture.

**Figure 13.8**  The view when the image picker has exited and control has returned to our code.

**Figure 13.9**  The view that the user will see when he/she selects picking an existing picture.

control returned to our code. Figure 13.9 shows the view that the user will see when he/she selects picking an existing picture.

## 13.6  Summary

In Section 13.1, you learned how to use the accelerometer. You learned how to subscribe to the acceleration information with a given update frequency. You also saw how to recognize several orientations of the device as well as specific movements. In Section 13.2, you learned how to play short sound files and how to configure a timer for scheduling tasks. In Section 13.3, you learned how to play video files from within your application. In Section 13.4, you learned how to obtain important information about the device. In Section 13.5 you learned how to use the camera for taking pictures. You learned that you do not have direct access to the camera or the image library, but rather you use a supplied controller (`UIImagePickerController`) that handles the user's interaction for taking and editing the picture. The controller provides you with the final image when the user finishes. The same controller was used to pick images stored in the user's library. We demonstrated these concepts using a simple application that allowed the user to either take a new picture or pick an existing one.

# APPENDICES

# A

# Saving and Restoring App State

Since at most one application can run at a given time, your application should give the user the illusion of being active all the time even if the user hit the Home button. To achieve that, your application should save its current state (e.g., which level of hierarchy it is currently displaying, the current search term, etc.) when the application is terminated, and restore that state when it is relaunched.

There are several ways in which you can maintain this state information. You can, for example, use the SQLite database or flat-files. A property list, however, is ideal for this situation and is the subject of this appendix.

To use property lists for capturing/restoring the state of an application, you need to follow the following guidelines:

- Represent the state in a dictionary or in an array.

- The state elements can be instances of NSDictionary, NSArray, NSData, NSDate, NSNumber, and NSString.

- Add the state elements to the dictionary or the array.

- Serialize the dictionary or the array into an NSData object using the NSPropertyList-Serialization class method.

- The NSData object represents the state information in either an XML or a binary format. For efficiency, use binary format.

- Write the NSData object into a local file in the Documents directory.

- To restore the state, load the written file into an NSData object and use the NSPropertyListSerialization class method to obtain the dictionary or the array.

In the following, we give an example of saving/restoring an application state using Property Lists. The state of the application is assumed to be captured by a dictionary. This dictionary has five elements: two NSStrings, one NSNumber, one NSArray, and one NSDate value.

Listing A.1 shows the application delegate method that demonstrates the Property List concept. The method builds the state of the application (a dictionary) and invokes saveAppState to save the state and then restoreState to restore it.

*iPhone SDK Programming*   Maher Ali
© 2009 John Wiley & Sons, Ltd

**Listing A.1**    The delegate method used in building the app state, saving it and then restoring it using Property Lists.

```
- (void)
applicationDidFinishLaunching:(UIApplication *)application {

    // build app state
    state = [[NSMutableDictionary alloc] initWithCapacity:5];
    [state setObject:@"http://www.thegoogle.com" forKey:@"URL"];
    [state setObject:@"smartphones" forKey:@"SEARCH_TERM"];
    [state setObject:[NSNumber numberWithFloat:3.14] forKey:@"PI"];
    [state setObject:[NSMutableArray arrayWithObjects:
            @"Apple iPhone 3G",
            @"Apple iPhone",
            @"HTC Touch Diamond",
            nil]
        forKey:@"RESULT"];
    [state setObject:[NSDate date]  forKey:@"DATE"];

    // save state of app
    [self saveAppState];

    // restore state of app
    [self restoreState];
}
```

Listing A.2 shows the `saveAppState` method. The method uses the class method `dataFromPropertyList:format:errorDescription:` of the class `NSProperty-ListSerialization` to obtain an `NSData` object of the serialized dictionary. There are two formats you can use: binary format specified using `NSPropertyListBinaryFormat_v1_0` or XML format specified using `NSPropertyListXMLFormat_v1_0`. You can also give a reference to an `NSString` object that can be used to signal back an error message. It is your responsibility to release that object if an error should occur. Once you have obtained the `NSData` object, you can write it to a local file.

**Listing A.2**    Saving the state of the application in a property list.

```
-(void) saveAppState{
    NSString *theError;
    NSData  *theData = [NSPropertyListSerialization
                    dataFromPropertyList:state
                    format:NSPropertyListXMLFormat_v1_0
                    errorDescription:&theError];
    if(theData){
        NSString *fileName = [NSHomeDirectory()
            stringByAppendingPathComponent:@"Documents/state.plist"];
```

```
  [theData writeToFile:fileName atomically:YES];
}
else{
  NSLog(@"Error saving app state: %@", theError);
  [theError    release]; // need to release
}
}
```

Listing A.3 shows the contents of the XML file `state.plist` used to store the application's state. The number of bytes used to store the state in XML format is 543 while it is 204 when the binary format is used.

**Listing A.3**    The property list in XML format.

```xml
<?xml version="1.0" encoding="UTF-8"?>
<!DOCTYPE plist PUBLIC "-//Apple//DTD PLIST 1.0//EN"
"http://www.apple.com/DTDs/PropertyList-1.0.dtd">
<plist version="1.0">
<dict>
  <key>DATE</key>
  <date>2008-09-04T17:47:28Z</date>
  <key>PI</key>
  <real>3.1400001049041748</real>
  <key>RESULT</key>
  <array>
    <string>Apple iPhone 3G</string>
    <string>Apple iPhone</string>
    <string>HTC Touch Diamond</string>
  </array>
  <key>SEARCH_TERM</key>
  <string>smartphones</string>
  <key>URL</key>
  <string>http://www.thegoogle.com</string>
</dict>
</plist>
```

Listing A.4 shows the method used to restore the application's state. First, the file is read into an `NSData` object using the techniques in Chapter 9. After that, the class method `property-ListFromData:mutabilityOption:format:errorDescription:` is used to obtain the dictionary object. The parameter `mutabilityOption` is used to specify the mutability of the objects returned. If you specify `NSPropertyListImmutable`, then the dictionary, as well as all of its entries, will be returned as immutable. If you specify `NSPropertyListMutable-ContainersAndLeaves`, then the dictionary and all of its entries will be created as mutable objects. The option `NSPropertyListMutableContainers`, which we use here, generates mutable objects for arrays and dictionaries only.

**Listing A.4** Restoring the state of the application in a property list.

```
-(void) restoreState{
  NSString   *theError;
  NSPropertyListFormat   format;

  NSString *fileName = [NSHomeDirectory()
      stringByAppendingPathComponent:@"Documents/state.plist"];
  NSData      *theData = [[NSData alloc]
      initWithContentsOfFile:fileName];
  if(theData){
    [state release];
    state = [NSPropertyListSerialization
            propertyListFromData:theData
            mutabilityOption:NSPropertyListMutableContainers
            format:&format
            errorDescription:&theError];
    if(state){
      [state retain];
    }
    else{
      NSLog(@"Error retrieving app state: %@", theError);
      [theError   release]; // need to release
    }
    [theData release];
  }
}
```

# B
# Invoking External Applications

Your iPhone application can programatically invoke other iPhone applications. Moreover, you can open your iPhone application to be invoked by other iPhone applications. To accomplish that, you specify a new URL scheme in the application's bundle, and the system will register that new scheme once the application is installed.

To invoke another iPhone application, you use the UIApplication instance method openURL: and pass in the URL of that application. The following code fragment will open the Maps application and display a specific address.

```
NSString  *address = @"http://maps.google.com/maps?q=plano,tx";
NSURL *myURL = [NSURL URLWithString:address];
[[UIApplication sharedApplication] openURL:myURL];
```

To register a new URL scheme, you need to add it to the Info.plist file. In Fig. B.1, we show what needs to be added to register the new URL scheme lookup. The URL identifier can be any unique string.

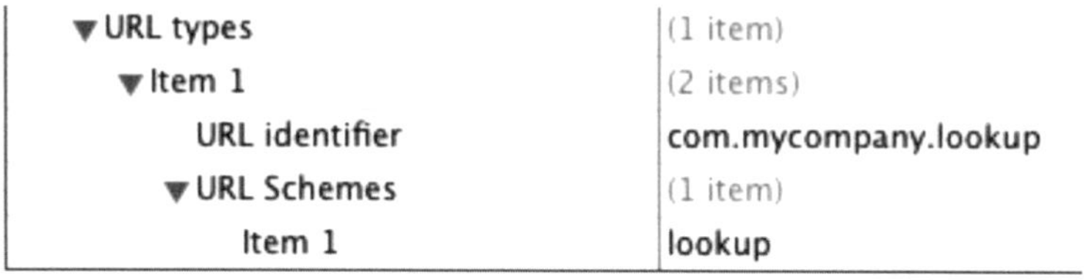

| | |
|---|---|
| ▼ URL types | (1 item) |
| ▼ Item 1 | (2 items) |
| URL identifier | com.mycompany.lookup |
| ▼ URL Schemes | (1 item) |
| Item 1 | lookup |

**Figure B.1**  Adding a new URL scheme in the Info.plist file.

To actually service the invocation, you need to implement the application delegate's method application:handleOpenURL:, which is declared as follows:

```
- (BOOL)
application:(UIApplication *)application
handleOpenURL:(NSURL *)url
```

You receive an instance of NSURL encapsulating the URL used in the invocation. You can use the many methods of NSURL in order to retrieve queries, parameters, and fragments according to your needs. For example, our `lookup` scheme can be invoked by either using the ZIP code or the city. To look up based on the ZIP code, you invoke it as follows: `lookup://www?zip#68508`. To invoke it using the city, you use `lookup://www?city#Lincoln`.

Listing B.1 shows an implementation of the `lookup` URL scheme handling. To retrieve the query, we use the `query` method of NSURL. This can be either `"city"` or `"zip"`. To retrieve the fragment, we use the `fragment` method. The implementation below, simply displays the important parts of the invocation URL. If you cannot process the request, you return NO. Otherwise, you service it and return YES.

**Listing B.1**   An implementation of the `lookup` url scheme handling.

```
- (BOOL)
application:(UIApplication *)application
handleOpenURL:(NSURL *)url{
  NSString *query = [url query];
  NSString *fragment = [url fragment];
  NSMutableString *output;
  if ([query isEqualToString:@"zip"]){
    output = [NSMutableString
      stringWithFormat:@"Looking up by zip code %@", fragment];
  }
  else  if ([query isEqualToString:@"city"]){
    output = [NSMutableString
      stringWithFormat:@"Looking up by city  %@", fragment];
  }
  else return NO;
  textView.text = output;
  return YES;
}
```

# REFERENCES AND BIBLIOGRAPHY

[1] http://geocoder.ibegin.com/downloads.php.

[2] ZIP code: http://en.wikipedia.org/wiki/ZIP code.

[3] B'Far, R, *Mobile Computing Principles: Designing and Developing Mobile Applications with UML and XML*, Cambridge University Press, 2004.

[4] Core Location Framework Reference, Apple documentation.

## Bibliography

[5] Beam, M and Davidson, JD, *Cocoa in a Nutshell: A Desktop Quick Reference*, O'Reilly, 2003.

[6] Brownell, D, *SAX2*, O'Reilly, 2002.

[7] Davidson, JD, *Learning Cocoa With Objective C*, 2nd edition, O'Reilly, 2002.

[8] Duncan, A, *Objective-C Pocket Reference*, 1st edition, O'Reilly, 2002.

[9] Garfinkel, S and Mahoney, MK, *Building Cocoa Applications: A Step-by-Step Guide*, 1st edition, O'Reilly, 2002

[10] Hillegass, A, *Cocoa® Programming for Mac® OS X*, 3rd edition, Addison-Wesley Professional, 2008.

[11] Kochan, S, *Programming in Objective-C*, Sams, 2003.

[12] Mott, T, *Learning Cocoa*, O'Reilly, 2001.

[13] Owens, M, *The Definitive Guide to SQLite*, Apress, Inc., 2006.

[14] Tejkowski, E, *Cocoa Programming for Dummies*, 1st edition, For Dummies, 2003.

[15] Williams, E, Aviation Formulary V1.43: http://williams.best.vwh.net/avform.htm.

[16] Collections Programming Topics for Cocoa, Apple Reference Library.

[17] Document Object Model (DOM): http://www.w3.org/TR/DOM-Level-2-Core/.

[18] Exception Programming Topics for Cocoa, Apple documentation.

[19] Introduction to the Objective-C 2.0 Programming Language, Apple documentation.

[20] Key-Value Coding Programming Guide, Apple documentation.

[21] libxml2: The XML C parser and toolkit: http://xmlsoft.org/.

[22] Threading Programming Guide, Apple Reference Library.

[23] The XML standard: http://www.w3.org/TR/REC-xml.

# INDEX

#import, 3
#include, 3

accelerometer, 351
alloc, 6
animation, 91
AudioServicesCreateSystemSoundID(), 356
AudioServicesDisposeSystemSoundID(), 357
AudioServicesPlaySystemSound(), 357

camera, 360
category, 15
CGPoint, 69
CGPointMake, 70
CGRect, 70
CGRectMake, 70
CGSize, 70
CGSizeMake, 70
Class, 5
class
    methods, 2
    object, 2
CLLocation, 327
    altitude, 328
    coordinate, 327
    horizontalAccuracy, 328
    timestamp, 328
    verticalAccuracy, 328
CLLocationManager, 325
    CLLocationManagerDelegate, 326
    desiredAccuracy, 326
    distanceFilter, 326
    startUpdatingLocation, 327
    stopUpdatingLocation, 327
copyWithZone:, 45

dealloc, 8

dynamic, 11

exception
    catch, 18
    finally, 18
    throw, 17
    try, 18
exceptions, 17

geocoding, 334
GPS, 325

id, 5
implementation, 1, 2
Info.plist, 375
instance
    methods, 2
interface, 1, 2

Key-value Coding, 24
KVC, 24

libxml2
    charactersSAXFunc(), 310
    xmlChildrenNode, 305
    xmlDocGetRootElement(), 303
    xmlNode, 303
    xmlNodeListGetString, 307
    xmlStrcmp(), 305

message, 2
modal view controller, 152
MPMoviePlayerController, 358
multithreading, 30
MVC, 125

nil, 5
Nill, 5
NSArray, 39
    arrayWithObjects:, 41, 48
    copy, 43
    NSMutableArray, 39
    objectAtIndex:, 43
    sortedArrayUsingSelector:, 52
NSAutoreleasePool, 7
NSBundle, 270
NSCopying, 45
NSData
    dataWithContentsOfFile:, 292
    writeToFile:atomically:, 294
NSDictionary, 58
    allKeys, 59
    allValues, 60
    dictionaryWithObjectsAndKeys:, 59
    isEqualToDictionary:, 59
    keysSortedByValueUsingSelector:, 60
    objectForKey:, 59
NSError, 22
NSException, 17
    exceptionWithName:reason:userInfo:, 20
    raise, 17
NSFileHandle, 271
    seekToFileOffset:, 271
NSFileManager, 258
    defaultManager, 258
    enumeratorAtPath:, 258
NSHomeDirectory(), 257
NSIndexPath, 208
    row, 209
    section, 209
NSInteger, 49
NSInvocationOperation, 31
NSMutableArray, 39
    removeObject:, 45
NSMutableDictionary, 58
    addEntriesFromDictionary:, 60
    removeObjectForKey:, 59
NSMutableSet, 53, 56
    addObject, 56
    removeObject:, 56
    unionSet:, 56
NSNull, 28
NSObject, 5
    alloc, 6

conformsToProtocol:, 9
    copy, 6
    dealloc, 8
    init, 6
    poseAsClass:, 17
    release, 6
    retain, 6
NSOperation, 31
NSPropertyListSerialization, 372
NSSelectorFromString(), 5
NSSet, 53
    anyObject, 56
    containsObject:, 56
    intersectsSet:, 55
    isSubsetOfSet:, 55
    NSMutableSet, 56
NSString, 5
    cStringUsingEncoding:, 302
    NSMutableString, 5
    stringWithContentsOfURL:encoding:error:,
        302
NSURL, 376
NULL, 5

posing, 17
property, 10
    assign, 11
    copy, 11
    dynamic, 11
    getter, 11
    nonatomic, 11
    readonly, 11
    setter, 11
    synthesize, 10
property list, 371
protocol, 8
    optional, 8
    required, 8

radio interface, 131
raise, 17
release, 6
retain, 6
retain count, 6
RSS, 298

SEL, 5
self, 6
SQL, 275

SQLite, 275
    BLOB, 289
    sqlite3_close(), 277
    sqlite3_column_XXX(), 285
    sqlite3_create_ function(), 287
    sqlite3_exec(), 277
    sqlite3_finalize(), 283, 285
    sqlite3_free(), 277
    sqlite3_malloc(), 277
    sqlite3_prepare_v2(), 284
    sqlite3_result_error(), 287
    sqlite3_result_XXX(), 289
    sqlite3_step(), 285
    sqlite3_value, 289
    sqlite3_value_type(), 289
    SQLITE_DONE, 283
    SQLITE_ROW, 283
static, 2
super, 6
synthesize, 10

tabbar, 131
table view, 205
target-action, xii, 103, 104

UIAccelerometer
    delegate, 353
    sharedAccelerometer, 352
    updateInterval, 352
UIAccelerometerDelegate, 354
    accelerometer:didAccelerate:, 354
UIActionSheet, 178
UIAlertView, 176
UIApplication
    openURL:, 375
    sendActionsForControlEvents:, 105
UIButton, 116
    buttonWithType:, 116
UIControl, 103
    controlEvents, 105
    enabled, 103
    highlighted, 103
    selected, 104
    state, 104
UIDatePicker, 121
UIDevice, 359
    model, 360
    orientation, 360

systemName, 359
systemVersion, 359
uniqueIdentifier, 359
UIEvent, 75
    allTouches, 76
UIImage
    imageNamed:, 135
UIImagePickerController, 360
    isSourceTypeAvailable:, 360
UIImagePickerControllerDelegate, 360
UINavigationController, 141
UINavigationItem, 149
UIPageControl, 120
UIPickerView, 161
    component, 161
    row, 161
UIResponder, 77
    touchesBegan
      withEvent:, 77
    touchesCancelled:withEvent:, 77
    touchesEnded:withEvent:, 77
    touchesMoved:withEvent:, 77
UIScreen, 71
UISegmentedControl, 117
UISlider, 113
    continuous, 114
    maximumValue, 114
    minimumValue, 114
UISwitch, 115
UITabBarItem, 133
    badgeValue, 133
UITableView, 205
    dataSource, 206
    dequeueReusableCellWithIdentifier:, 209
    setEditing:animated:, 214
    tableView:canMoveRowAtIndexPath:, 227
    UITableViewDataSource, 206
    UITableViewStylePlain, 206
UITableViewCell, 205, 209
    image, 211
UITableViewDelegate, 206
UITextField, 107
    UITextFieldDelegate, 111
UITextInputTraits, 108
UITextView, 172
UITouch, 76
UIView
    beginAnimations:context:, 92

commitAnimations, 92
locationInView:, 76
previousLocationInView:, 76
tapCount, 76
UIViewController, 125
dismissModalViewControllerAnimated:,
153
initWithNibName:bundle:, 126
interfaceOrientation, 126
leftBarButtonItem, 150
loadView, 129
modalViewController, 153
navigationItem, 149
parentViewController, 153
presentModalViewController:animated:, 153
rightBarButtonItem, 150
shouldAutorotateToInterfaceOrientation:,
131
tabBarItem, 132

view, 131
UIWebView, 180
stringByEvaluatingJavaScriptFromString:,
192
UIWebViewDelegate, 197

vibrate, 357
view
bounds, 73
center, 72
frame, 72
geometry, 69
subviews, 75
superview, 75

XML, 297
DOM, 301
RSS, 298
SAX, 307